日本語 N(
NihonGO NOW!

NihonGO NOW! is a beginning-level courseware package that takes a performed-culture approach to learning Japanese. This innovative approach balances the need for an intellectual understanding of structural elements with multiple opportunities to experience the language within its cultural context.

From the outset, learners are presented with samples of authentic language that are context-sensitive and culturally coherent. Instructional time is used primarily to rehearse interactions that learners of Japanese are likely to encounter in the future, whether they involve speaking, listening, writing, or reading.

Level 1 comprises two textbooks with accompanying activity books. These four books in combination with audio files allow instructors to adapt a beginning-level course, such as the first year of college Japanese, to their students' needs. They focus on language and modeled behavior, providing opportunities for learners to acquire language through performance templates. Online resources provide additional support for both students and instructors. Audio files, videos, supplementary exercises, and a teachers' manual are available at www.routledge.com/9781138304147.

NihonGO NOW! Level 1 Volume 1 Textbook is ideally accompanied by the *Level 1 Volume 1 Activity Book*, which provides core texts and additional practice for beginning-level students.

Mari Noda is Professor of Japanese at The Ohio State University.

Patricia J. Wetzel is Emerita Professor of Japanese at Portland State University.

Ginger Marcus is Professor of the Practice of Japanese Language at Washington University in St. Louis.

Stephen D. Luft is Lecturer of Japanese at the University of Pittsburgh.

Shinsuke Tsuchiya is Assistant Professor of Japanese at Brigham Young University.

Masayuki Itomitsu is Associate Professor of Japanese at Linfield College.

日本語 NOW!
NihonGO NOW!

Performing Japanese Culture
Level 1 Volume 1
Textbook

Mari Noda, Patricia J. Wetzel, Ginger Marcus,
Stephen D. Luft, Shinsuke Tsuchiya,
and Masayuki Itomitsu

Routledge
Taylor & Francis Group

LONDON AND NEW YORK

First published 2021
by Routledge
2 Park Square, Milton Park, Abingdon, Oxon OX14 4RN

and by Routledge
52 Vanderbilt Avenue, New York, NY 10017

Routledge is an imprint of the Taylor & Francis Group, an informa business

British Library Cataloguing-in-Publication Data
A catalogue record for this book is available from the British Library

Library of Congress Cataloging-in-Publication Data
Names: Noda, Mari, author.
Title: Nihongo now! : performing Japanese culture / Mari Noda, Patricia J. Wetzel, Ginger Marcus, Stephen D. Luft, Shinsuke Tsuchiya, Masayuki Itomitsu.
Description: New York : Routledge, 2020. | Includes bibliographical references. | Contents: Level 1, volume 1. Textbook—Level 1, volume 1. Activity book—Level 1, volume 2. Textbook—Level 1, volume 2. Activity book. | In English and Japanese.
Identifiers: LCCN 2020026010 (print) | LCCN 2020026011 (ebook) | ISBN 9780367509279 (level 1, volume 1 ; set ; hardback) | ISBN 9780367508494 (level 1, volume 1 ; set ; paperback) | ISBN 9781138304123 (level 1, volume 1 ; textbook ; hardback) | ISBN 9781138304147 (level 1, volume 1 ; textbook ; paperback) | ISBN 9781138304277 (level 1, volume 1 ; activity book ; hardback) | ISBN 9781138304314 (level 1, volume 1 ; activity book ; paperback) | ISBN 9780367509309 (level 1, volume 2 ; set ; hardback) | ISBN 9780367508531 (level 1, volume 2 ; set ; paperback) | ISBN 9780367483241 (level 1, volume 2 ; textbook ; hardback) | ISBN 9780367483210 (level 1, volume 2 ; textbook ; paperback) | ISBN 9780367483494 (level 1, volume 2 ; activity book ; hardback) | ISBN 9780367483364 (level 1, volume 2 ; activity book ; paperback) | ISBN 9780203730249 (level 1, volume 1 ; ebook) | ISBN 9780203730362 (level 1, volume 1 ; ebook) | ISBN 9781003051855 (level 1, volume 1 ; ebook) | ISBN 9781003039334 (level 1, volume 2 ; ebook) | ISBN 9781003039471 (level 1, volume 2 ; ebook) | ISBN 9781003051879 (level 1, volume 2 ; ebook)
Subjects: LCSH: Japanese language—Textbooks for foreign speakers—English. | Japanese language—Study and teaching—English speakers.
Classification: LCC PL539.5.E5 N554 2020 (print) | LCC PL539.5.E5 (ebook) | DDC 495.682/421—dc23
LC record available at https://lccn.loc.gov/2020026010
LC ebook record available at https://lccn.loc.gov/2020026011

ISBN: 978-1-138-30412-3 (hbk)
ISBN: 978-1-138-30414-7 (pbk)
ISBN: 978-0-203-73036-2 (ebk)

Typeset in Times New Roman
by Apex CoVantage, LLC

Visit the eResources: www.routledge.com/9781138304147

For Galal, Liz, Marvin, Jeneal, Alyssa, and Sheldon

Contents

Act 5   お願^{ねが}いしてもいいですか。
May I ask a favor of you? 187

Acknowledgments

This textbook could not have come into being without the assistance and cooperation of many people and organizations. We have tried to list them all below.

For helping with the audio file production and editing: Larry Mollard (Washington University in St. Louis), Paul Kotheimer (The Ohio State University), and Teppei Fukuda (Portland State University).

For performing in the audio program for the Scenes: Aki Hirano, Keiji Iwamoto, Yamato Kitahashi, Yuka Kishiue, Kaho Sakaue, Yuya Sano, Kie Uchiyama, Shoichi Ueda, and Yui Yamato (participants in the 2018 ALLEX Foundation Summer Program); Mami Chujo, Yumeho Hashimoto, Asako Higurashi, Nao Kakizakai, Masaya Mizutani, Mirai Nagasawa, Mayu Okawara, Hiroaki Onuki, Shiori Saito, Rina Sato, Eun Yon Seong, Tetsuko Sugawara, Mizuho Tanaka, Yosuke Yamauchi, Takuma Yoshida, Chiaki Yoshikawa, and Yuji Yuasa (participants in the 2019 ALLEX Foundation Summer Program); Nozomi Imai (Vanderbilt University); Shunichi Maruyama (The Ohio State University); Kanako Yao (Washington University in St. Louis).

For performing in the audio program for the *Activity Book*: Junzo Oshimo and Noriko Kanisawa Kowalchuck (University of Pittsburgh).

For funding support for production of the audio program for the *Activity Book*: The Asian Studies Center, University of Pittsburgh.

For video production: Hiroki Ohsawa (Hiroki Ohsawa Productions), director, producer, script writer, editing, and casting; Yuk Hong Law, director of photography; The Diddy-Diddys, music; Daiki Minagawa, assistant producer; Tailun Zhang, production sound mixer/boom operator; Saaya Minami, production assistant; Yukari Narahara, graphic designer; Norio Hozaki, Tokorozawa unit location manager.

For performing in the video series: Konomi Tanikawa, Coralie, Takatoshi Kurosawa, Saki Ohwada, Kenji Iida, Hiroko Shinkai, Yui Nikaido, Hiromasa Ishibashi, Ryuki Endo, Kirio Yoshimura, Emi Soma, Kiyomi Ohsawa, Ichio Ohsawa, Mika Ogata, Taro Makimura, Yoshio Shimada, Ririko Izawa, Ayana Hirata, Sachika Hayashi, Tohko Maehara, Goichiro Yoneyama, Kana Yoshimura, Fuzuki Iguchi, Yuki Okusato, Ayano Niwa, Saki Kawamura, Antonella Borrelli, Kirara Sakai, Haruka Fujishiro, Shihomi Hamaya, Mitsuji Higashimoto, Anna Nagai, Takamichi Masui, Takeshi Nishimagi, and members of the Aikido Kobayashi Dojo Tokorozawa Dojo.

For arranging and providing locations for the video production: Shinsei Service, LLC; Asobiba 101, Mr. and Mrs. Ohsawa, Mr. and Mrs. Saito, Monjayaki Okonomiyaki Warabe,

Hiroaki Kobayashi and Aikido Kobayashi Dojo, Naomi Noda, Natsumi Ito, and Waseda University Tokorozawa Campus.

For funding support for the video production: US Department of Education Title VI grant to The Ohio State University East Asian Studies Center.

For script rehearsal video production: Andy Watabe (Brigham Young University).

For funding support for the script rehearsal video production: the College of Humanities, Brigham Young University.

For the illustrations: Haruna Shikata, who created the main characters and facial expression icons; Sylvia Yu (Washington University in St. Louis), who created the mascots; Elizabeth Callahan (Brigham Young University), who assisted with the creation of illustrations for the *Activity Book*; Shawna Lawlor (Brigham Young University), who created the models for symbol production practice; Ayaka Horii (Linfield College), who created the models for symbol production practice in an earlier draft; Sarah Rigall (Brigham Young University), who assisted with editing the illustrations and reading/writing activities.

For funding support for illustrations, editing reading/writing activities, and creating the models for symbol practice: the College of Humanities and the Department of Asian and Near Eastern Languages, Brigham Young University.

For funding support for illustrations: The Asian Studies Center, University of Pittsburgh.

For reading and commenting on the earlier drafts of Scene scripts: Sachiko Takabatake Howard, Noriko Kanisawa Kowalchuck, Junzo Oshimo (the University of Pittsburgh); Teppei Kiyosue, Yuko Kuwai, Hiromi Tobaru, Shun Maruyama, Ying Zhang, and Eri Terada (The Ohio State University).

For field testing and commenting on the field test versions of the *Main Text*, *Activity Book*, and audio files: Sachiko Takabatake Howard, Noriko Kanisawa Kowalchuck, and Junzo Oshimo (University of Pittsburgh); Yuko Kuwai, Hiromi Tobaru, Shun Maruyama, Yeri McClain, Ying Zhang, Lindsay Stirek, Kayo Puthawala, and Shoichi Ueda (The Ohio State University); Alan Wortham and Sarah Cox Smith (Brigham Young University); Makoto Morioka and Mariko Kain (Columbus State Community College); Cong Li (Duke-Kunshan University); Joseph Mesics (Johnsbury Academy); Karen Curtin (Portland State University); James-Henry Holland and Kyoko Ishida Klaus (Hobart and William Smith Colleges); and all of the students who studied with the earlier drafts and provided invaluable feedback.

For funding support for the lesson plan development associated with field testing: US Department of Education Title VI grant to The Ohio State University East Asian Studies Center.

Proofreading: Elizabeth Hengeveld, Hiroko Yoshii (University of Missouri, St. Louis), Mami Chujo, and Chiaki Yoshikawa.

Many thanks to the editors at Routledge for encouraging us to launch this project.

To our life partners, Galal Walker, Elizabeth Hengeveld, Marvin Marcus, Jeneal Luft, Alyssa Tsuchiya, and Sheldon Safko, for their unflagging support and trust in our ability to carry out this project.

We are very grateful to all of the above for assisting us with every aspect of the production of these materials. Any errors or omissions are solely the responsibility of the authors.

Prologue

Objectives and expectations

We assume that your objective in studying Japanese is to be able to use the language to interact with people in a culturally coherent way. This objective coincides with the goals of this material—to help learners become able to use Japanese to participate in Japanese culture. In other words, you will be able to follow Japanese cultural norms to express yourself in ways that are in line with your own intentions and to comprehend the intentions of others. Primarily we address verbal expressions, both spoken and written, though we also attend to non-verbal expressions such as body language, facial expressions, and even silence.

We assume that you have no previous background in the formal study of Japanese, though it is quite likely that most beginning learners have had some level of exposure to Japanese language and behavior. Some of the "Scenes" you encounter may already be familiar to you. We expect that you will engage yourself actively in all of the Scenes, assuming roles of the actors in the Scenes and understanding the circumstances that determine how actors carry out their intentions through language. Important factors to notice are the time and place of the Scene, the roles of the participants in the Scene, and the influence of any bystanders. We refer to this kind of active engagement as "performance." The vocabulary and the sentence structures you learn are simply tools you will need to perform successfully in Japanese culture. Your objective in using *NihonGO NOW!* is to continuously expand your repertoire for performing in Japanese culture.

Means

NihonGO NOW! is a program to enhance your performance in Japanese through the resources of the *Textbook*, the *Activity Book*, and online materials. *NihonGO NOW!* supports self-managed learning, but a Teachers' Manual, available online, provides resources for instructors. The program is organized into 24 "Acts" (幕) or learning units. Each Act consists of a Speaking and listening (S/L; 話す・聞く) section and a Reading and writing (R/W; 読み書き) section. In a typical Act, there are six Scenes (場) focusing on listening and speaking and two to three Scenes for reading and writing.

Practicing listening and speaking will require extensive work with audio materials. You need to train your brain to process sequences of sounds, either in production or reception, quite automatically, always connecting them to intentions expressed in context. Expect to use a significant portion of your study time with audio materials. Use visual materials (video clips, illustrations, photographs) and text to enhance your audio-centered study. Reading and writing will require processing of text. We also provide audio materials to enhance your study of written texts.

Here are the resources provided in this program and how to utilize them for effective and efficient study of Japanese. All audio and video materials are available online.

Textbooks: 2 volumes, 12 Acts in each volume. Each Act presents several Scenes.

Elements of a Scene (場) in the *Textbook*

Elements	What you should do
Scene title	Read the English equivalent and look at the Japanese. Focus on what the Scene is about.
場面 Setting: a short description of the Scene.	Read and know the circumstances in which this performance is set, what roles the speakers have, and what they are doing. How would you perform in this Scene? Consider any bystanders who may be there, even if they are not actively speaking.
台詞 Script (in S/L section): what the actors do in this performance.	1. Listen to the audio and visualize what you are hearing without looking at the textbook. 2. View the video (if available). Did your visualization come close to the Scene you see? What do you think is going on? 3. Read the English equivalent. How close were you in guessing what is going on? What things can you already say in Japanese? What do you need to learn that is new? 4. Look through the Japanese and confirm what looks familiar to you and what appears to be new. Romanization is provided for Acts 1 through 4 to help you with this process. Do not try to decode everything by looking at the Japanese script. Use your ears! 5. Work with the audio files to learn to perform the Scene (see procedures in the audio files section below.) 6. Practice repeating the lines, using the Build-up audio file. Use the reverse build-up technique on the Build-up audio, where you begin at the end of a sentence and add elements preceding it step-by-step. 7. Use Role Play audio files to practice role play, paying attention to the communicative purpose of what you are saying. Practice until you can play each role without stopping the audio file. 8. Perform the script in the appropriate context (in class).

Elements	What you should do
テキストText (in R/W section): what you read as part of your performance.	1. View the Text layout and skim it for general content. What message is being conveyed? Scan for key items you would expect to see. 2. Listen to the audio as you follow the text. How close were you in guessing what is going on? What parts could you already read? What sequences did you need to learn that are new? 3. Read the English equivalent to confirm your understanding. 4. If appropriate, read the Text out loud. 5. Consider what you would do in response to reading this Text.
単語と表現 Vocabulary and expressions: The items that are shaded are used in the Scene Script. Others may be substituted in the script to create new performances.	1. Go through the list and know how each item is used or might be substituted in the Scene. 2. Work with the audio to learn how to say the items. Repeat each item while looking at the English provided in the text. Review and repeat those items that are more challenging. 3. Imagine a new Scene, for which you can use the additional vocabulary. Try performing that new Scene.
文字と例 Symbols and examples (in R/W Section): new symbols along with short phrases in which the new symbols are used. For the most part, the R/W section only uses vocabulary and expressions that have been practiced in the S/L sections of the same or preceding Acts. When new vocabulary and expressions are introduced (with the "+" mark in the R/W section), study them and imagine the contexts in which they may be used. Items marked with # are for reference only, and those marked with ¥ mark are familiar words that contain unintroduced kanji.	1. Look at each symbol, paying attention to the stroke shape and the overall composition. You may want to trace it and write it on your own a few times. 2. Listen to the audio files as you view the examples. 3. Read the English equivalent provided. 4. Look at the examples while saying the words you see out loud. Avoid isolating symbols in the examples. Think of contexts in which these sequences may be found in writing. 5. Read the examples out loud. Can you do this at a normal speaking speed?
拡張 Expansion: suggestions for expanding your vocabulary that are specific to your personal interests and professional specialization.	* Not every Scene has this section. Once you have a handle on the performance according to the script provided, follow the suggestion to discover how expressions that are specific to your interest are rendered in Japanese. Substitute these items in the script to create new Scenes. This will expand and personalize your performance repertoire.

Elements	What you should do
舞台裏 Behind the Scenes (BTS in S/L Section): explanations about productive features of the language, cultural themes, and strategies for participating in Japanese culture.	1. Read the BTS title and recall how the feature was rendered in the Scene script. 2. Read the explanation. This should help you understand how the Scene is structured, what strategies you can use, and how you can use the language productively. 3. Go over the examples. Adding these examples to your repertoire will expand your performance power immensely.
解説 Between the Lines (BTL in R/W Section): features of the written language and strategies for participating in Japanese culture through text.	These explanations appear throughout the section. Read them carefully. This should help you understand how the symbols are used in Japanese writing as well as strategies for using the written language in your performance.

Elements of a Scene (場) in the *Activity Book*

The *Activity Book* provides Practice (練習) and Assessment (評価) activities and pages on which to write down your reactions or responses for practice activities.

練習 Practice: activities you should do in preparation for Scene rehearsal (in class). They focus on the new forms introduced, but also provide valuable opportunities for review and use of familiar things in new contexts.	Most activities in the S/L section and many in the R/W section entail working with audio. Follow the directions provided. Aim for fluency and accuracy as you interpret and express intentions. 　　Always visualize the Scene in your mind. Where are you? What role are you playing? What do others in the Scene look like? What are you all doing? What intentions are expressed and interpreted? The more concrete you can make these images, the more effective the practice will be.
理解練習 Comprehension Practice	Read the context provided, then listen to the audio files and answer questions. Write your answers in the Activity Book.
実演練習 Performance Practice	Read the context provided, then practice appropriate responses, using the pattern provided in the examples. The audio files may provide a cue. After your speech, check the model provided in the audio file and repeat it to confirm. There are often multiple ways to do or say the same thing. The model shows how you can use what you have learned to manage the performance effectively. 　　If English descriptions or illustrations provide the cue, the model may include a response to the speech. Listen to both the model and the response.
腕試し Tryout: activities to test your knowledge of performance outside of class	* Not every Scene has this section. Follow the instructions and try using your skills in the real world at the right moment. You and the people you interact with will be the judge of your level of performance. Report to your instructor how well your Tryout went.

読み練習　Reading Practice:	1. Read the items quietly while listening to the audio files and imagining Scenes in which they may be used. 2. Read them again silently without the help of the audio. What intensions are expressed? 3. Read each item out loud. Can you do this at a normal speaking speed with full comprehension of what you are saying?
文字練習　Symbol Practice	Do this before class in which writing is practiced. Practice handwriting the symbols step-by-step.
書き練習　Writing Practice	Do this before class in which writing is practiced. 　Practice writing words and phrases and composing texts in the appropriate Japanese script. Some of your "writing" practice will entail inputting Japanese on an electronic device. For other practice, write in the space provided in the Activity Book or use appropriate writing sheets, such as 原稿用紙 *genkooyooshi* (the writing sheets with a set number of cells) as instructed by your teacher.
評価 Assessment: review activities that test your ability to participate in the culture.	
聞いてみよう Listening Comprehension: Similar to Comprehension Practice, but the content is more comprehensive and challenging.	Read the context provided, then listen to the audio file and answer questions. Write your answers on the answer sheet provided in the Activity Book.
使ってみよう Dry Run: speaking practice based on contextual cues.	Read the context outlined in the textbook and try to express it (always thinking about culture) using the strategies you have learned. Listen to the audio to see if your version was similar to the sample. There may be multiple ways to do the same thing in addition to the sample provided.
読んでみよう Contextualized Reading	1. Read the context and imagine what text you might expect to see in it. 2. Look at the overall contour of the text. What kind of information would you expect to see in different locations within the text? 3. Read the questions and consider where you might find the information necessary to answer them. 4. Read the text, working with words and phrases rather than isolated symbols. This "chunking" is an important strategy for reading. 5. Write your answers in the Activity Book.

書_かいてみよう Contextualized Writing	1. Read the context and imagine the overall contour of what you would produce. 2. Identify what you will need to convey through writing. 3. Compose. If you don't remember the exact symbol, use a place holder and finish composing. Then review, if necessary, to replace the place holders with appropriate symbols.
書_かき取_とり Dictation	1. Listen to the audio. Listen until you have a good understanding of what you are hearing. 2. Repeat what you heard silently in your mind with full comprehension of what you are saying. Imagine the context in which you might be putting it into writing. 3. Write what you are able to say and understand.
知_しってる? What do you know?: questions to check your understanding of the BTS/BTL items.	Write your answers on the answer sheet provided in the Activity Book.

Audio files are available online for Scene Scripts, Vocabulary and Expressions, Comprehension Practice, Speaking Practice, Comprehension, and Dry Run in the Speaking/Listening section. For the Reading/Writing section, audio files are available for Text, Symbols and Examples, Reading Practice, and Dictation. For speaking practice, always speak—do not whisper—at a comfortable volume and try to build up your speed until you are able to speak at a natural tempo. Think concretely about the context in which these performances work.

Video files online depict the Scenes. Use these to situate the Scenes clearly in the cultural context. Ask yourself who is involved. Do you know the characters and their backgrounds? Why are they doing what they are doing? As you practice with the audio, imagine these Scenes.

Symbol practice sheets are found in Appendix A in the Activity Book.

Check the website for additional learning resources that will become available at www.routledge.com/9781138304147, such as an English-Japanese glossary, a list of BTS and BTL, and a full list of different types of verbs, classifiers, and conjugations. Links to useful resource sites are also available online.

The Teacher's Manual and additional resources for teachers are also available online. They include additional practice and assessment ideas, along with points to focus on in class, and responses to frequently asked questions.

Special Symbols used in the reading and writing section:

#: for your reference only. These expressions won't appear in practice activities until they are introduced in the Speaking and Listening portion.

+: new expression that is to be learned. These may appear in practice activities.

¥: for those expressions that have already been introduced but when written in Japanese include kanji that have not yet been introduced. The kanji representation is for reference only.

Main places and characters

Humans have an amazing ability to join and adapt to multiple social circles and adjust their behaviors to the expectations of each of these circles, taking on different roles as they do. Even if the circles within which you use Japanese may be somewhat limited now, the potential for expanding those circles has no limit. *NihonGO NOW!* presents Scenes that take place in various circles of interaction that are representative of circles that you are likely to experience. Your objective is to become able to handle the many situations depicted in these Scenes while also allowing the Japanese people in these Scenes to feel comfortable interacting with you.

Not all of the Scenes may seem immediately relevant to all learners. For example, if you are a college student, you might find the business Scenes somewhat remote. If you are a professional and have already completed your higher education, the college Scenes may seem less than useful. However, developing the experiential knowledge or handling these Scenes adds to your capacity to move from one circle to another within the Japanese context. So you should practice the roles, including those of the Japanese people in each Scene. You should strive to perform smoothly and accurately all of the Scenes depicted in Level 1. Some of the Scenes in Level 2 are used to practice narration. In that case, your aim is to assume that you have engaged in the performance presented and focus on narrating what happened. Remember also that expressions used in every Scene may be transferred to other Scenes with adjustments, linguistic or non-linguistic.

The circles of people and places—what can be called 'sagas'—that you can experience through this material are depicted in the following diagrams.

サーシャ・モリス (25)
Saasha Morisu
Sasha MORRIS

An intern at the Ogaki Trading （大垣商会）company in
Tokyo. Originally from Missouri, she graduated from Clinton
University in Oregon. She shares an apartment with her Japanese
friend, Eri.

神田健太 (32)
KANDA Kenta

八木礼子部長 (53)
Reiko YAGI-bucho

山田恵理 (26)
YAMADA Eri

An office worker at the
Ogaki Trading; he helps
interns.

Head of the division at
Ogaki Trading where Sasha
and Kenta work. She has
three children—a son who is
the oldest and twins, a boy
and a girl.

Sasha's roommate. A graduate
student at Fukuzawa
University's School of Human
Science. Assists Sakamoto-
sensei in the Japanese language
program. Originally from Kyoto.

ブライアン・ワン (20)
Buraian Wan
Brian WANG

A student at Clinton University, participating in study abroad at Fukuzawa University, having a home stay with the Shirai family in Saitama.

白井一郎 (16)
しらいいちろう
SHIRAI Ichiroo

Brian's host brother. A high school student, he goes to the community Aikido Club with Brian.

坂本優子先生 (47)
さかもとゆうこせんせい
Sakamoto Yuuko-sensei
Professor SAKAMOTO

Professor of Japanese at Fukuzawa University, Brian's Japanese language teacher. She is also Eri's academic advisor.

川村博 (21)
かわむらひろし
KAWAMURA Hiroshi

A junior at Fukuzawa University. He volunteers as Brian's language partner. Also a member of the university swimming club.

鈴木彩乃 (27)
すずきあやの
SUZUKI Ayano

A recently promoted black belt at the Aikido club where Brian and Ichiro train. She is a biology teacher at a local high school.

エイミー・ジョンソン (20)
Eimii Jonson
Amy JOHNSON

A student studying Japanese and
business at Clinton University. She is
a member of the Japanese Language
Club and works part time on campus.

松浦 孝 (21)
MATSUURA Takashi

A Japanese student from
Fukuzawa University on study
abroad at Clinton University
in Oregon, where he belongs
to the Japanese Language
Club.

We have two mascots for this course: Go-kun and Nyau-chan.

プロローグ

目的と期待できる成果

学習者の目標は文化に呼応した形で日本語を用いて人と交わることと言えます。同様に、本教材の目標は、学習者による日本語を用いて文化に根ざした様々な活動への参加を支援することにあります。学習者が日本の文化的な規範に沿いながら自らの意図を表現し、他の人の意図を解釈できることを目指しています。主に言語表現を扱いますが、ボディーランゲージや顔の表情、あるいは無言でいることを含む非言語表現も扱います。

　本シリーズの第1巻は、過去にフォーマルな日本語学習経験を有さない学習者を対象としています。もちろん、多くの学習者は何らかの形で日本語の言語行動に触れているでしょう。本シリーズの「シーン」の中には、既に見たこと、聞いたことのあるような場面もあるかもしれません。そのような場面も含め、学習者に期待するのはすべての「シーン」に能動的に関わり、登場人物を取り巻いて行動を左右する状況を理解しながら、その人物を演じることです。ここで重要になるのは、シーンの展開する時間的状況、場所的状況、人物の立場、さらに傍観者の影響です。このような要素と実際の行動によって成り立つ能動的な関わりを、「パフォーマンス」と呼んでいます。シーンを通して学ぶ語彙や文法は、日本文化に呼応した「パフォーマンス」を支える道具に過ぎません。『日本語 NOW!』の目標は、学習者による日本文化におけるパフォーマンスの領域を継続的に広げていくことにあります。

手順

『日本語 NOW!』は教科書、アクティビティブック、オンライン教材の三本柱で学習者のパフォーマンスを広げるサポートをします。これらの学習リソースを使った独学も可能ですが、教師マニュアルを含む教師のためのサポートもオンラインで展開します。このプログラムは24幕 (Acts) の単元から成ります。各幕は、話す・聞く (S/L) と読み書き (R/W) のセクションによって構成され、通常、ひとつの幕に、6つの話す・聞くの場 (Scene) と、1〜3の読み書きのテキスト(Scene) が紹介されています。

話す・聞くの練習には音教材が欠かせません。学習者は、多種多様な状況のもとで音情報を瞬時にプロセスして意図を素早く表現したり理解する力を習得しなければなりません。授業に備えた自習時間の大半は音教材を使った学習に当てることになります。その時、動画やイラスト、写真、文字などの視覚教材の使い方次第で、学習の効果も変わってきます。読み書き練習はテキストをプロセスする練習です。このためにも音教材を用います。

　本シリーズが提供する学習リソースと、その有効的な使い方は以下の通りです。動画、音教材、その他のサポート教材はオンライン上で提供します。

　4巻から成る教科書の各幕(Act)はいくつかのシーン(場、Scene)を提供しています。

教科書のシーン(場)の内容と使い方

要素	学習者がすること
シーンのタイトル	英語のタイトルを読んでから日本語を見て、どのようなシーンかを考える。
セッティング(Setting)	読んで、場の状況(時間、場所、登場人物の立場、傍観者)を理解し、自分がその状況にいたらどのような行動をとるか、考えてみる。
セリフ(Script)、登場人物の行動	1. 教科書を見ずに音声ファイルの声を聞いて登場人物の行動を視覚想定化してみる。 2. 付録の動画がある場合はそれを観て、1で想定した場面や状況を調整する。 3. セリフの英語版を読んで、1、2で想定した登場人物の行動を振り返る。知っている日本語で言える部分、新たに学習する必要のある部分を頭の中で分けてみる。 4. 日本語(あればローマ字)のセリフを見ながら、オーディオを聞き、3で行った仕分けを頭の中でチェックする。日本語のセリフや単語を書き取ることはしない。ローマ字は第1〜第4幕のみに提示されている。 5. 音教材を使って、パフォーマンスの準備をする。 　a. リピート(B-up)音声ファイルを用いて、各文の最後の部分から始め、徐々に前にある要素を付け足しながら滑らかに言えるまで練習する。 　b. Role play音声ファイルを用いて、登場人物のそれぞれのセリフを相手との掛け合いの形で練習する。セリフは行動の一部と考え、顔の表情やボディランゲージ、間合いなども考慮する。 6. 状況に合わせてパフォーマンスをする。(教室ではそのリハーサルを行う)

テキスト(読み書きセクションのText)	1. 全体のレイアウトを見て内容の予測をする。 2. 音声ファイルがあればそれを聞きながら文字を追い、1の予測を修正する。よく理解した部分と、新たに学習すべき部分を頭の中で整理する。 3. テキストの英語を読み、全体の理解を確認する。 4. 声を出して読むタイプのテキストの場合は音読してみる。 5. このテキストを読んだあとで、どのような行動をするか考えてみる。
単語と表現 (話す・聞くセクションの Vocabulary and expressions)	1. リストを見て、それぞれの単語・表現がシーンの中でどのように使われているか、あるいはどのように使えるかを考える。 2. 音声ファイル (Vocab) を聞いて意味を確かめながらリピート練習をする。 3. 追加単語をシーンに応用して新たなパフォーマンスを試みる。
文字と例(読み書きセクションのSymbols and examples)新出文字を用いた例文は既習の語彙表現のみを使っている。例外的に新たな語彙表現が導入される場合は＋印で、参考として未習事項を紹介する場合は#印、紹介された語彙で未習漢字を含む語彙は¥印で表示している。	1. 紹介された文字を見る。文字全体の構成やそれぞれの画の形態に注意を払う。文字をトレースしてもよい。 2. 音声ファイルを聴きながら例文を目で追う。 3. 例文の英語を読んで意味を確認する。 4. 例文を見て知っている言葉を口に出してみる。単語や文単位で見るようにし、例文から文字だけを単独で取り出さないようにする。それぞれの例文が使われる状況を想定してみる。 5. 例文を声に出して読む。普通に話す程度の速さで読めることを目指す。
拡張(話す・聞くのExpansion) 個々の専門や生活に特化した語彙表現を基本の語彙表現に加える。	*すべてのシーンにあるわけではない。 スクリプトに沿ったパフォーマンスができるようになったら、提示されたストラテジーを使い、周りの日本語話者との交流を通して、個別に必要な語彙表現を増やす。
舞台裏(話す・聞くセクションのBehind the Scenes, BTS)文法、文化事項や談話のストラテジーの説明	4. BTSのタイトルを読んで、シーンのどの部分がそのBTSに該当するかを考える。 5. BTSの説明を読む。シーンの構成や話者のストラテジーを学んで、より広い語用の可能性を模索する。 6. BTSにある例文を読み、口に出してみて、どのような場面で使えるかを考える。

解説(読み書きセクションの Between the lines, BTL)書き言葉独特の表現やストラテジーについての解説	注意して読む。紹介されている文字の使い方や書き言葉のストラテジーを学ぶ。

　教科書と対応したアクティビティブックには、練習と評価のセクションがあり、練習によっては答えを記入するスペースがあります。

アクティビティブックの内容

練習(Practice)授業のリハーサルに備える活動。新出事項に焦点を当てつつ、既習事項も新しい状況で使うことによって復習を兼ねながらパフォーマンス力を高める。	ほとんどの話す・聞くのセクションの練習と、一定の読み書き練習は、音声ファイルを使用しながら行う。淀みなく意図を理解したり、表現したりすることを目指す。 練習は、常にパフォーマンスのシーンを意識しながら行う。置かれている場面や状況、登場人物の立場や表現、そして表現の裏にある意図などの要素を、より具体的にイメージする。
• 　理解練習（Comprehension practice）	提示された状況を読んで理解した上で音声ファイルを聞き、答えを記入する。
• 　実演練習（Performance practice）	提示された状況を読んで理解した上で、音声ファイルの会話の例にしたがって会話の一方の発話をする。その後、音声ファイルにあるモデルを聴いて、必要に応じて会話をやり直す。意図が同じでも、実際の発話には複数の可能性があることが多い。音声ファイルに示すものは、これまで学習したことを有効に使えるサンプルである。
腕試し(Tryout)習得できたパフォーマンスを教室の外で使ってみる。	*すべてのシーンにあるわけではない。 指示にしたがって、習得したパフォーマンスのスキルを教室外の適当な場面で使ってみる。出来不出来の評価は学習者を含む当事者に委ねられる。 腕試しの成果を担当の教師に報告する。
読み練習（Reading practice）	1. 音声ファイルを聴きながらテキストを目で追う。どのようなシーンで見るものか、考える。 2. 音声ファイルを聞かずに黙読する。どのような意図が表現されているのか考える。 3. 音読してみる。内容をよく理解しながら、普通に話す程度の速さで読めることを目指す。
文字練習（Symbol practice）	授業で書き練習を行う前にしておく。 表示された手順に従って文字を書く練習をする。

書き練習（Writing practice）	授業で書き練習を行う前にしておく。 手書き、または電子端末を使い、日本語の表記を用いて作文をする。手書きの場合は、教師の指示に従って、アクティビティブックの付録にある練習シートや原稿用紙などを用いる。
評価 Assessment	
聞いてみよう（Listening Comprehension）	状況説明を読み、音声ファイルの会話を聴いて質問に答える。答えはアクティビティブックの付録にあるシートに記入する。
使ってみよう（Dry run）	状況説明を読み、学習したストラテジーを意識しながら提示された意図を表現してみる。音ファイルのサンプルを聞いて、自分の表現と比較する。一つの状況でも複数の対処法がある。音声ファイルにあるものは一つのサンプルに過ぎないので、教師は学生が考えたやり方を聞いて評価を付けたり、別の方法を提示したりする。
読んでみよう（Contextualized reading）	1. 状況説明を読んで、その状況でどのようなテキストを目にするか想起する。 2. 全体のレイアウトを見て、どこに、どのような種類の情報が表示されているか考える。 3. 問題を読み、テキストのどの部分に答えがあるか見当をつける。 4. テキストを読む。文字単位ではなく、単語、文単位の情報を汲み取るようにする。 5. 答えをアクティビティブックの所定の箇所に記入する。
書いてみよう（Contextualized writing）	1. 状況説明を読んで、これから書くテキストの全体像を想定する。 2. 書き言葉で意図を表現するために、何が必要か、確認する。 3. 作文する。特定の文字が思い出せない場合は、文字の場所を空けておきながら、文章全体をまず仕上げる。その後、読み返しながら、空白部分に適当な文字を挿入する。
書き取り（Dictation）	1. 音声ファイルの声を聞いて内容をよく理解する。 2. 聞いて理解したことを頭の中で確認しながら、その内容を書き記す状況を考える。 3. 自分で理解し、言える内容を表記する。
知ってる？（What do you know?） BTS/BTL の理解度チェック	アクティビティブックの付録にある記入用紙に答えを記入する。

音声ファイルは全てオンラインでアクセスできます。シーンパフォーマンスの準備をしたり、練習をしたりする場合、ひそひそ声を使わず、はっきりした発声を心がけ、自然なペースで発話できるようにしてください。また、そのようなパフォーマンスをする状況をなるべく具体的に考えて描いてみると良いでしょう。

　動画ファイルもオンラインでアクセスできます。動画は、それぞれのシーンの文化的状況を具体的に把握するために使います。誰がどのような立場で行動しているのか、何故そのような行動をしているのか考え、音声ファイルを用いた練習の時に、そのイメージを思い浮かべてください。

　プログラムサイト[Insert URL content from publisher]には順次新しい学習リソース、教師用リソースを掲載していきます。

主要な登場人物と場所的背景

私たちは同時に多くのグループに属し、それぞれのグループの中で異なる立場を維持しつつ、グループ間を絶えず移動しながら生活しています。学習者が日本語を使うグループは、最初はごく限られているかもしれませんが、その可能性は無限に広がっています。『日本語 NOW!』は学習者が遭遇するであろう複数のグループを想定し、そこで起こるシーンを提示しています。これらのシーンで起こり得る様々な状況に柔軟に対応し、そこで遭遇する日本語話者と円滑に交流していくことが、本シリーズを用いる日本語学習者の目標です。

　提示される全てのシーンが、全ての学習者の生活に密着しているとは限りません。大学生にとって、ビジネスシーンは無関係のように思えるかもしれません。逆に、社会人にとっては、大学のシーンは過去のものと感じられるかもしれません。しかし、これらのシーンでの行動を体験的に学ぶことは、学習者が複数のグループ間を自由に行き来できるようになることと密接に繋がっています。日本人の役を含め、一見、個々の学習者の「今の自分」とはかけ離れた役どころでも、シーンに登場する全ての役を演じる練習が、日本語能力を深めます。最初の12幕のシーンでは、全ての役を淀みなく演じられるよう練習してください。後半12幕は、ナレーションを含みます。ナレーションでは、シーンのセリフそのままではなく、ナレーションサンプルの構成とストラテジーを使って、起こったことを他の人に話す練習をします。

　特定の人々や特定の場所で起こることをサガと言います。『日本語 NOW!』で扱うサガは、以下の図にまとめられます。

サーシャ・モリス (25)

大垣商会東京支社のインターン。ミズーリ出身。オレゴン州クリントン大学卒業。日本人の友人の恵理とアパート同居。

神田健太 (32)

大垣商会の会社員。インターンのサポート役。

八木礼子部長 (53)

大垣商会の部長。長男と双子の次男と長女の母親。

山田恵理 (26)

サーシャのルームメート。福沢大学人間科学部の大学院生。日本語のプログラムで坂本先生のアシスタントを務める。京都出身。

ブライアン・ワン (20)

クリントン大学の学生。福沢大学
に留学中。埼玉県在住の白井家で
ホームステイ中。

白井一郎 (16)

ブライアンのホームステイ先の息
子。高校生。ブライアンとともに
地元の合気道クラブに通う。

坂本優子先生 (47)

福沢大学日本語の教授。ブ
ライアンの日本語の教師。
恵理の指導教官。

川村博 (21)

福沢大学3年生。ボラン
ティアでブライアンのラ
ンゲッジパートナー。大
学の水泳部部員。

鈴木彩乃 (27)

ブライアンと一郎の通
う合気道クラブで黒帯
を取得。近辺にある高
校の生物学教師。

エイミー・ジョンソン (20)

クリントン大学の大学生。日本語と
ビジネスを専攻。日本語クラブのメ
ンバー。キャンパスでバイト中。

松浦孝 (21)
福沢大学の学生。留学中のク
リントン大学（オレゴン州）
で日本語クラブのメンバー。

NOW!にはゴー君、ニャウちゃんというマスコットキャラクターが登場します。

序幕 *Jomaku*
じょまく
Introduction

Instructional expressions part 1

Listen to the audio files and practice responding to these instructions with an appropriate action. You need not learn to say these expressions yourself, but need to react promptly when you hear your instructor say them.

はい。	Ha˥i.	Okay.
始めましょう。	Ha⌐jimemasho˥o.	Let's begin.
聞いてください。	Ki⌐ite kudasa˥i.	Please listen.
言ってください。	I⌐tte kudasa˥i.	Please say it.
答えてください。	Ko⌐ta˥ete ku⌐dasa˥i.	Please answer.
もう一回言ってください。	Mo⌐o ik-kai itte kudasa˥i.	Please say it again.
みんなで言ってください。	Mi⌐n'na˥ de i⌐tte kudasa˥i.	Please say it all together.
一人ずつ言ってください。	Hi⌐tori-zu˥tsu i⌐tte kudasa˥i.	Please say it one at a time.
もっと大きな声で話してください。	Mo˥tto ⌐o˥oki na ⌐ko˥e de ha⌐na˥ shite ku⌐dasa˥i.	Please talk louder.
本を見ないでください。	Ho˥n o ⌐mi˥nai de ku⌐dasa˥i.	Please don't look at the book.
携帯を見ないでください。	Ke⌐itai o mi˥nai de ku⌐dasa˥i.	Please don't look at your phone.
書いてください。	Ka˥ite ku⌐dasa˥i.	Please write it.
終わります。	O⌐warima˥su.	That's all for today (used at the end of a class).

Basic greetings

Work with the audio files until you are able to use these phrases intentionally and you are comfortable responding to others appropriately when you hear them use the phrases.

おはようございます。	O⌐hayoo gozaima˥su.	Good morning (formal).
こんにちは。	Ko⌐n'nichi wa.	Hello.
こんばんは。	Ko⌐nban wa.	Good evening.
ありがとうございました。	A⌐ri˥gatoo go⌐zaima˥shita.	Thank you (for what you have done).

Basic greetings

a *Ohayoo gozaimasu* is the first greeting of the day. If you know the person well, *ohayoo* is fine. You should always greet your teacher or other superiors with the full form, *ohayoo gozaimasu,* because it is more polite. It is also expected that lower-ranking people initiate the greeting (speak first) to their superiors.

b *Konnichi wa* is used at other times of the day, before evening. But *konnichi wa* is not used between family members or friends. (See *otsukaresama* in Act 1 Scene 11.)

c *Konban wa* is the standard greeting when you meet people in the evening.

d *Arigatoo gozaimashita* is used to thank someone for what they have done. This is an appropriate thing to say to your instructor after class, before leaving the classroom.

お辞儀 *Ojigi* Bowing

All languages have gestures and body language that are peculiar to the culture. Japanese are well known for bowing—when they are introduced, when they say goodbye, and when they leave a room or office. Depending on the gravity of the situation, the bow might be a quick nod of the head (acknowledging a colleague in the hall) or a formal bow (when meeting a superior for the first time; when accepting a diploma). It is important to remember that your eyes should look down, not at the person you are addressing.

拡張 *Kakuchoo* Expansion
<ruby>かくちょう</ruby>

1 Observe someone bowing, either as they interact with you or with someone else. Pay attention to how deeply they bow, how many times they bow, the social situation (i.e., the type of relationship that the people who are bowing have with each other), and the immediate situation (i.e., why they are interacting with each other; for example, thanking, apologizing, greeting, etc.).
2 Ask someone how deeply they would bow in various situations, such as (a) greeting a friend, a teacher, or a boss; (b) being introduced to someone else; (c) thanking someone for something small (e.g., picking up something for you that you dropped) or something big (e.g., staying at someone's home for several days).

Japanese sounds and romanization

This book will present Japanese in two formats—romanization (*roomaji*) (the use of the Roman alphabet to represent Japanese sounds) and Japanese script. The Japanese writing system is extremely complex, and it can be helpful for beginning students to use romanization as a reminder of what Japanese sounds like when first learning how to speak. You will see Japanese represented in romanization for the first four Acts. At that point, you will have learned *hiragana*, and that will allow you to move to reading only in Japanese.

The romanization used here is a variation of one called Hepburn with slight modifications.

a. The mora

The mora (mora-like unit) is the basic unit of pronunciation in Japanese. The writing system is based on it, and Japanese literature, especially poetry, has mora count at its very core. All Japanese words are made up of morae that consist of:

a vowel (5 vowels in all: *a, i, u, e, o* in the left-most column in the chart below);

or

a consonant plus a vowel (62 possible combinations in the top five rows and middle columns below);

or

a consonant plus a /y/ plus a vowel (33 possible combinations in the last three rows below) (note that /s/ plus/ /y/ is pronounced /sh/, /z/ plus /y/ is pronounced /j/, and /t/ plus /y/ is pronounced /ch/);

or

moraic *n* (in the last column on the right below). This /n/ is the only consonant that constitutes a mora all by itself in Japanese. It also assimilates to whatever follows, so before /m/ or /b/ it is pronounced /m/ (*shinbun* 'newspaper' is pronounced shimbun), before /t/ or /d/ it is pronounced /n/ (*hontoo* 'true' is pronounced *hontoo*), and before /k/ or /g/ it is pronounced /ng/ (*ginkoo* 'bank' is pronounced *gingkoo*). At the end of an utterance or before a vowel, it is pronounced with the tongue raised at the back of the mouth without making contact.

The morae of Japanese

a	ka	ga[1]	sa	za	ta	da	na	ha	pa	ba	ma	ya	ra	wa	
i	ki	gi	shi	ji	chi		ni	hi	pi	bi	mi		ri		
u	ku	gu	su	zu	tsu		nu	fu	pu	bu	mu	yu	ru		
e	ke	ge	se	ze	te	de	ne	he	pe	be	me		re		
o	ko	go	so	zo	to	do	no	ho	po	bo	mo	yo	ro		n
	kya	gya	sha	ja	cha		nya	hya	pya	bya	mya		rya		
	kyu	gyu	shu	ju	chu		nyu	hyu	pyu	byu	myu		ryu		
	kyo	gyo	sho	jo	cho		nyo	hyo	pyo	byo	myo		ryo		

The vowels are pronounced as follows:

a as in /father/
i as in /peak/
u as in /food/
e as in /egg/
o as in / tote/

In the column headed by *sa* note that *sh* (*shi, sha, shu, sho*) is pronounced with your tongue somewhere between your teeth and your alveolar ridge—not as far back as English /she/ and not as far forward as English /see/.

In the column headed by *ta*, note that *ch* (*chi, cha, chu, cho*) is similar. Try saying "cheese" with your tongue further forward and smiling.

Note that the Japanese /r/ is a flap of the tongue against the roof of your mouth, and that there is no l/r or b/v distinction in Japanese. So English *right* and *light* sound the same when borrowed into Japanese: *raito*. Similarly, *love* and *rub* collapse into *rabu*.

Finally, Japanese *fu* is pronounced by blowing air softly between rounded lips, not at all like English *fu* which finds your top teeth against your lower lip.

b. Long vowels and long consonants

Unlike English, Japanese has long—in terms of duration—vowels and consonants. (This should not be confused with long and short vowels in English). One-mora *chi* (血) 'blood' is not the same as two-mora *chii* (地位) 'rank.' *Obasan* (おばさん) 'aunt' should not be confused with *obaasan* (おばあさん) 'grandmother.' In the first member of each pair (*chi* and *obasan*) the vowel is short and clipped; in the second member of each pair (*chii* and *obaasan*) the vowel is longer in duration.

Here are some other word pairs that differ only in the length of the vowel:

2 morae	3 morae
shujin (主人)'husband'	*shuujin* (囚人) 'prisoner'
hire (鰭)'fin'	*hirei* (非礼) 'impoliteness'
riko (利己) 'self-interest'	*rikoo* (理工) 'science and technology'

Similarly, consonants can be long in Japanese. *Oto* 'sound' is two morae or two beats while *otto* 'husband' is three morae since the /t/ is held for an additional beat.

Here are some other word pairs that differ only in the length of the consonant:

2 morae	3 morae
hato 'dove'	*hatto* 'hat' (borrowed from English)
kona 'flour'	*konna* 'this kind of'

c. Pitch accent

As you listen to Japanese, you will notice that words are not distinguished by accent the way they are in English. English has what is called 'stress accent.' The difference between all of the following pairs

CONtent (noun)	conTENT (adjective)
INsult (noun)	inSULT (verb)
DIScharge (noun)	disCHARGE (verb)
TRUSTy (adjective)	trusTEE (noun)

is one of loudness. The first words in the pairs have their stress on the first mora. The second words in the pairs have their stress on the second mora. Stress accent is important at both the word level and the sentence level in English. Japanese on the other hand has "pitch accent" rather than stress accent. The pitch can change from mora to mora, and this distinguishes words. The word $_a{}^{me}$ whose second mora is pronounced with higher pitch means 'candy'; $^a{}_{me}$ with the first mora pitched higher means 'rain.' Here are more examples of word pairs in Japanese that differ only in pitch accent.

$_{ka}{}^{me}$ 'jug'	$^{ka}{}_{me}$ 'turtle'
$_{ha}{}^{shi}$ 'bridge'	$^{ha}{}_{shi}$ 'chopsticks'
$_{ka}{}^{ta}$ 'form'	$^{ka}{}_{ta}$ 'shoulder'

xlii

In this material, when we show pitch, the following convention will be used: a horizontal line above the text indicates that the next pitch rises until you see a vertical tail ˥ to indicate that the next pitch falls. (This is similar to the way that Japanese accent dictionaries indicate accent for speakers of Japanese.) The words above will be represented in the following way using these marks:

ka˹me 瓶(か˹め)   ka˥me 亀(か˥め)

ha˹shi 橋(は˹し)   ha˥shi 箸(は˥し)

ka˹ta 形(か˹た)   ka˥ta 肩(か˥た)

All Scenes in Act 1 through 4 will include the pitch profile. Here are some examples from Scene 1:

> Bu˹ra˥ian desu. This means that the pitch of /ra/ is higher than all of the other morae in this phrase.
> Yo˹roshiku onegai-shima˥su. This means that the pitch rises on the second mora /ro/ and falls on the last mora /su/. You may not hear the fall in pitch, because the /u/ of /su/ is usually voiceless, but it will be audible in other contexts.

Pay attention, too, to how pitch accent interacts with sentence intonation. In English, question intonation often rises across the sentence. When you say, "Do you understand?" the intonation rises consistently. In Japanese, the same question, Wa˹karima˥su ka? has pitch accent along with rising question intonation at the end on ka:

```
     karima    a
wa       su k
```

It is also possible that pitch may rise and never come down in Japanese. Intonation for the greeting konnichi wa does not fall, which never happens in English:

```
   nnichi wa
ko
```

Finally, you should be aware that pitch accent differs from dialect to dialect, and sometimes generation to generation. What you see here is a standard Tokyo pitch profile, but you should not be surprised to hear differences among speakers.

Now go to the Activity Book for 練 習 Renshuu Practice and 腕試し Udedameshi Tryout.

Note

1 Sometimes the /g/ sound of Japanese is a hard sound, as in give. Sometimes it is a softer sound like the /ng/ in singer. This is a matter of dialect. The soft /g/ never starts a word.

ねが
よろしくお願いします。

Yoroshiku onegai shimasu.

Nice to meet you.

ことわざ　*Kotowaza*　Words of wisdom[1]

いち ご いち え
一期一会　*Ichigo-ichie*
'Once in a lifetime' or '*carpe diem*' (seize the day).

◆ 話す・聞く *Hanasu/kiku* **Speaking and listening**

Scene 1-1　はい。 *Hai.* Present (i.e., I'm here.)

Brian is at an orientation meeting and the group's Japanese teacher, Professor Sakamoto, is taking attendance.

 ## The script

坂本先生	ブライアン
ブライアン・ワンさん。	はい。

Sakamoto-sensei	*Buraian*
Bu⌐raian Wa¹n-san.	*Ha⌐i.*

Professor Sakamoto	**Brian**
Brian Wang.	Present.

 ## 単語と表現 *Tango to hyoogen* Vocabulary and expressions

Names

ブライアン・ワン	*Buraian-Wan*	Brian Wang
モリス	*Morisu*	Morris
サーシャ	*Saasha*	Sasha
神田	*Kanda*	Kanda [family name]
白井	*Shirai*	Shirai [family name]
坂本	*Sakamoto*	Sakamoto [family name]

3

Titles

NAME 〜さん	NAME-*san*	Mr. or Ms. NAME
NAME 〜先生	NAME-*sensei*	Prof./Dr. NAME

Special expressions

はい	*hai*	present (in roll call); here you are (handing something over); got it (accepting something)
ええ	*ee*	yes (suggesting agreement or indicating understanding; less formal than *hai*)

Behind the Scenes

Behind the Scenes (BTS's) give you information that will help you make sense of individual expressions. BTS's contain notes about when, where, and how to use the language in a culturally appropriate way.

BTS 1 はい *Hai*

Hai has a number of uses including 'that's right,' 'here you are' (handing something over), 'got it' (accepting something that is handed to you or acknowledging a request), or, as is the case in this exchange, 'present' or 'here' in roll call. When someone calls your name in Japanese, it is customary to respond with a crisp *hai* to show your respect (especially to superiors). A less formal way of indicating agreement or understanding is *ee*. Either is appropriate in speaking to higher-ups.

BTS 2 Titles 〜さん -*san* and 〜先生 -*sensei*: うち *uchi* and そと *soto*

-*san* is a title that attaches to names in Japanese, and is roughly equivalent to Ms., Mrs., or Mr. Because English titles sound much more formal than -*san*, this book will use -*san* in translations from the Japanese. -*san* can be used with both given and family names, so Shirai Reiko might be called '*Shirai-san*' at work and '*Reiko-san*' by her acquaintances in the neighborhood. The convention for names in Japan is surname plus given name, so Shirai is a surname and Reiko a given name.

The title -*san* is never added to your own name or the names of people in your in-group when speaking to outsiders. Japanese people recognize a clear distinction between people who are in-group (*uchi*) and people who are out-group (*soto*), and this is reflected

よろしくお願いします。

everywhere in the language. In-group might be my company (in contrast to people from other companies), my family (in contrast to other's families), or just myself (in contrast to others in the situation). The boundaries of *uchi* and *soto* change from situation to situation, depending on who else is present. You will be hearing more about this crucial distinction in future Acts.

Dropping titles from other people's names is called *yobisute* (呼び捨て) in Japanese, and happens only within *uchi* (between close friends and family) or from supervisor to subordinate (especially when the supervisor wants to call attention to the relationship, such as when giving direct orders or reprimanding).

-sensei is a title of respect for anyone in a teaching or leadership role. It can also be used alone (without a name) to address or refer to these people. Like *-san*, *-sensei* is not attached to your own name. In addressing people, titles associated with occupation are used regularly either alone or in combination with the individual's last name. You will be learning more of them in the coming Acts.

Now go to the Activity Book for 練習 *Renshuu* Practice and 腕試し *Udedameshi* Tryout.

Notes

1 This lesson and all others will start off with a *kotowaza*. *Kotowaza* are Japanese proverbs or short sayings that give insight into Japanese culture. They are used regularly in Japanese discourse. We have selected one *kotowaza* for each of the chapters to get us going. You should talk about these phrases in class and with your Japanese friends.

Scene 1-2　はい、どうぞ。 *Hai, doozo.* Here you go.

Professor Sakamoto hands out a packet of materials to the students.

 The script

さかもとせんせい 坂本先生	ぶらいあん ブライアン
はい、どうぞ。	ありがとうございます。

Sakamoto-sensei	*Buraian*
Ha⌐i, do⌐ozo.	*A⌐ri⌐gatoo gozaimasu.*

Professor Sakamoto	**Brian**
Here you go (take it).	Thank you.

単語と表現 *Tango to hyoogen* Vocabulary and expressions

Special expressions

はい、どうぞ。	*hai, doozo*	Here you go (take it, do it).
どうぞ。	*doozo*	Go ahead.
ありがとうございます。	*arigatoo gozaimasu*	Thank you (for what you do/will do).
ありがとう。	*arigatoo*	Thank you. (informal)

BTS 3 More on はい *hai*

Here you see another use of *hai* to get the attention of another person, especially when there is an upcoming action that requires their awareness. You have heard this in the Instructional Expressions. Teachers often use this to signal that they are moving onto the next activity in class.

  Doozo by itself is best translated as 'go ahead.' When you offer something to someone—something to eat, a seat, an invitation to go through a door first—it is common to use the word *doozo* '(please,) go ahead.' See (*doozo*) *yoroshiku onegai-shimasu* below.

BTS 4 ありがとうございます。 *Arigatoo gozaimasu.* Thank you.

Arigatoo (gozaimasu) is used to thank someone for what they are doing or are going to do. *Arigatoo (gozaimashita)* is used to thank someone for what they did. *Gozaimasu/gozaimashita* makes *arigatoo* more polite, so you should always use the full form with your teacher or other superiors.

Now go to the Activity Book for 練習 *Renshuu* Practice and 腕試し *Udedameshi* Tryout.

1-2 よろしくお願いします。

7

Scene 1-3 お願いします。 *Onegai-shimasu.*
Please help me with this.

Professor Sakamoto is asking each student to sign a document.

The script

坂本先生	ブライアン (and other students)
すみません。お願いします。	はい。

Sakamoto-sensei	*Buraian* (and other students)
Suᴿmimaseˈn. Oᴿnegai-shimaˈsu.	Haˈi.

Professor Sakamoto	Brian (and other students)
Excuse me. Please help me with this.	Got it.

単語と表現 *Tango to hyoogen* Vocabulary and expressions

Special expressions

すみません・すいません	*su(m)imasen*	excuse me; I'm sorry; thank you
お願いします	*onegai-shimasu*	please help me with this

Behind the Scenes

BTS 5 すみません・すいません。 *Su(m)imasen.* Excuse me.

Sumimasen (or its slightly more informal alternative *suimasen*) has a variety of functions. It is used in this Scene as an attention getter. If you are in a shop and don't see the proprietor or a salesperson around, you can call "*Sumimasen!*" and someone will come to help you. It may also be used to offer a casual apology. It may be translated as 'thank you' when humbly accepting an offer, for example, or 'I see' when you acknowledge a reprimand without necessarily admitting guilt.

BTS 6 お願いします。 *Onegai-shimasu.*
Please help me with this.

The phrase *onegai-shimasu* by itself is an all purpose request for assistance: 'please help me with this' or 'please give me a hand here.' In the next Scene you will see *onegai-shimasu* in combination with *yoroshiku* (*yoroshiku onegai-shimasu*) meaning 'nice to meet you' or literally 'please treat me favorably').

Now go to the Activity Book for 練習 *Renshuu* Practice and 腕試し *Udedameshi* Tryout.

Scene 1-4 ブライアンです。 *Buraian desu.*
I'm Brian.

Brian Wang meets his host family for the first time. The host family knows his name in advance, so Brian introduces himself using his given name.

The script

ブライアン	白井さん（お母さん）
ブライアンです。	白井です。どうぞよろしく。
よろしくお願いします。	

Buraian	*Shirai-san (okaasan)*
Buˈraˈian desu.	*Shiˈrai deˈsu. Doˈozo yoroshiku.*
Yoˈroshiku onegai-shimaˈsu.	

Brian	Mrs. Shirai (the mother)
I'm Brian.	I'm Shirai. Nice to meet you.
It's nice to meet you.	

単語と表現 *Tango to hyoogen* Vocabulary and expressions

Special expressions

NAME です。	NAME *desu.*	I am NAME.
どうぞよろしく。	*Doozo yoroshiku.*	Nice to meet you.
よろしくお願いします。	*Yoroshiku onegai-shimasu.*	Nice to meet you.
どうぞよろしくお願いします。	*Doozo yoroshiku onegai-shimasu.*	Nice to meet you.

10

拡張 *Kakuchoo* Expansion

Use English to do this task. Ask a Japanese person to say your family name and given name(s) in Japanese and familiarize yourself with how they sound. Check to make sure that the way they are pronounced in Japanese does not coincide with any words or phrases in Japanese with inappropriate connotations.

Behind the Scenes

BTS 7 自己紹介 *Jikoshookai* Self-introduction

All cultures have ritual language—words and phrases that are virtually automatic in a given situation. Business people say 'How do you do?' when they meet. We say 'thanks' or 'thank you' when someone holds the door for us. Japan is well known for its emphasis on saying the right thing at the right time. Saying what's expected puts your listeners in the right frame of mind for what follows. Ritual expressions make people feel comfortable; they reassure Japanese people that you understand how Japan works.

Here you learn the simplest form of self-introduction, [NAME *desu*] 'I am NAME.' In ordinary circumstances, Japanese introduce themselves using their family name (*Wan desu*), and sometimes, but not always, in combination with their given name (*Buraian Wan desu*). When you are meeting peers or higher-ups (at work, in university clubs), this will be the usual convention. In Scene 1, Brian uses his given name because he is introducing himself to his host mother in Japan, who already knows Brian's family name.

You should do your best to "Japanize" the pronunciation of your name (adapt it to the Japanese sound system) because this is what Japanese do. It also makes it easier for Japanese listeners to understand. It is also a good idea to slow down when you say your name since your Japanese listeners are likely to be unfamiliar with English pronunciation.

BTS 8 名前 *Namae* Names

Remember that the convention for naming in Japan is family name first, given name second. Thus the members of the Tanaka family are Tanaka Ken (father), Tanaka Toshiko (mother), and Tanaka Naomi (daughter). What happens when foreigners go to Japan? How should they introduce themselves? What follows are guidelines for names. Don't be surprised to find exceptions and alternative conventions. a. Western names are expected in Western order: Sasha Morris is *Saasha Morisu*. Again, watch for exceptions. b. Chinese and Korean names are expected to follow the same convention as they do in their native languages—which is the same as Japan. Thus Liu Jing (Chinese) and Pak Yonsuk (Korean)

11

consist of family name plus given name. c. The kanji that are used for Chinese names frequently have different pronunciations in China and Japan. The kanji for the surname Wang in China (王) is pronounced '*Oo*' in Japanese. The name Zhang (張) in Chinese is pronounced '*Choo*' in Japanese. Chinese speakers should select the option that they feel most comfortable with. If you are an American of Chinese heritage, you have a choice. You can use the Chinese pronunciation or the Japanese pronunciation for your name. Similarly, you can use the Western order (given name first, family name second) or the Japanese order.

BTS 9 (どうぞ) よろしく (お願いします)。
(Doozo) yoroshiku (onegai-shimasu).

The phrase *(doozo) yoroshiku (onegai-shimasu)* literally means something like '(Treat me) favorably please.' It can be used in any number of circumstances where the other person will have some control over your fate: when you ask a favor, when you are going to be tested, when you join a group activity, and at the start of a meeting. More specifically, *(doozo) yoroshiku (onegai-shimasu)* marks the official beginning of a relationship, which is why it is so common in introductions. The longer form (with *doozo* 'by all means' and *onegai-shimasu* 'please') is more formal. Note that Brain, who is younger, uses the full phrase to his host mother, but the host mother uses the shorter form.

Now go to the Activity Book for 練習 *Renshuu* **Practice and** 腕試し *Udedameshi* **Tryout.**

Scene 1-5 では。 *De wa.* Well, then.

The orientation program is over and Professor Sakamoto signals that it's all right to leave.

The script

<ruby>坂本先生<rt>さかもとせんせい</rt></ruby>	<ruby>学生<rt>がくせい</rt></ruby>
では。	ありがとうございました。<ruby>失礼<rt>しつれい</rt></ruby>します

Sakamoto-sensei	*Gakusei*
De¹ wa.	*A⌐ri¹gatoo go⌐zaima¹shita. Shi⌐tsu¹rei-shi⌐ma¹su.*

Professor Sakamoto	Students
Well, then.	Thank you. Excuse me.

<ruby>単語<rt>たんご</rt></ruby>と <ruby>表現<rt>ひょうげん</rt></ruby> *Tango to hyoogen* Vocabulary and expressions

Special expressions

では。	*De wa.*	Well, then.
<ruby>失礼<rt>しつれい</rt></ruby>します。	*Shitsurei-shimasu.*	Excuse me.

Behind the Scenes

BTS 10 Signaling a turning point: では *De wa* Well, then

In American English, "have a good day (weekend)" signals the end of a transaction. In a Japanese interaction, *de wa* or its informal equivalent *ja(a)* (see Scene 9) signals major transition points in an interaction. Visitors may say *de wa* as they rise from their seats to take their leave; a team leader may declare the end of a meeting with *de wa*, after which

13

team members are to disperse to begin their respective tasks, and it may be used to signal that a presenter is going to move on to another topic. In this Scene, Professor Sakamoto says *de wa* to signal the end of an orientation event.

BTS 11 失礼します。 *Shitsurei-shimasu.* Excuse me.

Shitsurei-shimasu is used when entering a room, excusing yourself from any sort of meeting, or when interrupting. Here Brian responds to Professor Sakamoto's signal of ending with an expression of thanks for the orientation that just took place and excuses himself.

Shitsurei-shimasu, borrowings such as *baibai* 'bye-bye' or the more casual *bai* 'bye,' and *de wa* 'well then' or its informal form *ja(a)* (see Scene 9 below) are used when leaving. You have almost surely heard the word *sayonara*. *Sayonara* is a formal phrase for a clear ending to an interaction. It is increasingly reserved for a farewell that is perceived to be final, suggesting death or irrevocable breaking of relationships, as in a divorce. While it may continue to be taught in kindergarten and in the lower grades of elementary school as a formal goodbye for the day, it is not used when you part with friends for the day or when you leave work at the end of the day.

Shitsurei-shimashita is used as you leave or any time you have done something that might be perceived as rude.

Now go to the Activity Book for 練習 *Renshuu* Practice and 腕試し *Udedameshi* Tryout.

Scene 1-6 いただきます。 *Itadakimasu.* I humbly receive. (Ritual expression used before meals)

Brian joins the Shirai family for breakfast in the kitchen.

The script

お母さん	ブライアン
ブライアンさん、おはよう。	おはようございます。
どうぞ。	あ、いただきます。
	ごちそうさま。

Okaasan	*Buraian*
Bu⌐ra⌐ian-san, o⌐hayoo.	*O⌐hayoo gozaima⌐su.*
Do⌐ozo.	*A, i⌐tadakima⌐su.*
	Go⌐chisoosama.

Mother	Brian
Brian, good morning.	Good morning.
Go ahead.	Oh, thank you. (lit. 'I'll receive it' [humble].)
	Thank you. (lit. 'It was a feast.')

単語と表現 *Tango to hyoogen* Vocabulary and expressions

Special expressions

| おはよう。 | *Ohayoo.* | Good morning (informal). |
| いただきます。 | *Itadakimasu.* | I humbly receive (eating ritual). |

ごちそうさま。	*Gochisoosama.*	Thank you. (lit. 'It was a feast.')
ごちそうさまでした。	*Gochisoosama deshita.*	Thank you. (lit. 'It was a feast.' (formal))

Behind the Scenes

BTS 12 Morning greetings

Notice that Mrs. Shirai, the host mother, says *ohayoo* to Brian, but Brian, still new to the family and much younger, says *ohayoo gozaimasu* back to her. Both of these mean 'good morning.' The difference is that you use the shorter form to in-group members (family, close friends) or lower ranking people, but the longer form to those you don't yet know well or to higher-ups. You should always use the longer form, for example, with your teacher, even though your teacher may use the short form in greeting you.

BTS 13 Eating rituals

Before you begin to eat or when you receive a gift in Japan, it is customary to say *itada-kimasu.* This literally means 'I humbly receive' (with no religious connotation). Likewise, when you are finished eating, it is customary to say *gochisoosama (deshita)* 'it was a feast' to show your appreciation for the food. Even when they are eating alone, Japanese people can often be heard whispering *itadakimasu* to themselves, simply out of habit. It is appropriate to repeat *gochisoosama (deshita)* at the end of a dinner party where you were a guest, even if you have finished the meal some time earlier.

Now go to the Activity Book for 練習 *Renshuu* Practice and 腕試し *Udedameshi* Tryout.

よろしくお願いします。

Scene 1-7 僕、一郎。 *Boku, Ichiroo.* I'm Ichiro.

The Shirai family's teenage son, Ichiro, comes into the room to greet Brian.

The script

一郎	ブライアン
あ、ブライアン？	はい。ブライアンです。
どうも！僕、一郎。	一郎君？どうぞよろしく。

Ichiroo	*Buraian*
A, Buˈraiˈan?	*Haˈi, Buˈraiˈan desu.*
Doˈomo! Boˈku, Iˈchiroo.	*Iˈchiroo, kun? Doˈozo yoroshiku.*

Ichiro	Brian
Oh, Brian?	Yes, I'm Brian.
Hello! I'm Ichiro.	Nice to meet you.

単語と表現 *Tango to hyoogen* Vocabulary and expressions

Nouns

僕	*boku*	I (masculine)
私	*watashi*	I (gentle)
あなた	*anata*	you
一郎	*Ichiroo*	[given name]

Special expressions

ブライアン?	*Buraian?*	(Is it/Are you) Brian?
どうも。	*Doomo.*	Hello.
僕、一郎。	*Boku, Ichiroo.*	I'm Ichiro. (casual)
一郎君	*Ichiroo-kun*	Ichiro (addressing or referring to)

Behind the Scenes

BTS 14 Names and titles

There is a good deal of variety in the names that you will encounter in Japan, as well as the kanji that are used to write them, which is why exchanging business cards is important. Variety is especially noticeable among given names. Here are some common given names for men and women (kanji are omitted because there is a wide range of possibilities):

Male names	Female names
Akira	Keiko
Hiroshi	Ai
Kazuo	Kazuko
Takashi	Miho
Shoo	Kaoru
Daiki	Manami
Kenta	Miki
Masao	Masako
Makoto	Shiori
Takeshi	Kana

Addressing and referring to people in Japanese can be much more complicated than it is in English. You have seen three titles that can be added to names, usually family names, in

Japanese: *-san, -kun,* and *-sensei.* More will come up in later Acts. Among friends, the use of the given name alone is common in college, but becomes less so at the workplace. Japanese people often use the given name without a title for foreigners, even at the workplace. In this Scene, Ichiro is younger than Brian, but calls Brian by his given name without any title. You should always append *-san* to the names of those who are older than you (even by as little as one year) or who are your superiors. Pay careful attention to how Japanese people use names and titles in groups that you join.

BTS 15 Words for self and others

Direct reference to people, including oneself, in Japanese is much more complex than it is in English. The noun *watashi* 'I' is introduced here, but it is only one of many forms that people can use in referring to themselves. Others include:

> *watakushi*—more formal than *watashi*
> *atashi*—an informal form used primarily by women
> *boku*—a form used primarily by boys and men; it can also be used to refer to little
>   boys (meaning "you")
> *ore*—a rougher form used by older boys and men

It is therefore a matter of sometimes delicate maneuvering to decide how to refer to yourself. It depends on your relationship with the other(s) in the context as well as the circumstances you find yourself in. In this Scene you also see a good example of the stylistic difference between the host, Ichiro, who is less formal (*Boku, Ichiroo*) and the visitor, Brian, who maintains formal style (*Buraian desu*).

Likewise there are a number of words for referring to "you," the most common of which is *anata.* But this is not to say that the use of *anata* is common. This term should never be used with superiors, and overuse can indicate a romantic relationship. Keep in mind that a more common way to refer to the other person is [Name + *-san*] or [Name + *-title*] (mentioned in the preceding BTS).

BTS 16 どうも *Doomo* Hello

Doomo literally means 'in every way.' It precedes many phrases in Japanese to strengthen the impact: *Doomo arigatoo gozaimasu* 'thank you very much,' *Doomo shitsurei-shimashita* 'Please excuse me,' *Doomo sumimasen* 'I'm very sorry' or 'Thank you very much.' When it is used alone, it might mean any of these, or it may be a greeting ('hello'). In this Scene, Ichiro says *doomo* before identifying himself.

Now go to the Activity Book for 練習 *Renshuu* Practice and 腕試し *Udedameshi* Tryout.

Scene 1-8 行<ruby>い</ruby>ってきます。 *Itte kimasu.* See you later.

Brian is leaving for school.

The script

お母<ruby>かあ</ruby>さん	ブライアン<ruby>ぶ ら い あ ん</ruby>
行<ruby>い</ruby>って(い)らっしゃい。	行<ruby>い</ruby>ってきます。

Okaasan	*Buraian*
⌐*tte (i)rasshai.*	⌐*tte kima*⌐*su.*

Mother	Brian
See you later.	See you later.

単語と表現<ruby>たん ご ひょうげん</ruby> *Tango to hyoogen* Vocabulary and expressions

Special expressions

行<ruby>い</ruby>って(い)らっしゃい。	*Itte (i)rasshai.*	See you later. (lit. 'Go and come back.')
行<ruby>い</ruby>ってきます。	*Itte kimasu.*	See you later. (lit. 'I'll go and come back.')

Behind the Scenes

BTS 17 Leaving

When you leave your home base (home, office, workplace) intending to return, it is customary to say *itte kimasu*. This literally means 'I'll go and come back,' but is probably closer to 'see you later' in English.

The person who stays behind acknowledges the other's departure by saying *itte (i)rasshai*. This literally means 'go and come back,' but is probably closer to 'see you later' or 'have a good day' in English.

Now go to the Activity Book for 練習 *Renshuu* **Practice and** 腕試し *Udedameshi* **Tryout.**

Scene 1-9 じゃあね。 *Jaa ne.* See you.

Ichiro, Brian's homestay brother, is also leaving for school.

The script

<ruby>一郎<rt>いちろう</rt></ruby>	<ruby>ブライアン<rt>ぶ ら い あ ん</rt></ruby>
じゃあね。<ruby>バイバイ<rt>ば い ば い</rt></ruby>。	じゃ、また。

Ichiroo	*Buraian*
Ja¹a ne. Ba¹i bai.	*Ja¹ maˈta.*

Ichiro	Brian
See you later. Bye-bye.	See you again.

<ruby>単語<rt>たん ご</rt></ruby>と<ruby>表現<rt>ひょうげん</rt></ruby> *Tango to hyoogen* Vocabulary and expressions

Special expressions

じゃ(あ)ね。	*Ja(a) ne.*	See you later (informal).
じゃ(あ)。	*Ja(a).*	So (informal).
<ruby>バイバイ<rt>ば い ば い</rt></ruby>。	*Baibai.*	Bye-bye (informal).
<ruby>バイ<rt>ば い</rt></ruby>。	*Bai.*	Bye (informal).
じゃまた。	*Ja mata.*	See you again (informal).
じゃまたね。	*Ja mata ne.*	See you again (informal).
また。	*Mata.*	(See you) again (informal as a parting expression).

BTS 18 Parting for the day: じゃ（あ）ね・バイバイ・じゃ（あ）、また *ja(a) ne, bai bai* and *ja(a), mata*

Ichiro's *jaa ne* and *baibai* are informal phrases used when people part and plan to meet again. Brian is also beginning to drop his formality, using the informal *ja(a) mata*. Be careful not to use these phrases to superiors such as your teacher.

Now go to the Activity Book for 練習 *Renshuu* Practice and 腕試し *Udedameshi* Tryout.

1-9

よろしくお願いします。

Scene 1-10 失礼します。 *Shitsurei-shimasu.* Excuse me.

Sasha arrives at the office to meet Kanda-san. Here you see another use of *doozo yoroshiku* at the onset of a project that people will be working on together.

The script

神田	サーシャ
モリスさん?	あ、神田さんですか?サーシャ・モリスです。
こんにちは。神田です。	どうぞよろしくお願いします。
こちらこそ [Pointing at a chair] どうぞ。	失礼します。 [Takes the seat]

Kanda	Saasha
Moˈrisu-san?	*A, Kaˈnda-san deˈsu ka? Saˈasha Moˈrisu desu.*
Koˈnnichi wa. Kaˈnda deˈsu.	*Doˈozo yoˈroshiku onegai-shimaˈsu.*
Koˈchira koˈso. [Pointing at a chair] Doˈozo.	*Shiˈtsuˈrei-shimasu. [Takes the seat]*

Kanda	Sasha
Morris-san?	Are you Kanda-san? I'm Sasha Morris.
Hello. I'm Kanda.	It's nice to meet you.
The pleasure is mine. [Pointing at a chair] Go ahead.	Excuse me. [Takes the seat]

単語と表現 Vocabulary and expressions

Special expressions

あ、	A,	Oh,
神田さんですか?	Kanda-san desu ka?	Are you Kanda-san?
こちらこそ	kochira koso	(the pleasure/fault/etc.) is mine

Behind the Scenes

BTS 19 Question intonation

Listen carefully, as always, to the audio files for all of the Scenes. In this Scene and in Scene 7, you hear people's names used as questions:

Scene 7: *Buraian?*
Scene 10: *Morisu-san?*
Scene 10: *Kanda-san desu ka?*

Note how question intonation interacts with pitch accent.

BTS 20 Repeating your name in a self-introduction

When you introduce yourself in Japanese, it is typical to repeat your name, even if the other person has mentioned it already. Learn how your name is pronounced in Japanese and enunciate clearly. This is helpful to your Japanese listeners who may not be familiar with English.

You should also watch for signals that people are not equal in status. Here, for example, Sasha defers slightly to Kanda—by using the formal *desu* (explained in Act 2) and by saying *doozo yoroshiku onegai-shimasu* (literally 'please treat me favorably'). This is because she (Sasha) is the newcomer and will be indebted to Kanda for help in adjusting to Japan. Kanda implicitly acknowledges this by omitting formal signals.

BTS 21 Responding to どうぞ *Doozo* (Please), go ahead

When you hear *doozo* '(please), go ahead,' accepting this offer depends on the context. If you are going to sit down or enter an someone else's space (such as an office), *shitsurei-shimasu* 'excuse me' is appropriate. If you are accepting something such as food or drink, *itadakimasu* 'I receive (humble)' or *arigatoo gozaimasu* 'thank you' is appropriate. Observe that in this Scene, Sasha waits for Kanda's signal (*doozo*) and says *Shitsurei-shimasu* before taking a seat. You will soon learn how to request permission to do something that in your own culture you might take for granted.

Now go to the Activity Book for 練習 *Renshuu* Practice and 腕試し *Udedameshi* Tryout.

Scene 1-11 お疲れ様です。 *Otsukaresama desu.* Hello.

On her way back from lunch, Sasha runs into Yagi-san, the division chief, in the corridor.

The script

サーシャ	八木
お疲れ様です。	お疲れ様。

Saasha	*Yagi*
O⌐tsukaresama de¬su.	*O⌐tsukaresama.*

Sasha	Yagi
Hello (lit. 'Good work.')	Hello.

単語と表現 *Tango to hyoogen* Vocabulary and expressions

Nouns

八木	*Yagi*	[family name] (Ms. Yagi is Sasha's supervisor)

Special expressions

お疲れ様です。	*Otsukaresama desu.*	Good work. Hello.
お疲れ様。	*Otsukaresama.*	Good work. Hello. (informal).

Behind the Scenes

BTS 22 お疲れ様 *Otsukaresama*

You frequently hear *otsukaresama (desu)* (literally, 'you must be tired') as a parting greeting when people leave their work or study places for the day. It is also a sign of appreciation when someone finishes a project or assignment. But you will also hear it as a generic greeting when meetings end, as people see each other in the hall, or as they get together after work to eat and drink. *Otsukaresama desu* is used to ensure that everyone feels recognized and part of the group (company, class, club).

Now go to the Activity Book for 練習 *Renshuu* Practice and 腕試し *Udedameshi* Tryout.

Scene 1-12 お疲れ様でした。 *Otsukaresama deshita.*
Good work.

Sasha is done for the day and says goodbye to her co-workers.

The script

サーシャ	神田
お先に失礼します。	お疲れ様でした。
	八木
	お疲れ様。

Saasha	*Kanda*
Oˈsaki ni shitsuˈrei-shiˈmaˈsu.	Oˈtsukaresama deˈshita.
	Yagi
	Oˈtsukaresama

Sasha	Kanda
I'll be leaving.	Good work.
	Yagi
	Good work.

単語と表現 *Tango to hyoogen* Vocabulary and expressions

Special expressions

お先に失礼します。	*Osaki ni shitsurei-shimasu.*	I'll be leaving (ahead of you).
お先に。	*Osaki ni.*	(I'll be x-ing) ahead of you.
お疲れ様でした。	*Otsukaresama deshita.*	Good work.

Behind the Scenes

BTS 23 Finishing up for the day

When you leave a place where others are still working, it is customary to acknowledge that you are going home ahead of them. *Osaki ni shitsurei shimasu* literally means 'I excuse myself ahead of you.' Those who stay behind acknowledge the hard work of those who are leaving with *otsukaresama (deshita)* 'you worked hard.' Note that this phrase is in the past because the work is over. *Osaki ni* is also more generally used to acknowledge that you are going ahead of someone—through a door, in line, for lunch, etc.

Now go to the Activity Book for 練習 *Renshuu* Practice and 腕試し *Udedameshi* Tryout.

Scene 1-13 ただいま。 *Tadaima.* I'm home.

Sasha returns home and her roommate, Eri, is already there.

The script

さあしゃ サーシャ	えり 恵理
ただいま。	あ、お帰りなさい。お疲れ様。

Saasha	*Eri*
Ta⌐daima	*A, o⌐kaeri nasai. O⌐tsukaresama.*

Sasha	Eri
I'm home.	Oh, welcome back. Good job (today).

単語と表現 *Tango to hyoogen* Vocabulary and expressions

Nouns

えり 恵理	*Eri*	[female given name] (Eri is Sasha's house mate.)

Special expressions

ただいま。	*Tadaima.*	I'm home; I'm back.
お帰りなさい。	*Okaeri nasai.*	Welcome back.

よろしくお願いします。 1-13

Behind the Scenes

BTS 24 ただいま *Tadaima* and おかえりなさい *Okaeri nasai*

When you return home, it is customary to announce your arrival with *tadaima* 'I'm home' or 'I'm back' (literally 'just now'). The people who are at home ahead of you, or who are waiting, greet you by saying *okaeri nasai* 'welcome back' (literally, 'come back').

Now go to the Activity Book for 練習 *Renshuu* **Practice and** 腕試し *Udedameshi* **Tryout.**

1-13
よろしくお願いします。

31

Scene 1-14 おやすみなさい。 *Oyasumi nasai.* Good night.

Sasha is ready to go to bed.

サーシャ さ あ しゃ	恵理 え り
おやすみなさい。	おやすみなさい。

Saasha	*Eri*
O[「]yasumi nasai.	*O[「]yasumi nasai.*

Sasha	Eri
Good night.	Good night.

単語と表現 *Tango to hyoogen* Vocabulary and expressions
たん ご ひょうげん

Special expressions

| おやすみなさい。 | *Oyasumi nasai.* | Good night. |

BTS 25 おやすみなさい。 *Oyasumi nasai.* Good night.

Oyasumi nasai may be used when you go to bed at home or when you part from friends at the end of the evening. It is good homestay etiquette to say this to each family member before retiring into your room for the night.

Now go to the Activity Book for 練習 *Renshuu* Practice and 腕試し *Udedameshi* Tryout.

Then do 評価 *Hyooka* Assessment activities.

Between the lines

Between the Lines (BTL's) give you information that will help you understand the Japanese writing system.

BTL 1 Japanese script

The contemporary writing system for Japanese has a long, complex, and often contentious history. Many readers will probably know that Japan began importing its writing system from China in the 4th century. Many changes happened as this script was adapted to an unrelated and very different language. Suffice it to say that modern Japanese is written using a combination of *kanji* (characters mostly borrowed from China) along with *hiragana* and *katakana* (two mutually independent syllabaries derived from the Chinese characters). Each kana symbol represents a mora, such as *a, ka, sa, ta, na*—in contrast to an alphabetic system where each symbol represents one sound. If we divide language into content words (nouns, verbs, adjectives) and function words (particles, inflectional endings, and the like), then in general the conventions for kanji, hiragana, and katakana are as follows:

- Kanji: used to represent content words or parts of content words.[1]
- Hiragana: used to write function words or elements such as inflections, and/or words for which there is no accepted kanji. The question of whether a word is written in kanji or hiragana is purely a matter of convention and is decided by Japan's Ministry of Education, Culture, Sports, Science, and Technology (文部科学省 *Monbukagakushoo*).
- Katakana: used to represent borrowed words or in situations where the goal is to make the language stand out (onomatopoeia, brand names), much like italics in English.

The mixture of these three in written Japanese is called *kanji-kana-majiri-bun*. Here is an example of how it works:

ジョンソンさんは今日東京に行きます。	*Jonson-san wa kyoo Tookyoo ni ikimasu.*	Johnson-san will go to Tokyo today.

The shaded content words—*kyoo* 'today,' *Tookyoo* 'Tokyo,' and the *i-*of *ikimasu* 'go'—are written in kanji. The name 'Johnson' (underlined) is written in katakana because it is borrowed. All other elements—title *-san*, particles *wa*, *ni*, and the inflection *-kimasu*—are written in hiragana because they are function words or elements.

It is also very common to see two other kinds of script in Japanese texts. One is Arabic numerals and another is Roman letters (the Western alphabet). For example:

入り口２０ｍ先	*iriguchi 20 m saki*	entrance 20 meters ahead
Ｍサイズ	*M saizu*	size: medium

Finally, Japanese are well known for their use of emoticons or *emoji*, including ones that are constructed from keyboard characters. The combination (^_^), for example, is used to indicate laughter, while (*_*) indicates surprise.

Now go to the Activity Book for 読み練習 *Yomi-renshuu* Reading Practice.

BTL 2 Kanji readings

Since kanji were borrowed from China over time, they were very often borrowed more than once from different regions in China, which means they may have more than one pronunciation or "reading." The character 明 (which means something like 'bright' or 'light'), for example, was borrowed once with the pronunciation *mei* (as in *Meiji* of Meiji Era—the age of enlightenment)*,* then with the pronunciation *myoo* (as in *myoonichi* 'tomorrow') and then again with the pronunciation *min* ('the Ming Dynasty'). What's more, kanji were assigned to Japanese words whose meanings are similar to the Chinese words that are represented. So the same character 明 is used to write the Japanese word *akarui* 'bright.' Most kanji have one or more Japanese readings in addition to their Chinese reading(s). The Japanese readings are called *kun-yomi* (訓読み) and the Chinese readings are called *on-yomi* (音読み).

BTL 3 縦書きと横書き *Tategaki* and *Yokogaki*

Traditionally, Japanese is written vertically from top to bottom, right to left. This is called *tategaki*. Here is an example:[2]

野菜ひとつからこんなにも豊かな料理。いろんな味で、野菜丸ごとヤサイクル。部位が違えば、味も違う。たとえば大根一本とっても、その味わいは本当に多彩です。実も皮も、根も葉も、丸ごと使い切る"ヤサイクル"で、野菜をもっと豊かに味わってみませんか。それは、ゴミを減らしてCO2を削減する、地球にもやさしいおいしさ。いろんなところを、いろんな味で食べるエコ。味の素KKは、いつでもお手伝いします。

More and more, Japanese people elect to write—either by hand or in word processing—from left to right horizontally. This is called *yokogaki* and the same text would look like this:

野菜ひとつからこんなにも豊かな料理。いろんな味で、野菜丸ごとヤサイクル。部位が違えば、味も違う。たとえば大根一本とっても、その味わいは本当に多彩です。実も皮も、根も葉も、丸ごと使い切る"ヤサイクル"で、野菜をもっと豊かに味わってみませんか。それは、ゴミを減らしてCO2を削減する、地球にもやさしいおいしさ。いろんなところを、いろんな味で食べるエコ。味の素KKは、いつでもお手伝いします。

You will be practicing both *tategaki* and *yokogaki* in this textbook.

よろしくお願いします。

BTL 4 振^ふり仮^が名^な Furigana

Hiragana has another use, and that is to assist readers with the pronunciation of kanji. Since kanji are not "phonetic" and change pronunciation depending on context, it can be very difficult to remember how to pronounce all of the kanji. In cases where a writer or publisher wants to help readers know how to pronounce kanji, hiragana will be placed above (or in *tategaki* to the side of) the kanji to indicate their reading. This use of kana is called *furigana* (also sometimes *rubi*).

Examples

1.	坂田 さか た	Sakata	[family name, place name]
2.	坂田 さか だ	Sakada	[family name, place name]
3.	須田 す だ	Suda	[family name]
4.	佐賀 さ が	Saga	[family name, place name]
5.	赤坂 あかさか	Akasaka	[family name, place name]
6.	テスト て す と	tesuto	test

In the speaking-listening sections, you will see furigana for much of the Japanese that you see. In the reading-writing sections, you will see furigana when you are not expected to know how to pronounce the Japanese.

There are several websites and other add-ons to web browsers that provide furigana to webpages. Ask your teacher or do a search for furigana providers to find the appropriate add-on(s) for your browser.

BTL 5 原稿用紙^{げんこうよう し} *Genkooyooshi*

Genkooyooshi refers to Japanese practice paper that is divided into individual small squares (200–400 per sheet) for writing characters. *Genkooyooshi* is used extensively in Japan, not just by novices learning to write for the first time. In the past, students at all levels turned in their writing assignments on vertically-aligned *genkooyooshi*. Word processing and printing have made this unnecessary in large part, but primary and secondary school students are still asked to turn in assignments written on *genkooyooshi*. *Genkooyooshi* templates in both vertical and horizontal format are available for word processing as well. When you use *genkooyooshi*, each symbol, including punctuation and Roman letters, is allotted one space. Each regular-sized symbol should be placed centrally in each cell. The positioning of punctuation marks and reduced-size symbols differs depending on whether you use vertical or horizontal *genkooyooshi*. When using a vertical format, these symbols should occupy the right half of the cell, usually the upper right area. For horizontal format,

1-15R よろしくお願^{ねが}いします。

the small symbols and punctuation marks occupy the bottom half of the cell, usually the bottom left area.

Notes

1 Content words (nouns, verbs, adjectives) are associated with creating an idea. They are the largest (almost limitless) class of words in a language. Function words (in English: prepositions, articles, and verb endings) are grammatical markers that show the relationships among other words in a sentence. They are a closed set.
2 Both the vertical and the horizontal texts are used with permission from the Ajinomoto Co. Ltd.

だいじょうぶ
大丈夫です。

Daijoobu desu.

It'll be fine.

せんり　みち　いっぽ
千里の道も一歩から　*Senri no michi mo ippo kara*
A journey of a thousand miles begins
with a single step.

◆ 話す・聞く *Hanasu/kiku* Speaking and listening

Instructional expressions part 2

PERSON に言ってください。	PERSON *ni i⌐tte kudasa˥i.*	Please say it to PERSON.
PERSON に聞いてください。	PERSON *ni ki⌐ite kudasa˥i.*	Please ask PERSON.
PERSON にもう一度聞いてください。	PERSON *ni mo⌐o ichi-do kiite kudasa˥i.*	Please ask PERSON again.
PERSON に答えてください。	PERSON *ni ko⌐ta˥ete ku⌐dasa˥i.*	Please answer PERSON.
日本語で話しましょう。	*Ni⌐hongo de hanashimasho˥o.*	Let's speak in Japanese.
読んでください。	*Yo˥nde ku⌐das˥ai.*	Please read it.
見てください。	*Mi˥te ku⌐dasa˥i.*	Please look at it.
頑張りましょう。	*Ga⌐nbarimasho˥o.*	Let's do our best.

Practice responding to these prompts with the appropriate behavior.

大丈夫です。

41

Scene 2-1　わかりますか？ *Wakarimasu ka?*
Do you understand?

Kanda-san has assigned a job to Sasha and checks if she is okay with it.

 The script

神田（かんだ）	サーシャ（さあしゃ）
それ、わかりますか？	はい、大丈夫（だいじょうぶ）です。
すごいですね!	いえいえ。
じゃ、よろしく。	はい。頑張（がんば）ります。

Kanda	Saasha
So⌐re¬, wa⌐karima¬su ka?	Ha¬i, da⌐ijo¬obu desu.
Su⌐go¬i desu ne!	⌐I¬e¬ie.
Ja¬, yo⌐roshiku.	Ha¬i. Ga⌐nbarima¬su.

Kanda	Sasha
Do you understand that?	Yes, it's fine.
Amazing, isn't it!	No, no.
So then, thanks.	Yes, sure. I'll do my best.

42

単語と表現 *Tango to hyoogen* Vocabulary and expressions

Nouns

それ	*sore*	that (thing near you)
これ	*kore*	this (thing)
あれ	*are*	that (thing over there)
どれ	*dore*	which (thing)
大丈夫	*daijoobu*	fine, safe, all right
平気	*heiki*	calm, unconcerned, all right

Verbs

わかります（わからない）	*waka-imasu (wakar-anai)*	understand
できます（できない）	*deki-masu (deki-nai)*	can do, become complete
します（しない）	*shi-masu (shi-nai)*	do, play (a game or sport)
来ます（こない）	*ki-masu (ko-nai)*	come
頑張ります（頑張らない）	*ganbar-imasu (ganbar-anai)*	will do my best

Adjectives

すごい	*sugoi*	amazing
いい	*ii*	good
よろしい	*yoroshii*	good (polite)

Sentence particles (see BTS 3)

ね	*ne*	[sentence particle indicating agreement]
か?	*ka?*	[question particle]
ね?	*ne?*	[particle checking on whether the other person is following]

Special expressions

はい	*hai*	yes; here you are
ええ	*ee*	yes (casual)
いえいえ	*ieie*	no no
いえ	*ie*	no
いいえ	*iie*	no
よろしく	*yoroshiku*	thanks; please treat me favorably

大丈夫です。

BTS 1 Core Sentences: Verb/Adjective/Noun *desu* (non-past, formal)

A major distinction in Japanese is between words that do not change form (such as Nouns and Particles) and those that do change form (or inflect). Japanese has three kinds of inflecting forms: Verbs, Adjectives, and [Noun *desu*]. These constitute the Core Sentences of Japanese.

Unlike English, there is no subject required in a Japanese Sentence—as long as you know who or what you are talking about. Therefore, a Core Sentence—a Verb, an Adjective, or a Noun *desu*—is a complete Sentence all by itself. Unless it is understood otherwise from the context that we are talking about someone or something else,[1] statements are about the speaker and questions are about the addressee.

a. Verb

A Verb is a word that has a number of forms, two of which are *-masu* and *-masen*. The *-masu* form is non-past affirmative and the *-masen* form is non-past negative. An alternative form of *-masen* is *-(a)nai desu*. The *-(a)nai desu* form is more common in spoken language (except for invitations) while the *-masen* form is more typical of written Japanese.

Notice that "non-past" includes both present and future in English. So *shimasu* may mean 'I do it' (as a rule or habitually) or it may mean 'I will do it.' (Note that it does not mean 'I am doing it now.') *Shinai desu* may mean 'I don't do it' or 'I won't do it.'

します。	*Shimasu.*	I do/play (it).
しません・しないです。	*Shimasen. / Shinai desu.*	I don't do/play (it).

b. Adjective

An Adjective is a word that has a number of endings, two of which are *-i* and *-ku* added to the Adjective stem. You see these endings in the non-past affirmative and non-past negative forms of Adjectives.

Non-past affirmative	すごいです。	*Sugoi desu*	It's amazing.
Non-past negative	すごくないです。	*Sugoku nai desu*	It's not amazing.
	すごくありません。	*Sugoku arimasen*	It's not amazing.

Note that there are two alternatives for the non-past negative form. Either of these is acceptable, but native speakers usually say that the *arimasen* alternative sounds a bit more formal. Note also that the negative form of *ii desu* is *yoku nai desu/yoku arimasen.* So the *-ku* form of *ii* is *-yoku.*

c. Noun *desu*

The last type of Core Sentence will be called [Noun *desu*]. Nouns combine with *desu* to form Sentences.

大丈夫です。	*Daijoobu desu.*	It's all right.
平気です。	*Heiki desu.*	I'm not concerned.

There are two alternatives for the negative of Noun *desu*:

日本語じゃないです。	*Nihongo ja nai desu.*	It's not Japanese.
日本語じゃありません。	*Nihongo ja arimasen.*	It's not Japanese.

Again, the *arimasen* alternative sounds a bit more formal.

The *-mas-* (*-masu, -masen*) and *desu* that you see in these Core Sentences tell you that these Sentences are in formal style. Formal style is used between people who don't know each other well, in relationships that are recognized culturally as being formal (doctor-patient, teacher-student, boss-subordinate), or in situations that are considered to require careful language—in other words when people feel social distance between themselves and the people they are talking to. You also saw formal and informal alternatives for greetings in Act 1.

BTS 2 これ、それ、あれ、どれ *Kore, sore, are, dore*
This, that (near you), that (over there), which

Kore, sore, and *are* are representative of a pattern that you will see elsewhere in Japanese. Unlike English, which makes a two-way distinction between *this* (close to me or us) and *that* (away from me), Japanese makes a three-way distinction among:

これ	*kore*	this thing/these things (close to me or that I'm about to mention)
それ	*sore*	that thing/these things (close to you), that thing/these things (you/we just mentioned)
あれ	*are*	that thing/these things (away from both of us), that thing/these things (we both know about)

だいじょうぶ
大丈夫です。

The question word for this series is *dore* 'which one?' or 'which thing?' when you are asking about three or more items. In Act 2 you will learn how to ask 'which one out of two?' Note that the accent of *ko⌐re, so⌐re,* and *a⌐re* is different from that of *do⌐re.*

BTS 3 Sentence particles か *ka* and ね *ne*

Sentence Particles are short words that end a Sentence and affect the meaning of the Sentence. Two of these appear in this conversation.

With rising intonation, the Particle *ka* changes a statement to a question. Even though Japanese does not typically use question marks, for clarity this will be represented here with a question mark (?). You will not see this question mark in the Reading/Writing section.

来ますか?	*Kimasu ka?*	Are you coming?
しませんか?	*Shimasen ka?*	You don't do it?

With falling intonation, the Particle *ne* tells listeners that you agree with them or that you assume they agree with you. This will be represented here with an exclamation point (!).

すごいですね!	*Sugoi desu ne!*	That's amazing, isn't it!

With slightly rising intonation, *ne* is used to check whether the other person agrees or is following. This will be represented here with a question mark (?).

わかりますね?	*Wakarimasu ne?*	You understand, right?

BTS 4 Noun + Sentence

Nouns can hook up to Sentences in a number of relationships, including subject, object, time, and place. Especially when initiating an interaction or bringing up a topic in conversation, the Noun is mentioned and a comment is made without specifying what the grammatical relationship (subject, object, time, etc.) is between the two.

これ、わかりますか?	*Kore, wakarimasu ka.*	Do you understand this?
ひろしさん、できないですね!	*Hiroshi-san, dekinai desu ne!*	Hiroshi can't do it, can he!
すず き せんせい 鈴木先生、すごいですね!	*Suzuki-sensei, sugoi desu ne!*	Prof. Suzuki is amazing, isn't she!
あしたできますか。	*Ashita dekimasu ka.*	Can you do it tomorrow?

46

| これ、お願いします。 | *Kore, onegai-shimasu.* | Please give me this one. |
| 駅、行きますか。 | *Eki, ikimasu ka.* | Are you going to the station? |

BTS 5 Affirming and negating

As you have already seen, it is dangerous to translate *hai* simply as 'yes.' Hai has many uses, including 'here you are,' 'present' (when your name is called for attendance), as well as acknowledging what the other person has said ('keep going'). In response to a question, *hai* means 'what you said (or assumed) is right' whether preceded by an affirmative or a negative.

Q: わかりますね?	*Wakarimasu ne?*	You understand, right?
A: はい、わかります。	*Hai, wakarimasu.*	Yes, I understand.
Q: 来ないですね?	*Konai desu ne?*	You won't come, right?
A: はい、すみません。	*Hai, sumimasen.*	That's right. I'm sorry.

In the latter example, English speakers are more likely to say, 'No, I can't. I'm sorry.'

Ee is slightly less formal than *hai*. It is only used in a response to questions, not in the sense of 'here,' 'present,' 'here you are,' 'moving on,' etc., that you saw for *hai*.

You can disagree with or negate what the other person says with *ie* and the longer (and more emphatic) form *iie*. You should be cautious about directly contradicting or disagreeing with superiors. But one situation in which denial is appropriate is when you are complimented. In this conversation, Sasha responds *ieie* to Kanda-san's praise of her ability to understand so quickly. Humility is a virtue in Japan, and Japanese people tend to deny compliments.

Now go to the Activity Book for 練習 *Renshuu* Practice and 腕試し *Udedameshi* Tryout.

Note

1 In the cases where identity, gender, and number are not specified, this book will arbitrarily assign these in examples. So *shimasu* may be translated as 'she does,' 'he does,' or 'they do.'

Scene 2-2　ちょっと …… *Chotto . . .* It's a little . . .

Kanda-san approaches Sasha about a task she is yet to perform.

The script

<ruby>神田<rt>かん だ</rt></ruby>	<ruby>サーシャ<rt>さ あ しゃ</rt></ruby>
<ruby>電話<rt>でん わ</rt></ruby>、しますか?	<ruby>今<rt>いま</rt></ruby>ですか?いえ、あのう、ええと、ちょっと ……。
あ、いいですよ!じゃあ、あとで。	すみません。

Kanda	*Saasha*
Deˈnwaˈ, shiˈmaˈsu ka?	*Iˈma desu ka? Iˈeˈ, aˈnooˈ, eˈeto, choˈtto . . .*
A, iˈi desu yo! Jaˈa, ˈaˈto de.	*Suˈmimaseˈn.*

Kanda	Sasha
Will you make the phone call?	Now? No, umm, uhh, it's just . . .
It's all right. So then, maybe later.	Sorry.

<ruby>単語<rt>たん ご</rt></ruby>と<ruby>表現<rt>ひょうげん</rt></ruby> *Tango to hyoogen* Vocabulary and expressions

Nouns

<ruby>今<rt>いま</rt></ruby>	*ima*	now
きょう・<ruby>今日<rt>きょ う</rt></ruby>	*kyoo*	today
あした・<ruby>明日<rt>あ した</rt></ruby>	*ashita*	tomorrow
これから	*kore kara*	(from) now
<ruby>電話<rt>でん わ</rt></ruby>	*denwa*	telephone

携帯・ケータイ	keitai	cell phone, mobile phone
勉強	benkyoo	study
(お)仕事	(o)shigoto	work, job
宿題	shukudai	homework
テスト	tesuto	test
レポート	repooto	report
教科書	kyookasho	textbook
ミーティング	miitingu	meeting

Verbs

行きます(行かない)	ik-imasu (ik-anai)	go
います(いない)	i-masu (i-nai)	be, exist (animate)
書きます(書かない)	kak-imasu (kak-anai)	write
始めます(始めない)	hajime-masu (hajime-nai)	begin (something)
終わります(終わらない)	owar-imasu (owar-anai)	end

Sentence particles

よ	yo	[sentence particle indicating certainty]

Special expressions

あのう	anoo	umm (hesitation noise)
ええと	eeto	uhh (hesitation noise)
すみませんでした・すいませんでした。	su(m)imasen deshita	Sorry. Thank you (for what has happened).
ちょっと	chotto	a little
あとで	ato de	later

拡張 *Kakuchoo* Expansion

Are there any tasks or events that occur regularly in your workplace or school that are not mentioned here? What are they called in Japanese?

Behind the Scenes

BTS 6 Sentence particle よ *yo*

In this conversation, you see another Sentence Particle: *yo*. The Particle *yo* is assertive; it indicates certainty. It tells listeners that this is new information or that you don't believe they are thinking the same thing you are. The assertive-sounding *yo*, with falling intonation, can be rude when used to superiors, but in the right context it can be just the right thing to say. If your senior colleague says that he is worried about the report he'd produced, you could encourage him by saying *Ii desu yo.* 'It's just fine.'

BTS 7 "Echo" questions

You may notice in the conversations here and in your classroom practice that Japanese people keep the conversation going by asking a lot of clarifying questions that follow up on what the other person just said. Sometimes the question takes up (or echoes) what the other speaker just said.

A: 電話しますか?	*Denwa shimasu ka?*	Will you call?
B: 電話ですか?ええ、します。	*Denwa desu ka? Ee, shimasu.*	Call? Yes, I will.

At other times, the question is an attempt to clarify what was left out.

A: しますか?	*Shimasu ka?*	Are you going to do it?
B: これですか?	*Kore desu ka?*	You mean this?
A: いいですね?	*Ii desu ne?*	It's okay, isn't it?
B: これですか?	*Kore desu ka?*	You mean this?

Speakers might use an echo question when they actually don't understand what was just said. But they might also use it to show deference and concern for the other person—'I want to get this right.'—without expecting an answer. English speakers use these questions now and then, but they are far more common in Japanese. This may be because Japanese people are especially solicitous of others in a conversation. Echo questions are a sign that you are actively listening to what the other person is saying.

BTS 8 Buying time (hesitation noises)

All languages have hesitation noises. These are quasi-words that fill pauses, show deliberation, or buy time before you answer or make a commitment. Using the correct hesitation noises can make a big difference between natural-sounding Japanese and awkward, foreign-sounding speech. Here you learn two hesitation words: *ano* and *eeto*. *Ano* (sometimes lengthened to *anoo*) is a hesitation noise used when you want to make sure you have the other person's attention because you are about to say something or when you want to soften the impact of what you are about to say because it could be interpreted as negative or unpleasant. *Eeto* is typically used to indicate that you are searching for or don't know what to say or to hold the floor while you are trying to come up with what it is that you want to say next.

BTS 9 ちょっと *Chotto* A little

The word *chotto* literally means 'a little.' *Chotto wakarimasu* means 'I understand a little.' *Chotto tabemasu* means 'I eat a little.' But you may hear *chotto* in a variety of other situations where 'a little' just doesn't make sense in English. Here are some examples.

a. To soften the impact of what you say

It is all right to say *onegai-shimasu* 'please (help me)' when asking someone for assistance. But by adding *chotto*, you can make the request sound softer and less demanding.

ちょっとお願いします。　　*Chotto onegai-shimasu.*　　Would you (just) give me a hand here?

When you go to your professor's office, before going in you probably want to ask permission, you'd want to use the polite *yoroshii*, rather than *ii*, and adding *chotto* makes your intrusion less abrupt.

ちょっとよろしいですか？　　　　*Chotto yoroshii desu ka.*　　　　Is it all right?

b. Refusing

Often *chotto* all by itself indicates hesitation or reluctance.

A: 今しますか？　　　　*Ima shimasu ka.*　　　　Are you going to do it now?
B: ええと …… ちょっと。　　*Eeto . . . Chotto.*　　　Ummm . . . it's just.

This *chotto* should have downward intonation and be a bit drawn out, indicating that you are giving the matter consideration. In this sense it can also be used as a polite refusal.

c. Avoiding the unpleasant

Related to (b) above is the use of *chotto* (with slowed articulation and often a tilt of the head) to avoid saying something negative or unpleasant (criticism, disagreement, etc).

51

In this conversation Sasha doesn't want to tell Kanda-san directly that she hasn't made a phone call. You may also hear Japanese people say *chotto* under their breath when they see or hear something they don't approve of.

d. Getting someone's attention

When you call a waiter or a salesperson, it is appropriate to say *Chotto su(m)imasen.* This is often shortened to *Chotto*. Similarly, if you see someone drop something on the street or some other public place, you can get his or her attention by saying *Chotto (su[m]imasen).*

Now go to the Activity Book for 練習 *Renshuu* Practice and 腕試し *Udedameshi* Tryout.

Scene 2-3 おいしそうですね。 *Oishisoo desu ne.*
It looks delicious.

After lunch, Kanda-san offers Sasha some sweets that he brought back for everyone at the office from a recent business trip.

 The script

神田 (かんだ)	サーシャ (さあしゃ)
クッキー、お好きですか?	え?何ですか?
クッキーです。これ、よかったら食べませんか?	わあ、おいしそうですね。
どうぞ。	いいですか〜?じゃあ、いただきます。…… おいしい!…… おいしいクッキーですねえ。
どうも。	ごちそうさまでした。

Kanda	Saasha
Ku˥kkii, o˩suki de˥su ka?	E? Na˥n desu ka?
Ku˥kkii desu. Ko˩re, yo˥kattara ta˩bemase˥n ka?	Waa, o˩ishiso˥o desu ˩ne˩e!
Do˥ozo.	I˥i desu ka~? Ja˥a, i˩tadakima˥su . . . O˥ishii! . . . O˩ishii kuk˥kii desu ˩ne˩e.
Do˥omo.	Go˩chisoosama de˥shita.

Kanda	Sasha
Do you like cookies?	What? What is it?
They're cookies. If you'd like, please have one of these.	Wow, they look delicious, don't they.
Go ahead.	Is it all right? Well, then, I'll have one . . . Delicious! . . . They're delicious, aren't they!
Thanks.	Thank you. (lit. 'It was delicious.')

53

だいじょうぶです。

単語と表現 *Tango to hyoogen* Vocabulary and expressions

たんご ひょうげん

Nouns

(お)好き	(o)suki	liking, fondness, love
大好き	daisuki	very likeable, like very much
何	nan[1]	what
何	nani	what
クッキー	kukkii	cookie
ケーキ	keeki	cake
ご飯	gohan	cooked rice or a meal
朝ご飯	asagohan	breakfast
(お)昼ご飯	(o)hirugohan	lunch
晩ご飯	bangohan	dinner
(お)弁当	(o)bentoo	meal in a box
(お)すし・寿司	(o)sushi	sushi
焼き鳥	yakitori	yakitori (chicken shish kebab)
うどん	udon	wheat noodles
そば	soba	buckwheat noodles
カレーライス	kareeraisu	curry rice
ラーメン	raamen	ramen
お茶	ocha	tea
(お)水	(o)mizu	water
ビール	biiru	beer
ウーロン茶	uuroncha	oolong tea
紅茶	koocha	black tea
コーヒー	koohii	coffee
ミルク	miruku	milk
ジュース	juusu	juice
食べ物	tabemono	food
飲み物	nomimono	drink
(お)薬	(o)kusuri	medicine
おいしそう	oishisoo	look(s) delicious
おもしろそう	omoshirosoo	look(s) interesting
きれい	kirei	pretty, clean

Verbs

食べます(食べない)	*tabe-masu (tabe-nai)*	eat
飲みます・呑みます(飲まない)	*nom-imasu (nom-anai)*	drink, swallow (i.e. medicine)
いただきます(いただかない)↓²	*itadak-imasu (itadak-anai)*	eat; receive (humble)
読みます(読まない)	*yom-imasu (yom-anai)*	read

Adjectives

おいしい	*oishii*	delicious
おもしろい	*omoshiroi*	interesting

Sentence particles

ねえ	*nee*	[sentence particle assuming shared attitude/opinion]

Special expressions

わあ	*waa*	wow
え?	*e?*	what?
よかったら	*yokattara*	if it's all right
よろしかったら	*yoroshikattara*	if it's all right (polite)

拡張 *Kakuchoo* Expansion

What are some of the Japanese foods that you eat frequently? Find out what they are called and learn to say them accurately.

Behind the Scenes

BTS 10 Sharing snacks

It is customary in Japan for people to bring treats or snacks to the office or study group meeting. This kind of sharing builds group morale and cohesion. Especially if you have a chance to travel or visit a special place, it is viewed as a thoughtful gesture to bring something back for your friends and colleagues. These are consumed with tea, usually in the afternoon during break time. In this conversation, Kanda-san has offered Sasha cookies that were a gift from some visitors.

だいじょうぶ
大丈夫です。

BTS 11 Negative questions as invitations

A common use of negative Verbs is as invitations. It sounds rather stuffy in English to invite someone this way ('Won't you eat some?') but in formal style the *-masen* form (not the *-nai desu* form) is the most common form of invitation in Japanese. (See BTS 25.)

食べませんか？	*Tabemasen ka?*	Won't you eat some?
飲みませんか？	*Nomimasen ka?*	Won't you drink some?

BTS 12 遠慮 *Enryo* Restraint

In some cultures, people feel very comfortable accepting or rejecting offers of food and drink or invitations. Japanese tend not to be like that, especially around people they don't know well. When your Japanese hosts offer you something to eat or drink, it is typically polite to hold off accepting right away or tell them not to go to any trouble—at least at first. This is called *enryo* "restraint." It is a good example of virtues in Japan that center on deference to others. In this conversation, Sasha responds with surprise (*E?* 'Huh?') and asks Kanda-san what he is talking about (*Nan desu ka?* 'What do you mean?'). She then acknowledges his invitation, and says that they look delicious (*oishisoo desu nee*). After additional urging by Kanda-san, she asks if it is really all right to have one. It is quite likely that she heard his offer of cookies in the first place, but by asking questions and deferring her acceptance she shows restraint. Note that Kanda-san invites her to eat a cookie, even as she defers. This is the other side of *enryo*—urging the other person to go ahead and have some even when they show reluctance.

BTS 13 Adjective + Noun

Adjectives can combine directly with Nouns to form a Noun phrase. Examples: *ii keitai* 'nice cell phone' and *sugoi repooto* 'amazing report.' The resulting combination does everything that a Noun does. Therefore, it is possible to say *Ii keitai desu* 'It is a nice cell phone.' and *Subarashii repooto ja nai desu ka?* 'Isn't it a wonderful report?'

BTS 14 Sentence Particle ねえ *nee*

Nee indicates that what you are talking about is impressive and you share the other person's sentiments or that you assume they share yours. Sasha looks at the treat that Kanda-san has brought and says *Oishisoo desu nee.* 'They look delicious, don't they!' To review:

56

- *ne* with falling intonation tells listeners that you have discovered or realized something and want to share it.
- *ne* with slightly rising intonation is used to check whether the other person agrees or is following.
- *nee* with falling intonation indicates that you share the other person's sentiments or that you assume they share yours.

BTS 15 Informal affirmative (non-past) form of Adjectives

Recall the formal affirmative forms for Adjectives:

おいしいです。 *Oishii desu.* It's delicious.

You can drop the *desu* for an informal equivalent:

おいしい。 *Oishii.* It's delicious.

In this conversation, when Sasha exclaims *Oishii*! 'It's delicious!' she is only expressing the reaction without directing it to anyone in particular. What she says next, *Oishii kukkii desu nee.* 'They're delicious, aren't they!' is a comment directed to Kanda-san in the appropriate formal style.

Now go to the Activity Book for 練習 *Renshuu* Practice and 腕試し *Udedameshi* Tryout.

Notes

1 *Nan* occurs before /d/ and /n/; *nan* or *nani* occurs before /t/; *nani* occurs everywhere else.
2 The downward pointing arrow here means that this word in humble. This will be explained in more detail in later Acts.

Scene 2-4 いいですけど……。 *Ii desu kedo . . .*
It's okay, but . . .

Kanda-san checks if Sasha is available to do some task.

The script

神田 *かんだ*	サーシャ *さあしゃ*
今忙しいですか? *いまいそが*	私ですか?いや、いい ですけど……。 *わたし*
じゃあ、これ、お願いします。 *ねが*	こちらですね?はい、わかりました。

Kanda	*Saasha*
Iˈma iˈsogashiˈi desu ka?	Waˈtashi deˈsu ka? Iˈya, iˈi desu kedo. . . .
Jaˈa, koˈreˈ, oˈnegai-shimaˈsu.	Koˈchira deˈsu ne? Haˈ iˈ, waˈ karimaˈ shita.

Kanda	Sasha
Are you busy right now?	Me? No, it's all right. . . .
Well then, I'll ask you to take care of this.	This, right? Got it.

単語と表現 *Tango to hyoogen* Vocabulary and expressions
たんご ひょうげん

Nouns

こちら	*kochira*	here, this, in this general area, in this direction, this alternative (of two), the speaker's side of a telephone conversation, this person (polite)
そちら	*sochira*	there (near you), that (near you), in that general area, in that direction (in your direction), that alternative (of two near you), the other side of a telephone conversation, that person (polite)

| あちら | *achira* | there (away from both of us), that thing (away from both of us), in that direction (away from both of us), that alternative (of two away from both of us), that place (that we both know about), that person over there (polite) |
| どちら | *dochira* | where, which, which direction, which (of two), which person/who (polite) |

Adjectives

| （お）忙しい | *(o)isogashii* | busy |

Sentence particles

けど	*kedo*	but
が	*ga*	but, and
け（れ）ど（も）	*ke(re)do(mo)*	but

Special expressions

| いや | *iya* | no (informal); uhh (hesitation noise) |
| わかりました。 | *Wakarimashita.* | Understood. Got it. |

Behind the Scenes

BTS 16 Core Sentence + けど *kedo* but

Kedo is used to contrast two Sentences or ideas. Often the second Sentence is left unsaid because it is clear from context or because the speaker does not want to state the obvious or the unpleasant, or the speaker would like the other person to say something in response. *Wakarimasu kedo* . . . 'I understand but . . .' is what you might say when you don't want to admit that you can't put into practice what has just been explained.

Some uses of *kedo* may not seem contrastive. For example, a speaker might introduce a topic using *kedo*:

Tesuto desu kedo . . . 'About the test . . .' is how you might start a conversation with your instructor on the content of an upcoming test.

Murakami desu kedo . . . 'I'm Murakami, but . . .' This is what you might identify yourself when you go into a doctor's office for an appointment, or when you expect that the other person knows that you are expected.

The more formal forms of *kedo* (*keredo, kedomo, keredomo*) as well as *ga* are associated with formal speech or writing. These will appear in later lessons and in the reading-writing sections of this textbook.

BTS 17 The こちら *kochira* series

In this Scene you encounter *kochira, sochira, achira*, and *dochira*, another *ko-so-a-do* series. This set has multiple meanings (see Vocabulary and Expressions) which can be somewhat imprecise. You see in this Scene that they are polite equivalents of *kore, sore, are,* and *dore*. In the next three Scenes, you will see that they are also (a) polite equivalents of *koko, soko, asoko,* and *doko*, another *ko-so-a-do* series that indicates location, but more precisely, and (b) used to indicate general direction.

Note also that this series can be used in polite reference to people (*Sochira, Kanda-san desu ka*. 'Is that Kanda-san?'). In addition, *kochira* and *sochira* refer to the two sides of a telephone conversation. (*Kochira, Murakami desu* 'This is Murakami.')

Now go to the Activity Book for 練習 **Renshuu Practice and** 腕試し *Udedameshi* **Tryout.**

60

Scene 2-5 今どちらですか？ *Ima dochira desu ka?*
Where are you now?

Sasha is at her desk and sees that Kanda-san is not at his desk. When she calls him on his cell phone, she is surprised to find that he is, in fact, somewhere in the office.

The script

さあしゃ サーシャ	かんだ 神田
いま 今どちらですか?	ぼく かいしゃ 僕?会社ですが……。
かいしゃ え、会社ですか。あ、そうですか。	

Saasha	*Kanda*
I˺ma do˺chira desu ka?	*Bo˺ku? Ka˺isha de˺su ga . . .*
E, ka˺isha de˺su ka. A, so˺o desu ka.	

Sasha	Kanda
Where are you now?	Me? I'm in the office, but . . .
What, you're in the office! Oh, I see.	

単語と表現 *Tango to hyoogen* Vocabulary and expressions
たんご ひょうげん

Nouns

かいしゃ 会社	*kaisha*	office, company
がっこう 学校	*gakkoo*	school
うち	*uchi*	house, home
いえ いえ・家	*ie*	house, home
たく お宅	*otaku*	home (polite)

61

寮 りょう	*ryoo*	dormitory
アパート あぱあと	*apaato*	apartment
コンビニ こんびに	*konbini*	convenience store
駅 えき	*eki*	train station
トイレ と い れ	*toire*	toilet, bathroom, restroom
そう	*soo*	that way, so

拡張 *Kakuchoo* Expansion
かくちょう

Find out from a Japanese associate or friend what your workplace or study location might be called, and learn to say it accurately.

Behind the Scenes

BTS 18 Informal affirmative of [Noun です] [Noun *desu*]

Recall the formal affirmative forms for [Noun *desu*]:

きれいです。	*Kirei desu.*	It's clean.

You can drop the *desu* for an informal equivalent, including questions:

きれい。	*Kirei.*	It's clean.
今? いま	*Ima?*	Now?

Note that Kanda-san uses an informal question in this Scene: "*Boku?*" not "*Boku desu ka.*" This use of informal forms is very typical of self-directed statements; you would not talk to yourself in formal style. For example, if you read something interesting online, you would say to yourself "*Omoshiroi nee,*" not "*Omoshiroi desu nee.*" Kanda-san's question is as much directed to himself as it is to Sasha; he is verifying for both of them that he is the topic of discussion.

BTS 19 そう *Soo* That way

You will hear the word *soo* in many expressions. With rising intonation, the question *Soo desu ka?* 'Is that so?' indicates that you've heard new information and that you're

だいじょうぶです。 大丈夫です。

somewhat surprised or doubtful about whether it is really true. *Soo desu ne(e)* indicates that you agree with what the other person has said (or that you are carefully considering it—see BTS 28). *Soo desu yo* conveys certainty about what you're talking about.

BTS 20 Questions with falling intonation

In this Scene, Sasha's *Soo desu ka* (with falling intonation) means 'I see.' You will hear Japanese speakers use *Soo desu ka* frequently as they listen to others and take in information. This is part of being a good listener in Japan.

In general, questions with falling intonation are used to indicate that you understand what the other person said.

A: 寮ですよ。	*Ryoo desu yo.*	It's a dorm. (I'm living in a dorm')
B: あ、寮ですか。	*A, ryoo desu ka.*	Oh, (you're living in) a dorm.

BTS 21 Words for home: うち、家、お宅 *uchi, ie, otaku*

Words for home include *uchi* and *ie*, along with the more polite *otaku*. Each of these words has a much deeper cultural meaning that should not be ignored:

You saw *uchi* ('inside') in Act 1 in contrast to *soto* ('outside') to describe Japanese relationships. People who are *uchi* are insiders (family, friends) with whom one doesn't have to be careful about language, formal behavior, or pretense. With people who are *soto* (guests, clients, customers, strangers), one must be careful of how one talks and behaves. The distinction between *uchi* and *soto* is critical to understanding and using the Japanese language. *Uchi* also refers to 'home' in both the physical sense of a building and the concept of where one belongs.

The word *ie* refers to a home or a house (the building itself), but it is also the technical (and sometimes legal) term for the traditional family system. Conventions for the *ie* determine roles for family members (grandparents, parents, and children) along with succession and inheritance.

The word *otaku* is used to refer politely to someone else's house, but it can also be extended to refer to another person's company in client-client relations. It is often translated as 'you' when one businessperson asks the other what *otaku*'s position is on a particular question.

Otaku (usually written in katakana) is also a slang term for those who are hyper-involved (to the detriment of their involvement in the real world) in anime or some other subculture.

Now go to the Activity Book for 練習 *Renshuu* Practice and 腕試し *Udedameshi* Tryout.

Scene 2-6 どなたですか？ *Donata desu ka?*
Who is that?

Sasha is at a reception with her co-worker, Kanda-san. She is still getting used to identifying all the new faces she has met since her arrival, and relies on him to help her with names.

The script

さあしゃ サーシャ	かんだ 神田
あちら、どなたですか？	てらだ 寺田さんですよ。
あちらは？	さあ、ちょっとわからないですねえ。だれかなあ。
みずの 水野さんですか？	いやぁ、水野さんじゃないなあ。

Saasha	*Kanda*
A⌐chira, do¬nata desu ka?	Te⌐rada-san de¬su yo.
A⌐chira wa?	Sa¬a, cho¬tto wa⌐kara¬nai desu ⌐ne¬e. Da¬re ka ⌐na¬a.
Mi¬zuno-san desu ka?	I⌐ya(a), Mi¬zuno-san ja ⌐na¬i ⌐na¬a.

Sasha	Kanda
Who is that over there?	That's Terada-san.
How about over there?	Gosh, I just don't know. Who could it be?
Is it Mizuno-san?	Uhh, that's not Mizuno-san.

たんご ひょうげん
単語と表現 *Tango to hyoogen* Vocabulary and expressions

Nouns

どなた	*donata*	who (polite)
だれ だれ・誰	*dare*	who

だいじょうぶ
大丈夫です。

Sentence particles

| かなあ | *ka naa* | [sentence particle indicating a shared question] |
| なあ | *naa* | [sentence particle indicating shared agreement] |

Phrase particles

| は | *wa* | [particle for contrast] |

Behind the Scenes

BTS 22 Noun$_X$ は? Noun$_X$ *wa?* How about X?

In this Scene you see a new kind of Particle that attaches to Nouns and Noun phrases. The phrase Particle *wa* is used here for contrast. Sasha asks first about a person in the distance: *Achira, donata desu ka?* 'Who is that over there?' Then when she wants to pick out another person in contrast to the first, she uses *wa*: *Achira wa?* 'How about over there?' This *wa* can almost always be translated into English as 'how about.' Here is another example:

A: コーヒー、飲みませんね。	*Koohii, nomimasen ne.*	You don't drink coffee, do you.
B: ええ。	*Ee.*	Right.
A: お茶は?	*Ocha wa?*	How about tea?

BTS 23 Sentence Particles ねえ・なあ *nee* and *naa*

Naa is a casual equivalent of Sentence Particle *nee*. *Naa* tends to be more self-directed. So while *nee* assumes agreement from the other person, *naa* does not. In this conversation, Kanda-san says,

| さあ、ちょっとわからないで すねえ。だれかなあ。 | *Saa, chotto wakaranai desu nee. Dare ka naa.* | 'Gosh, I just don't know! Who could it be?' |

The first Sentence is in response to Sasha's question, while the second is much more a question to himself. *Naa* is less formal than *nee*, so be careful about seeking agreement with *naa* when you are talking to superiors. For the same reason, *naa* doesn't occur after *desu/-masu* forms.

2-6
大丈夫です。

65

BTS 24 Multiple Sentence Particles かなあ、かねえ
ka naa, ka nee

You will hear multiple Particles at the end of a Sentence (usually no more than two). The cumulative effect is, as might be expected, the combined meanings of the Particles.

だれかなあ。	*Dare ka naa.*	I wonder who it could be.

Here *ka* indicates a question and *naa* indicates that I assume you and I share the question.

いいですかねえ。	*Ii desu ka nee.*	I wonder if it's okay.

'I question whether it's all right and assume that you have the same doubt.'

BTS 25 Informal negatives

Here are the negative forms of the Core Sentences that you have seen so far:

Verb	食べないです 食べません	*tabenai desu* *tabemasen*	I don't eat
Nounです	きれいじゃないです きれいじゃありません	*kirei ja nai desu* *kirei ja arimasen*	it's not clean
Adjective	高くないです 高くありません	*takaku nai desu* *takaku arimasen*	it's not expensive

The second (*-masen*) alternative for each of these is a bit more formal (and thus more common in writing), and for Verbs is the preferred form for polite invitations. The *-nai desu* for any of these is also the basis of an informal equivalent. Simply drop *desu*. For verbs, it is this *-nai* form that is used for informal invitations.

Verb	食べない	*tabenai*	I don't eat
Noun です	きれいじゃない	*kirei ja nai*	it's not clean
Adjective	高くない	*takaku nai*	it's not expensive
	コーヒー、飲まない？	*Koohii, nomanai?*	Would you like to have coffee?

Now go to the Activity Book for 練習 *Renshuu* Practice and 腕試し *Udedameshi* Tryout.

Scene 2-7 安[やす]くないですねえ。 *Yasuku nai desu nee.*
It's not cheap, is it.

Sasha and Kanda-san are looking at restaurant reviews as they try to decide on a venue for a division party.

The script

さ あ しゃ サーシャ	かん だ 神田
ここ、どうですか?	いいけど……。
あ、ちょっと高[たか]いですか?	う～ん。安[やす]くないですねえ。
そうですねえ。あ、こっちは?	どこですか?ああ、いいですね。

Saasha	*Kanda*
Ko⌐ko, do⌐o desu ka?	*I⌐i kedo . . .*
A, cho⌐tto ta⌐ka⌐i desu ka?	*Uun. Ya⌐suku ⌐na⌐i desu ⌐ne⌐e.*
So⌐o desu ⌐ne⌐e. A, ko⌐tchi⌐ wa?	*Do⌐ko desu ka? A⌐a, i⌐i desu ⌐ne⌐e.*

Sasha	Kanda
How about this place?	It's good, but . . .
Oh, is it a little expensive?	Well, it's not cheap, is it!
Hmmm. Oh, how about this place?	Where? Oh, that's good, isn't it.

単語と表現 *Tango to hyoogen* Vocabulary and expressions

たんご ひょうげん

Nouns

ここ	*koko*	here
そこ	*soko*	there (near you), that place just mentioned
あそこ	*asoko*	over there, there (away from both of us), that place (that we both know about)
どこ	*doko*	where
どう	*doo*	how
こっち	*kotchi*	here, in this general area, in this direction, this alternative (of two)
そっち	*sotchi*	there (near you), in that general area, in that direction (in your direction), that alternative (of two near you)
あっち	*atchi*	there (away from both of us), in that direction (away from both of us), that alternative (of two away from both of us), that place (that we both know about)
どっち	*dotchi*	where, which direction, which (of two)

Adjectives

高い	*takai*	expensive
安い	*yasui*	inexpensive, cheap
大きい	*ookii*	big
小さい	*chiisai*	small
遠い	*tooi*	far
近い	*chikai*	close
難しい	*muzukashii*	hard, difficult
易しい	*yasashii*	easy
つまらない	*tsumaranai*	boring

Special expressions

う〜ん	*uun*	well (hesitation)
そうですね(え)	*soo desu ne(e)*	well, hmmm, right
ああ	*aa*	ahh, oh
とても	*totemo*	very

Behind the Scenes

BTS 26 どうですか? *Doo desu ka?* How is it?

Doo desu ka 'How is it?' or 'How about X?' can be used to present something for consideration (with the possibility of participation, purchase, opinion, and other relevant actions). It may also be used to ask about the other person's condition in general. It is never used as a greeting out of the blue to mean 'How's it going?'

BTS 27 Buying time: う～ん *uun,* いや（あ）*iya(a),* and そうですね（え）*soo desu ne(e)*

In this Scene you see two phrases that hold the conversational space open while a speaker tries to think of what to say next. *Uun* (pronounced *nnn* with the mouth closed as if you were humming) is similar to *eeto* but is more deliberate. It is used to indicate that you are searching for or don't know what to say or to hold the floor while you are trying to come up with what it is that you want to say next. The phrase *soo desu nee* indicates that the speaker is carefully deliberating about what to say and/or that she needs time to arrange her thoughts. In the previous Scene you also saw Kanda-san say *Iyaa, Mizuno-san ja nai naa* 'Uhh, that's not Mizuno-san.' This *iyaa* is not 'no' but a hesitation noise much like *unn*. After hesitations like this, listeners typically wait for the speaker to say something. This is a good way to "buy time" when you are trying to plan what to say in Japanese!

BTS 28 The ここ *koko* and こっち *kotchi* series

In this Act, we find two more new *ko-so-a-do* series that indicate location.

a　ここ、そこ、あそこ、どこ *koko, soko, asoko, doko*
b　こっち、そっち、あっち、どっち *kotchi, sotchi, atchi, dotchi*

The *koko, soko, asoko, doko* series is used to refer to specific location. Recall that the *kochira, sochira, achira, dochira* series also refer to location but in a vaguer sense—this general area, this direction.

The *kotchi* series is actually a casual equivalent of the *kochira, sochira, achira, dochira* series.

だいじょうぶ
大丈夫です。

Note again that the accent on the question word for both of these series is different from the others:

ko⌐ko, so⌐ko, aso⌐ko, do¬ko
ko⌐tchi, so⌐tchi, a⌐tchi, do¬tchi

Now go to the Activity Book for 練習 *Renshuu* **Practice and** 腕試し *Udedameshi* **Tryout.**

Scene 2-8 何かありますか？ *Nani ka arimasu ka?*
Is there something (for me to do)?

Sasha is about to leave, but asks Kanda-san if there is anything more to do.

The script

サーシャ	神田
何かすること、ありますか？	いや、別に。いいですよ！よかったらお先にどうぞ。
じゃあ、お先に失礼します。	お疲れ様でした。

Saasha	*Kanda*
Na˥ni ka su˥ru ko˥to, a˥rima˥su ka?	*I˥ya˥, be˥tsu ni. I˥i desu yo! Yo˥kattara o˥saki ni do˥ozo.*
Ja˥a, o˥saki ni shitsu˥rei-shi˥ma˥su.	*O˥tsukaresama de˥shita.*

Sasha	Kanda
Is there something I should do?	No, not particularly. It's all right! If you want to, go ahead (home).
Well then, I'll be leaving.	Good work.

単語と表現 *Tango to hyoogen* Vocabulary and expressions

Nouns

すること	*suru koto*	something to do

Verbs

あります（ない）	*arimasu (nai)*	exist (inanimate)

Special expressions

何か なに	*nani ka*	something
別に べつ	*betsu ni*	(not) particularly
じゃあ	*jaa*	well then

Behind the Scenes

BTS 29 Existence: あります *arimasu*
'There is/are' or 'I have'

Japanese makes a distinction between animate and inanimate existence. The Verb for <u>inanimate</u> existence—*arimasu* 'exist, have, be'—is introduced in this Act. Note that the negative of *arimasu* is *arimasen* or *nai desu*.

すること、ありますか?	*Suru koto arimasu ka?*	Is there something (I should) do?' (literally 'Do you have something to do?')
お弁当、ありますよ。 べんとう	*Obentoo arimasu yo!*	There is a boxed meal, you know.
宿題、ないですね? しゅくだい	*Shukudai, nai desu ne?*	You don't have homework, right?

BTS 30 先輩・後輩 *senpai/koohai*—junior/senior
せんぱい こうはい

In Japan, those who are veterans in a group or older are called *senpai* 'senior.' Newcomers or juniors are called *koohai*. It is important to understand how significant the *senpai-koohai* relationship is in Japan. There is a strong mentoring aspect to the *senpai-koohai* relationship, whether it is in school clubs and team sports or at work. American students are often surprised to find when they go to Japan that although they may be bigger and stronger than some of their Japanese classmates, they do not move immediately into the starting lineup of their sports club. They may be given menial tasks to do that all *koohai* members are expected to take on. And the *senpai-koohai* relationship lasts a lifetime. When there is a problem with a contract at work, one person may say, "I have a *senpai* in the Law Division who might be able to help us." In this conversation, Sasha seeks permission to leave from her *senpai*, Kanda-san, who is responsible for making sure that she is following protocol.

Now go to the Activity Book for 練習 *Renshuu* Practice and 腕試し *Udedameshi* Tryout.
れんしゅう　　　　　　　　　　　　　　　　うでだめ

Then do 評価 *Hyooka* Assessment activities.
ひょうか

Between the lines

BTL 1 平仮名^{ひらがな} Hiragana

The next three lessons introduce hiragana. This is the kana system that is used to write function words, inflections, and/or native Japanese (not borrowed) words for which there is no accepted kanji. Actually, it is possible to use hiragana to write anything in Japanese. But native speakers of Japanese who have even a minimal amount of schooling would not ordinarily write long strings of words or sentences in hiragana.

All hiragana symbols have their origin in more complicated *kanji*. Below is a chart that illustrates where each symbol came from. The top character in each block is the typeset version of the original kanji, the middle character is its cursive (handwritten) form, and the bottom character is the resulting *hiragana* symbol.

For the sake of authenticity, in these lessons anything that you see in hiragana is what Japanese people themselves would typically write in hiragana—or what the Ministry of Education, Sports, Science and Technology (文部科学省^{もんぶかがくしょう}) recommends be written in

无ゑん	和わわ	良らら	也せや	末まま	波はは	奈なな	太たた	左をさ	加かか	安めあ
	爲ゐゐ	利利り		美みみ	比ひひ	仁にに	知ちち	之しし	機きき	以りい
		留るる	由ゆゆ	武むむ	不ふふ	奴ぬぬ	川つつ	寸すす	久くく	宇うう
	恵ゑゑ	礼れれ		女めめ	部へへ	祢ねね	天てて	世せせ	計けけ	衣ええ
	遠をを	呂ろろ	与よよ	毛もも	保ほほ	乃のの	止とと	曽そそ	己ここ	於おお

Figure 2.1 Origin of *hiragana* characters

Source: https://commons.wikimedia.org/wiki/File:Hiragana_origin.svg

hiragana. These lessons also follow the convention for this textbook—that you will learn patterns and vocabulary first in the spoken form and then in the written form.

There are 46 hiragana symbols. They are often summarized in the chart called *gojuuon-hyoo* 'chart of fifty sounds'), although there are only 46 symbols included in the chart since some sounds are no longer used in modern Japanese.[1]

Gojuuon-hyoo 'Chart of fifty sounds'

ん	わ	ら	や	ま	は	な	た	さ	か	あ
n	wa	ra	ya	ma	ha	na	ta	sa	ka	a
		り		み	ひ	に	ち	し	き	い
		ri		mi	hi	ni	chi	shi	ki	i
		る	ゆ	む	ふ	ぬ	つ	す	く	う
		ru	yu	mu	fu	nu	tsu	su	ku	u
		れ		め	へ	ね	て	せ	け	え
		re		me	he	ne	te	se	ke	e
	を	ろ	よ	も	ほ	の	と	そ	こ	お
	o	ro	yo	mo	ho	no	to	so	ko	o

This chart employs vertical writing, so when read in order it is read top to bottom, right to left. That is: *a, i, u, e, o, ka, ki, ku, ke, ko,* etc. (あ、い、う、え、お、か、き、く、け、こ . . .). This order is called *gojuuon-jun* '*gojuuon* order'). This order is used to sort lists of names, items, etc., just as alphabetical order is used in English.

BTL 2 Punctuation (句読点)

<small>く とうてん</small>

You will see punctuation marks in Japanese that are different from English:

。 This marks the end of a sentence much as the period marks the end of an English sentence. In Japanese this is called *maru* (まる 'circle').

、 This marks a break in a sentence, much like the comma in English. But do watch for differences in where the comma is placed! In Japanese this is called 点 *ten* 'point, dot') or, more technically, *touten* (読点).

· · · · · · English uses three dots aligned at the bottom of a line to show that something is missing or unfinished. ("I understand but . . .") There is no set convention for this in Japanese but you often see two or more sets of three dots aligned in the center. This may or may not be followed by a *maru*: · · · · · ·。

74

「」 These square brackets are used to designate something as a quotation, just as " " are used in English: 「これです」

~ A tilde has many uses in Japanese. Often it shows that a mora is elongated for effect (わ〜 *waa*). In this textbook it will also be used to designate something as part of a word (Verb〜ましょう 'Verb~*mashoo*' for the -*mashoo* form of a Verb).

· A dot between two series of symbols (ブライアン・ワン 'Brian Wang') indicates that they are separate words. This is called *nakaten* (中点) and you will see it most commonly in Western names.

In addition to these, you will also see question marks and exclamation points in Japanese, although these are generally viewed as English borrowings.

BTL 3 Handwritten vs. print forms of characters

There is often a difference between the print form and the handwritten form of a character. As kana symbols are introduced below, you see first the print form, then the handwritten form. When you practice writing (see your Workbook), you should imitate the handwritten form.

Note

1 These symbols include ゐ (*wi*) and ゑ (*we*) in the w-column.

75

Scene 2-9R おいしそうですね！Looks delicious!

The following is a screenshot of a smart phone that Eri posted recently. What were Eri's friends saying about the post?

 テキスト Text

大丈夫です。

Eri Yamada: I'm about to eat (this)!
Yuko Sakamoto: Looks delicious!
Sasha: Oh, beautiful! Where is this?

文字と例 Symbols with examples

This Act introduces the first twenty-five hiragana symbols. For each symbol, you see representations in a font commonly used in print and a font that is closer to handwriting. Use the latter as your model for handwriting.

	Common Font	Romanization	Handwritten version
#1.	あ	*a*	あ
#2.	こ	*ko*	こ
#3.	そ*	*so*	そ
#4.	れ	*re*	れ
#5.	と	*to*	と

* This one-stroke symbol has a two-stroke variant: そ

Examples

これ	this (thing), this one, this item
それ	that (thing) (near you); that (one) (near you); the item (you just mentioned)
あれ	that (thing) away from both of us; that (one) away from us); the item (we both know)

BTL 4 Diacritics (*tenten/daku-on*, ゛)

The diacritical marks that you see attached to the symbols below are one kind of *dakuten* (濁点) or *nigoriten* (濁り点). Two small dots or slashes ゛ at the top right of a symbol change the consonant value of the mora from voiceless to voiced. In Japanese, these two marks are called *ten-ten* 点々 'dot-dot').

Voiceless		Voiced	
こ	*ko*	ご	*go*
そ	*so*	ぞ	*zo*
と	*to*	ど	*do*

From now on, voiced hiragana symbols will be introduced along with the voiceless ones.

#6.	か	ka	が	ga	か	
#7.	す	su	ず	zu	す	
#8.	た	ta	だ	da	た	
#9.	て	te	で	de	て	

Examples

1.	これです。	It's this one.
2.	それですか?	Is it that? Do you mean that one?
3.	あ、あれですか。	Oh, you mean that one.
4.	どれですか。	Which one is it?
5.	あれですが ...	I mean that one over there, but . . .
6.	だれですか。	Who is it?

#10.	さ*	sa	ざ	za	さ

* this is a three-stroke symbol.

#11.	ん	n			ん

Examples

1.	神田さん	Kanda-san
2.	あ、坂田さんですか。	Oh, is she Sakata-san?
3.	だれですか? 佐賀さん?	Who is it? Is it Saga-san?

#12	し	shi	じ	ji	し
#13	ま	ma			ま
#14	り*	ri			り

* When you write by hand, this is a two-stroke symbol.

Examples

1.	します。	She will do it. I do it.
2.	しますか。	Are you going to do it? Do they do it?
3.	仕事します。	I will work.
4.	あります。	There are some. I have it.
5.	あ、ありますか。	Oh, do you have it? Oh, does it exist?
6.	またあとで。	See you again later.
7.	仕事、ありますか。	Do you have a job? Is there anything I should do?

#15. き*   *ki*   ぎ   *gi*

#16. い   *i*

* this is a four-stroke symbol.

Examples

1.	今	right now
2.	行きます。	I'll go.
3.	ただいま。	I'm home.
4.	好きです。	I like it.
5.	大好きです。	I like it a lot.
6.	高いです。	It's expensive/high/tall.
7.	高いですか。	Is it expensive/high/tall?
8.	今しますか。	Are you going to do it right now?
9.	いただきます。	Thank you for the meal (*lit.* I humbly accept).
10.	あ、今仕事しますか？	Oh? You're going to work right now?

#17. せ   *se*   ぜ   *ze*

Examples

1.	しません。	I don't do it.
2.	行きません。	They won't go.
3.	ありません。	There aren't any.

4. これ、しませんか。	Would you like to do this?	
5. あれ、ありませんか。	That thing (that we both know), don't you have it?	
6. 神田さん。行きませんか。	Kanda-san. Won't you go?	

#18. **ち**   *chi*   **ぢ**¹   *ji*   **ち**

#19. **ら***   *ra*   **ら**

* When you write by hand, this is a two-stroke symbol.

Examples

1. こちら	this (direction/area/side); this alternative (of two)
2. そちらですか。	Is it that (direction/side/area)?
3. これ、あちらですか。	Is this (located) over there?
4. 寺田さん、どちらですか。	Where is Terada-san?
5. あ、赤坂さん。今、どちらですか。	(on the telephone) Oh, Akasaka-san, where are you right now?

#20. **ね**   *ne*   **ね**

#21. **よ**   *yo*   **よ**

In Japanese writing, there is rarely any distinction made between *ne* and *ne?* although you may see 「ね。」「ね!」and「ね?」. Even ***nee***, which can be rendered 「ねえ」、「ね ぇ」、「ね~」, etc. is sometimes written simply 「ね。」. We must rely heavily on the context to determine how ね is read and interpreted.

Examples

1. これですね。	It's this one, right?
2. 行きませんよ。	I won't go.
3. 高いですね。	It's expensive, isn't it.

4.	しませんね？		You won't do it, right?
5.	お願いします。		Please give me a hand.
6.	あ、あれですよ。		Oh, it's that one.
7.	寺田さん、こちらですね？		Terada-san is here/this direction, right?

#22.	う	*u*	う
#23.	え	*e*	え
#24.	お	*o*	お

Examples

1.	え？	Huh? Pardon?
2.	いえ	no
3.	家	house, home
4.	家	house, home
5.	お宅	house, home (polite)
6.	いえいえ。	No, no.
7.	すごいですね。	It's great/terrific/amazing, isn't it.

BTL 5 Long vowels

The long versions of あ, い, and う are written by repeating the same symbol: ああ, いい, うう. But the long version of お—even though it is pronounced /oo/—is written in hiragana おう and the long version of /e/—even though it is pronounced /ee/—is written えい. (There are exceptions to this convention, which will be pointed out as they come up. One of these can be seen in #2 below where う〜ん 'hmm' is written with a tilde.) Thus,

ああ	*aa*	
いい	*ii*	
うう	*uu*	
えい	*ei*	exceptions: ええ *ee* 'yes,' お姉さん *oneesan* 'older sister'
おう	*ou*	exceptions: 大きい *ookii* 'is big,' 大阪 *Oosaka* 'Osaka'

81

Examples

1.	どうぞ。	Please (go ahead/take it/have some).
2.	う～ん	[hesitation noise]
3.	先生	teacher, instructor, professor, doctor
4.	言います。	say, be called
5.	いいですか。	Is it OK? Is it good?
6.	どうですか。	How is it?
7.	そう、そう。	Yes, yes.
8.	そうですか。	Oh, really / Oh, okay.
9.	きれいですね。	It's pretty, isn't it!
10.	おいしいですね。	It's delicious, isn't it!
11.	おいしそうですね。	It looks delicious, doesn't it.
12.	今忙しいですか。	Are you busy right now?
13.	今ですか?いえ、いいですよ。	Now? No, it's fine.
14.	ごちそうさま(でした)。	Thank you for the meal.
15.	ありがとうございます。	Thank you (formal).
16.	ありがとうございました。	Thank you for what you have done (formal).

Summary of symbols in Act 2

The charts below summarize the 24 symbols introduced so far.

n	*w*	*r*	*y*	*m*	*h*	*n*	*t*	*s*	*k*	
ん *n*		ら *ra*		ま *ma*			た *ta*	さ *sa*	か *ka*	あ *a*
		り *ri*					ち *chi*	し *shi*	き *ki*	い *i*
								す *su*		う *u*
		れ *re*				ね *ne*	て *te*	せ *se*		え *e*
			よ *yo*				と *to*	そ *so*	こ *ko*	お *o*

b	d	z	g
	だ *da*	ざ *za*	が *ga*
	(ぢ) *ji*	じ *ji*	ぎ *gi*
		ず *zu*	
	で *de*	ぜ *ze*	
	ど *do*	ぞ *zo*	ご *go*

BTL 6 Tips for writing practice

a. Stroke types

All Japanese characters (*kana* and *kanji*) are composed of individual strokes that fall into different categories depending on how the stroke is started or ended.

1   Stop (*tome*): The stroke comes to a full stop, like the first stroke of あ, た, and よ.
2   Release (*harai*): The stroke becomes gradually thinner until it disappears, like the single stroke of し.
3   Hook (*hane*): The stroke ends with a hook, like the first stroke of こ, う, and ら.

All of these differences are visible in the printed and brush-written versions of the hiragana symbols, but the use of ballpoint pens might obscure many of them.

Where a stroke begins and ends is also critical and can even change the character; note that the long stroke of katakana *tsu* ツ starts at the top while the long stroke of *shi* シ starts at the bottom.

b. Stroke order

Attitudes toward calligraphy and handwriting show cultural differences. For the average American, good handwriting is largely a matter of legibility. However, there are prescriptive rules about the stroke order and stroke types of orthographic symbols in Japanese, and these rules are closely monitored and followed in Japanese schools.

Now go to the Activity Book for 練習 *Renshuu* **Practice.**

83

Then do 評価 *Hyooka* Assessment activities, including 読んでみよう *Yonde miyoo* Contextualized reading, 書き取り *Kakitori* Dictation, and 書いてみよう *Kaite miyoo* Contextualized writing.

Note

1 Note that じ and ぢ have the same pronunciation. The symbol ぢ is rarely used in modern Japanese.

第3幕
Act 3

何時ですか?

Nan-ji desu ka?

What time is it?

急がば回れ　*Isogaba maware*
More haste, less speed.
(Literally, 'If you are in a hurry, go the long way.')

◆ 話す・聞く *Hanasu/kiku* **Speaking and listening**
はな き

Scene 3-1 日本語で何といいますか？
に ほん ご なん
Nihongo de nan to iimasu ka?
What's it called in Japanese?

Amy Johnson, President of the Japanese Language Club at her university, welcomes a new student from Japan and introduces herself.

The script

エイミー え いみー	孝 たかし
ＪＬＣのジョンソンです。どうぞよろしくお願いします。 じぇええるしい じょんそん ねが	あ、福沢大学の松浦です。どうぞよろしくお願いします。 ふくざわだいがく まつうら ねが
	あの、ＪＬＣって……。 じぇええるしい
ジャパニーズ・ランゲージ・クラブのことです。学生のサークルですね。 じゃ ぱ に い ず ら ん げ え じ く ら ぶ がくせい さ あ く る	ああ、なるほど。
日本語で何といいますか? に ほん ご なん	そうですねえ。まあ、日本語クラブかなあ。 に ほん ご く ら ぶ
日本語クラブですね? に ほん ご く ら ぶ	ええ。

87

Eimii	Takashi
Je⌐e-eru-shi⌐i no Jo⌐nson desu. Do⌐ozo yo⌐roshiku onegai-shima⌐su.	A, Fu⌐kuzawa Da⌐igaku no Ma⌐tsu⌐ura desu. Do⌐ozo yo⌐roshiku onegai-shima⌐su.
	Ano, je⌐e-eru-shi⌐i tte. . . .
Ja⌐paniizu rangeeji ku⌐rabu no ko⌐to⌐ desu. Ga⌐kuseei no sa⌐akuru desu ne.	Aa, na⌐ruhodo.
Ni⌐hongo de na⌐n to i⌐ima⌐su ka?	So⌐o desu nee. Ma⌐a Ni⌐hongo-ku⌐rabu ka ⌐na⌐a.
Ni⌐hongo-ku⌐rabu desu ne?	E⌐e.

Amy	Takashi
I'm Johnson from JLC. Nice to meet you.	Oh, I'm Matsuura from Fukuzawa University. Nice to meet you.
	Uhh . . . JLC?
It means 'Japanese Language Club.' It's a student club.	Oh, I see.
What would it be called in Japanese?	Hmm. Let me think about it. I guess it'd be *Nihongo-kurabu*.
That's *Nihongo-kurabu*, right?	Yes.

単語と表現 *Tango to hyoogen* Vocabulary and expressions

Nouns

JLC	*Jee-Eru-Shii*	JLC (Japanese Language Club)
福沢大学	*Fukuzawa Daigaku*	Fukuzawa University
大学	*daigaku*	university, college
X大学	*X-Daigaku*	X University, X College
高校	*kookoo*	high school
大学院	*daigakuin*	graduate school
大垣商会	*Oogaki Shookai*	Ogaki Trading Company, Ltd.
アオイ出版	*Aoi Shuppan*	Aoi Publishing

日本語	*Nihongo*	Japanese (language)
英語	*Eigo*	English (language)
中国語	*Chuugokugo*	Chinese (language)
韓国語	*Kankokugo*	Korean (language)
フランス語	*Furansugo*	French (language)
スペイン語	*Supeingo*	Spanish (language)
ロシア語	*Roshiago*	Russian (language)
何語	*nanigo*	which language
学生	*gakusei*	student
サークル	*saakuru*	club
～会	*-kai*	organization, club, association, group
クラブ	*kurabu*	club
日本語クラブ	*Nihongo-kurabu*	Japanese Language Club
ジョンソン	*Jonson*	Johnson
ジャン¹	*Jan*	Zhang [Chinese family name]
張	*Choo*	Zhang [Chinese family name]
日本人	*Nihonjin*	Japanese (person)
アメリカ人	*Amerikajin*	American (person)
中国人	*Chuugokujin*	Chinese (person)
韓国人	*Kankokujin*	Korean (person)
フランス人	*Furansujin*	French (person)
スペイン人	*Supeinjin*	Spanish (person)
ロシア人	*Roshiajin*	Russian (person)
何人・なに人	*nanijin*	what nationality
日系人	*nikkeijin*	person of Japanese heritage
外国人	*gaikokujin*	foreigner
外人	*gaijin*	foreigner (can be derogatory)

Verbs

いいます いわない	*i-imasu (iw-anai)*	is called, say

Phrase particles

って	*tte*	[topic particle]

Special expressions

Xのこと	Noun$_X$ + *no koto*	it's a matter of X; it means X
なるほど。	*naruhodo*	Oh, I see now.
まあ	*maa*	I guess (non-committal)

拡張 *Kakuchoo* Expansion

1 Find out from a Japanese associate or friend the name of your school, university, or workplace in Japanese.
2 Do you speak languages other than those listed in the vocabulary section above? Make an intelligent guess as to what that language is called in Japanese and see if your guess was right by checking a reliable source.
3 Find out from a Japanese associate or friend how they would refer to your nationality if it isn't included in those provided here.
4 Find the Japanese expressions that correspond to various acronyms that are used frequently in your surroundings (e.g., JAL, JETRO, DNA) by telling what each acronym stands for in English, then asking what it is called in Japanese. You don't necessarily have to remember the full term in Japanese (that's what the acronyms are for!), but see if you can repeat the term once. Do this in Japanese.
5 Ask a Japanese exchange student or Japanese college graduate what kinds of circles and clubs there were at his or her home university. Do this in Japanese.
6 Ask a Japanese friend or acquaintance that is familiar with English what a certain word in English would be in Japanese.

Behind the Scenes

BTS 1 Pronouncing the alphabet

You should learn what the Roman alphabet sounds like in Japanese, since you may have to spell your name or provide other kinds of alphabetic information (email addresses, ticket confirmations, etc.). Listen to the accompanying sound file to help you learn the letters. All of these have the accent on the first mora.

<ruby>えい<rt></rt></ruby> a	*ei*	<ruby>えいち<rt></rt></ruby> h	*eichi*	<ruby>おお<rt></rt></ruby> o	*oo*	<ruby>ずいい<rt></rt></ruby> v	*vii*
<ruby>びい<rt></rt></ruby> b	*bii*	<ruby>あい<rt></rt></ruby> i	*ai*	<ruby>ぴい<rt></rt></ruby> p	*pii*	<ruby>だぶりゅう<rt></rt></ruby> w	*daburyuu*
<ruby>しい<rt></rt></ruby> c	*shii*	<ruby>じぇえ<rt></rt></ruby> j	*jee*	<ruby>きゅう<rt></rt></ruby> q	*kyuu*	<ruby>えっくす<rt></rt></ruby> x	*ekkusu*
<ruby>でいい<rt></rt></ruby> d	*dii*	<ruby>けい<rt></rt></ruby> k	*kei*	<ruby>あある<rt></rt></ruby> r	*aaru*	<ruby>わい<rt></rt></ruby> y	*wai*
<ruby>いい<rt></rt></ruby> e	*ii*	<ruby>える<rt></rt></ruby> l	*eru*	<ruby>えす<rt></rt></ruby> s	*esu*	<ruby>ぜっと<rt></rt></ruby> z	*zetto*
<ruby>えふ<rt></rt></ruby> f	*efu*	<ruby>えむ<rt></rt></ruby> m	*emu*	<ruby>ていい<rt></rt></ruby> t	*tii*		
<ruby>じい<rt></rt></ruby> g	*jii*	<ruby>えぬ<rt></rt></ruby> n	*enu*	<ruby>ゆう<rt></rt></ruby> u	*yuu*		

BTS 2 Nouns modifying Nouns: Noun_A の・な Noun_B Noun_A *no/na* Noun_B

When one Noun describes another, there are two possible patterns.

a. Nouns that use *no*

Some Nouns describe other Nouns with the Particle *no*: *watashi no keitai* 'my cell phone,' *nihongo no sensei* 'the Japanese teacher' (contrast *sensei no nihongo* 'the teacher's Japanese'). The relationship between the first and second Nouns varies, but it is always the second Noun that is being described in some way by the first. The resulting phrase may indicate possession (*watashi no keitai* 'my cell phone'), location (*Nihon no gakkoo* 'schools in Japan'), or it may serve to further specify which person or thing you mean (*Nihon no Ueno-san* 'the Ueno-san who is in Japan' (contrast *Amerika no Kanda-san* 'the Kanda-san who is in the US'). In this Scene you see this pattern used to describe people's affiliations—with their school, place of work, etc. Noun_A is the affiliation and Noun_B is the person or thing that can be identified in terms of Noun_A.

Here are some other examples.

<ruby>東京<rt>とうきょう</rt></ruby><ruby>大学<rt>だいがく</rt></ruby>の<ruby>松浦<rt>まつうら</rt></ruby>です。	*Tookyoo-daigaku no Matsuura desu.*	I am Matsuura from Tokyo University.
トヨタの<ruby>張<rt>ちょう</rt></ruby>です。	*Toyota no Choo desu.*	I am Cho from Toyota.
<ruby>高校<rt>こうこう</rt></ruby>の<ruby>先生<rt>せんせい</rt></ruby>じゃないですか?	*Kookoo no sensei ja nai desu ka?*	Aren't you a high school teacher?
<ruby>大学<rt>だいがく</rt></ruby>の<ruby>学生<rt>がくせい</rt></ruby>です。	*Daigaku no gakusei desu.*	She is a student at a university.
<ruby>学生<rt>がくせい</rt></ruby>の<ruby>サークル<rt>さあくる</rt></ruby>	*gakusei no saakuru*	student club

91

The number of Nouns (sometimes with Adjectives) that might describe another Noun is not limited (except by memory). Consider the following examples:

会社の神田さんのパソコン	*kaisha no Kanda-san no pasokon*	the computer of Kanda-san from the office
モリスさんのパソコンのキーボード	*Morisu-san no pasokon no kiiboodo*	the keyboard from Morris-san's personal computer
あの会社の古い名前	*ano kaisha no furui namae*	the old name of that company

b. Nouns that use *na*

A smaller set of Nouns describe other Nouns with the Particle *na*: *kirei na nihongo* 'beautiful Japanese,' *suki na sensei* 'the teacher that I like.' These will be called "*na* Nouns." All *na* Nouns are intangible, but not all intangibles are *na* Nouns. All *na* Nouns will be followed by (*na*) in the glossary to distinguish them from other Nouns.

大丈夫な薬	*daijoobu na kusuri*	medicine that is sure or safe
面白そうなサークル	*omoshirosoo na saakuru*	a club that looks interesting
きれいな日本語	*kirei na nihongo*	beautiful Japanese
失礼な英語	*shitsurei na eigo*	English that is rude

BTS 3 日本語で何といいますか?
Nihongo de nan to iimasu ka?
'What's it called in Japanese?' or
'What would it be called in Japanese?'

You will almost certainly want to ask what things are called in Japanese. This is what it means to be a language learner. In this question—*Nihongo de nan to iimasu ka?*—you see some familiar elements: *Nihongo* 'Japanese,' *nan* 'what,' *ka* (question Particle). You also see some elements that you haven't seen before: *iimasu* 'be called, say,' along with two new Particles: *de* and *to*. These will be analyzed later. For now, here is how this pattern is used.

宿題といいます。	*Shukudai to iimasu.*	It's called *shukudai* (homework).
日本語でマクドナルドといいます。	*Nihongo de Makudonarudo to iimasu.*	It's called *Makudonarudo* (McDonald's [restaurant]) in Japanese.

BTS 4 Phrase Particle って *tte*

In casual speech and informal written genres like email and text (not in formal writing!) you will very often hear (or see) Japanese speakers pick up a topic and comment on or ask about it with Phrase Particle *tte*.

日本の大学って高いですか？	*Nihon no daigaku tte takai desu ka?*	Are universities in Japan expensive?
張さんって北京大学の学生ですね？	*Choo-san tte Pekin-Daigaku no gakusei desu ne?*	Cho-san is a Peking University student, right?

The Particle *tte* with question intonation can also be used to echo what someone just said when you don't know what it means or aren't clear about what you are supposed to conclude.

ジェーエルシーって？	*Jee-eru-shii tte?*	(What do you mean by) JLC?
来ませんって？	*Kimasen tte?*	Isn't coming? (What do you mean by that?)
高いって？	*Takai tte?*	It's expensive? (What do you mean by "expensive?")

BTS 5 Noun$_x$ + のこと Noun$_x$ + *no koto*
a matter of Noun$_x$

The combination of a Noun plus *no koto* means something like 'a matter of N.' This is frequently used in explanations, as you see in this Scene when Amy explains what 'JLC' means:

Japanese Language Club *no koto desu*. It means 'Japanese Language Club.'
Combining the previous pattern [Noun *tte*] with this phrase, you might hear:

ジェーエルシーって Japanese Language Clubのことです。	*Jee-eru-shii tte Japanese Language Club no koto desu.*	JLC means Japanese Student Organization.
エミリーって、ってエミリー・リンさんのことですか？	*Emirii tte Emirii Rin-san no koto desu ka?*	By *Emirii*, do you mean Emily Lin?
アイエムエフって International Monetary Fund のことですけど、日本語で何といいますか？	*Ai-emu-efu tte, International Monetary Fund no koto desu kedo, Nihongo de nan to iimasu ka?*	IMF means International Monetary Fund, but what do you call it in Japanese?

BTS 6 ああ、なるほど。 *Aa, naruhodo.*
Oh, of course.

The word *naruhodo* has a number of English equivalents. It is a verbal response to the light suddenly dawning when you finally understand what the other person said—new information, an explanation, a joke—often something that is self-evident. English equivalents include 'I see,' 'that makes sense,' 'of course.' Here you see it in response to an explanation of "JLC."

Now go to the Activity Book for 練習 *Renshuu* Practice and 腕し試 *Udedameshi* Tryout.

Note

1 The kanji for a common Chinese last name (張) is pronounced "Zhang" in China (and the US), but "Choo" in Japan.

Scene 3-2　今何時ですか？ *Ima nan-ji desu ka?*
いまなんじ
What time is it now?

Amy Johnson is talking to Takashi, a Japanese student studying at her university. They are about to have a meeting, and Amy checks the time. (Remember, Japanese people expect things to start on time.)

The script

エイミー	孝
今 何時ですか?	2時半ごろじゃないですか? [after checking] あ、やっぱり、2時半ですね。
じゃあ、行きましょう。	ジェームス君と田中さんは?
あ、ジェームス君と田中さんですか? 今日はお休みです。	

Eimii	Takashi
Iˈma ˈnaˈn-ji desu ka?	Niˈ-jihan goˈro ja ˈnaˈi desu ka? [after checking] A, yaˈppaˈri, niˈ-jihaˈn desu ne.
Jaˈa, iˈkimashoˈo.	Jeˈemusu-kun to Taˈnaka-san wa?
A, Jeˈemusu-kun to Taˈnaka-san deˈsu ka? Kyoˈo wa oˈyasumi deˈsu.	

Amy	Takashi
What time is it now?	Isn't it around 2:30? [after checking] Oh, sure enough, it's 2:30.
Well, then, let's go.	What about James and Tanaka-san?
Oh, James and Tanaka-san? They are off today.	

単語と表現 *Tango to hyoogen* Vocabulary and expressions

Nouns

何時	*nanji*	what time
前	*mae*	before
過ぎ	*sugi*	past, beyond
授業	*jugyoo*	class
会議	*kaigi*	meeting
(お)休み	*(o)yasumi*	day off, vacation
病気	*byooki*	sick

Verbs

帰ります(帰らない)	*kaer-imasu (kaer-anai)*	return (home)
待ちます(待たない)	*mach-imasu (mat-anai)*	wait
勉強します(しない)	*benkyoo-shimasu*	study
仕事します(しない)	*shigoto-shimasu*	work
宿題します(しない)	*shukudai-shimasu*	do homework
授業します(しない)	*jugyoo-shimasu*	conduct a class
会議します(しない)	*kaigi-shimasu*	hold a meeting

Classifiers

Time expressions

1時	*ichi-ji*	1:00		13時	*juusan-ji*	13:00
2時	*ni-ji*	2:00		14時	*juuyo-ji*	14:00
3時	*san-ji*	3:00		15時	*juugo-ji*	15:00
4時	*yo-ji*	4:00		16時	*juuroku-ji*	16:00
5時	*go-ji*	5:00		17時 17時	*juushichi-ji/ juunana-ji*	17:00
6時	*roku-ji*	6:00		18時	*juuhachi-ji*	18:00
7時 7時	*shichi-ji/ nana-ji*	7:00		19時	*juuku-ji*	19:00

8時	hachi-ji	8:00	２０時	nijuu-ji	20:00
9時	ku-ji	9:00	２１時	nijuuichi-ji	21:00
10時	juu-ji	10:00	２２時	nijuuni-ji	22:00
１１時	juuichi-ji	11:00	２３時	nijuusan-ji	23:00
１２時	juuni-ji	12:00	２４時	nijuuyo-ji	24:00 (midnight)
			０時	rei-ji	0:00 (midnight)

Phrase particles

X は	X *wa*	as for X
X と Y	X *to* Y	X and Y

Special expressions

やっぱり	*yappari*	as expected, sure enough
TIME + ごろ	TIME + *goro*	about TIME
X 時半 (2:30)	*X-ji-han*	half past (hour X) (2:30)

拡張 *Kakuchoo* Expansion

1 Find the Japanese expressions to refer to objects in your surroundings that are essential to your daily activities, then practice saying the word until your partner seems comfortable with your pronunciation.
2 Find out which smartphone applications are most popular in Japan.

Behind the Scenes

BTS 7 [Noun + は] and [Noun + Phrase Particle + は] [Noun + *wa*] and [Noun + Phrase Particle + *wa*]

You saw the Phrase Particle *wa* in Act 2 Scene 6 as it introduces a Noun in contrast to some other (already understood) option. In the current Scene, Takashi asks about two other students: *Jeemusu-kun to Tanaka-san wa?* This illustrates the primary function of *wa* which is to pick a Noun out of some larger group of items that we most typically understand or know about from the context. For this reason, *wa* never follows a question word such as *nani* or *dore*. A good English translation of *wa* often involves bringing the *wa* Noun to the front of the sentence and then commenting on it (see the examples below). Here are examples illustrating four possible relationships between Nouns with *wa* and the rest of a Sentence:

• Time

あしたはできないですよ。	*Ashita wa dekinai desu yo.*	Tomorrow I can't do it (though I may be able to do it some other day).

• Subject

私は学生じゃありません。	*Watashi wa gakusei ja arimasen.*	I (at least) am not a student (although someone else may be).

• Object

すしは食べますけど……。	*Sushi wa tabemasu kedo . . .*	Sushi, I eat, but . . . (maybe not the other things that are Japanese).

• Quantity

ちょっとはわかりますけど……。	*Chotto wa wakarimasu kedo . . .*	I understand a little, but . . .

Particle *wa* is often called a topic particle, but recall that *tte* is also used to introduce a topic in speech or casual writing. (Keep in mind, too, that there are other ways of introducing a topic, such as *X desu ga . . .* 'About X . . .'). How is *wa* different from *tte*? For one thing, in using [Noun$_x$ *wa*], the speaker is clear about what defines or what is included in Noun$_x$. [Noun$_x$ *tte*], on the other hand, is vaguer—the speaker isn't exactly sure what defines the category. Secondly, *tte* suggests emotional or psychological involvement in Noun$_x$. Consider the following example with *tte* rather than *wa*, where *tte* shows heightened curiosity or excitement.

A: あちら、佐藤さんです。	A: *Achira, Satoo-san desu.*	A: That over there is Sato-san.
B: え?佐藤さん?佐藤さんって、あのCEOの佐藤さんですか?	B: *E? Satoo-san? Satoo-san tte ano CEO no Satoo-san desu ka?*	B: What? Sato-san? Sato-san means the Sato-san who is the CEO?

Moreover *tte* will never be used in the contrastive sense that *wa* has. In the following exchange, *tte* is not possible.

A: あ、これ、コーヒーじゃないですね。	A: *A, kore, koohii ja nai desu nee.*	A: Oh, this isn't coffee.
B: ああ、コーヒーはあちらです。	B: *Aa, koohii wa achira desu.*	B: Ah, the coffee is over there.

98

BTS 8 Verb stem 〜ましょう -*mashoo* forms

The -*mashoo* form is made by adding -*mashoo* to the Verb stem. The stem is the -*masu* form minus -*masu*. A Verb in its -*mashoo* form means 'let's' or 'why don't we/I.' Context usually makes clear which is intended.

飲みましょう。	*Nomimashoo.*	Let's drink it. / Why don't I drink it.
言いましょう。	*Iimashoo.*	Let's tell them. / Let's say it.
始めましょう。	*Hajimemashoo.*	Let's begin.

The addition of question Particle *ka* (-*mashoo ka*) with falling intonation invites the listener to agree to the suggestion—'shall we/I?'

食べましょうか。	*Tabemashoo ka.*	Let's eat, shall we?
言いましょうか。	*Iimashoo ka.*	Shall we/I tell/say it?
始めましょうか。	*Hajimemashoo ka.*	Let's begin, shall we?

It is also possible to combine a question word (such as *dore* or *doo*) with a -*mashoo* form (with or without *ka*) to pose a question that seeks collaboration.

どれ使いましょうか。	*Dore tsukaimashoo ka.*	Which one shall we use?
どうしましょう。	*Doo shimashoo.*	What shall I do?
そうしましょう。	*Soo shimashoo.*	Let's do it that way.

Note in this last example that Japanese uses *doo* 'how' rather than *nan* 'what.'

BTS 9 Time expressions and classifiers
〜時、〜時半
-*ji, -ji-han*

In Japanese, numbers rarely occur by themselves (except when doing math or listing numbers in a sequence—in a test or workbook exercise, for example). Instead they combine with "classifiers" that tell what is being counted. The classifier for naming hours on the clock is -*ji*. Especially for scheduling, Japan uses a 24-hour clock, so the afternoon hours continue after 12:00 *juuni-ji* (12:00 p.m.) with 13:00 *juusan-ji* (1:00 p.m.), 14:00 *juuyo-ji* (2:00 p.m.), 15:00 *juugo-ji* (3:00 p.m.), etc. with midnight being 0:00 or *rei-ji*. The question word for "what time" is *nan-ji*.

The numbers that combine with -*ji* are derived from Chinese, with the exception of 4:00 and 7:00. The Chinese-derived word for 4 is *shi,* which is homonymous with the word for death and is therefore unlucky (much as the number thirteen is avoided in Western cultures). *Shi* is used only when doing math or listing numbers in a sequence. Instead, with clock time, you hear the Japanese number, *yo-ji*. Similarly, the word for 7, *shichi,* is easily confused with *shi*, so the Japanese number *nana* often substitutes. Both *shichi-ji* and *nana-ji* are acceptable for 7:00.

今何時ですか?	*Ima nan-ji desu ka?*	What time is it now?
4時じゃありませんか?	*Yo-ji ja arimasen ka?*	Isn't it 4:00?

Half hours are indicated by adding *-han* to the hour: *ichi-ji-han* '1:30,' *ni-ji-han* '2:30,' etc.

4時半じゃありませんか?	*Yo-ji-han ja arimasen ka?*	Isn't it 4:30?

Uncertain or approximate time is indicated by adding *-goro* to the time. Examples:

授業、2時半ごろですね?	*Jugyoo, ni-ji-han goro desu ne?*	Your class is at about 2:30, isn't it?

Japanese people tend to be very particular about time (in a country where trains run consistently on schedule). People arrive promptly for appointments, events start at the scheduled time, and it is considered rude to be late for appointments. At the office, subordinates are expected to arrive early and be ready and waiting when events start.

BTS 10 Phrase Particle と *to*

The Particle *to* is used to connect Nouns to mean something very close to English 'and' or 'with.'

日本とアメリカ	*Nihon to Amerika*	Japan and America
マンガとアニメ	*manga to anime*	Comics and anime
鈴木先生と張さんと松浦 さん	*Suzuki-sensei to Choo-san to Matsuura-san*	Prof. Suzuki, Cho-san, and Matsuura-san

There is no limit to the number of Nouns connected, but the number rarely goes above three or four. A major difference between English 'and' and Japanese *to* is that *to* can be used to list <u>only Nouns</u>. It cannot be used to list Adjectives, Verbs, or any other kind of sentence.

BTS 11 やっぱり *Yappari*

The word *yappari* has a number of English equivalents: 'as expected,' 'sure enough,' 'I thought so,' 'now that I think about it.' The implication is that something happened as expected or that you have come to a conclusion after due consideration. In this Scene,

Takashi guesses that it's about 2:30, and after checking his watch sees that it is indeed 2:30 and says, *Yappari 2:30 desu.* 'Sure enough, it's 2:30.' If you hear about a particularly interesting class, then hear that it is your teacher, you might say, *Yappari Suzuki-sensei desu.* 'Just as you might expect, it's Prof. Suzuki.' Here are some other examples:

やっぱり難しいですか?	*Yappari muzukasii desu ka?*	Is it difficult (just as you thought it would be)?
やっぱりおいしいですね!	*Yappari oishii desu ne!*	It's delicious (just as we thought it would be), isn't it!
遠くないですか?う〜ん、やっぱりちょっと遠いですよ。	*Tooku nai desu ka? Unnn, yappari chotto tooi desu yo.*	Isn't it far? Hmmm, after all it is far!

There is a more formal equivalent of *yappari* that you are likely to see in writing: やはり *yahari*. You may also hear this in formal presentations. And there are two very informal forms of *yappari* that you are likely to hear especially from young people: やっぱ *yappa* and やっぱし *yappashi*. Be careful about using these when talking to superiors; they may see you as immature.

BTS 12 Negative questions with [Noun *desu*] or Adjectives

One use of negative questions (with rising intonation) is to indicate that you believe something might be the case.

A: 難しくないですか?	*Muzukashiku nai desu ka?*	Isn't it difficult?
B: ええ、難しいですよ。	*Ee, muzukashii desu yo.*	Yes, it certainly is!
A: 2時じゃないですか?	*Ni-ji ja nai desu ka?*	Isn't it 2:00?
B: ええ、2時ですね。	*Ee, ni-ji desu ne.*	Yes, it is, isn't it.

Note that the question is negative but the response in agreement will be affirmative in both exchanges.

This pattern is probably more frequent in Japanese than in English, because Japanese speakers tend not to make strong assertions unless they are absolutely sure. Even if you are sure, you run the risk of confrontation if the other person doesn't agree with you, so it's better to leave room for negotiation.

Now go to the Activity Book for 練習 *Renshuu* Practice and 腕試し *Udedameshi* Tryout.

Scene 3-3 「スマフォ」じゃなくて「スマホ」。
"Sumafo" ja nakute sumaho.
Not *"sumafo,"* sumaho.

Amy is asking Takashi about what something is called in Japanese.

 The script

エイミー	孝
それ、日本語で何といいますか?	これ?スマホですが……。
え?	スマホ。
スマホ?	そう。スマートホン、スマホ。
ああ、なるほど。スマフォですね?	「スマフォ」じゃなくて、スマホ。
スマホですか?	そう、そう。

Eimii	*Takashi*
So⌐re, ni⌐hongo de na˥n to i⌐ima˥su ka?	*Ko⌐re? Su⌐maho de˥su ga . . .*
E?	*Su⌐maho.*
Su⌐maho?	*So˥o. Su⌐maato˥hon, su⌐maho.*
Aa, na⌐ruhodo. Su⌐mafo de˥su ne?	*"Su⌐mafo" ja na˥kute, su⌐maho.*
Su⌐maho de˥su ka?	*So˥o, so˥o.*

Amy	Takashi
What do you call that in Japanese?	This? It's a *sumaho* . . .
What?	*Sumaho.*
Sumaho?	Right. *Sumaatohon, sumaho*
Oh, I get it. *Sumafo,* right?	Not "*sumafo,*" *sumaho.*
Is it *Sumaho?*	Right, right.

単語と 表現 *Tango to hyoogen* Vocabulary and expressions

Nouns

スマホ	*sumaho*	smartphone
鉛筆	*enpitsu*	pencil
ペン	*pen*	pen
シャーペン	*shaapen*	mechanical pencil
アプリ	*apuri*	app, application
ニュース	*nyuusu*	news

Special expressions

そう、そう。	*Soo, soo*	Right, right; Yes, yes.

拡張 *Kakuchoo* Expansion

What stationery items or gadgets do you and people around you use regularly? Find out from a Japanese associate or friend what they are called and practice their pronunciation.

Behind the Scenes

BTS 13 Conversational strategies

a. Question え? *E?* What?

The question word *E?* is used when you don't understand what the other person said and want them to repeat or explain. A more polite equivalent of this is *Hai?* Be careful, because the question *E?* can also be used to indicate disbelief.

b. Informal style

Note that although this conversation is basically formal, not every sentence ends in a *-masu* or *desu* form. This is very typical of Japanese conversation. Many factors trigger formality, or for that matter informality. Formality structures interactions—often a conversation will begin and end with formal forms with few signals of formality in the actual discussion. Since formality is a kind of social "mask," surprise or fear will cause it to drop away and you will hear informal forms (Amy's *E?* is an example of this.) If you are talking to your superior and s/he is the topic of conversation, you are likely to hear formal forms; by the same token, if the conversation becomes a heated discussion of the current budget situation, formality tends to drop away. Another way to think of this is that politeness and formality are not on-off switches. They can be turned up and down like dimmer switches. If speakers feel more formal for whatever reason, there will be more signals of formality in the conversation.

c. Noun₁ じゃなくて Noun₂ Noun₁ *ja nakute* Noun₂
Not A, but B

In this Scene, Takashi corrects Amy's pronunciation of *sumaho* 'smart phone.' You might expect the pronunciation of this word to maintain the /f/ sound of 'phone' in English, but it does not. (See the next note on loanwords.) In correcting her, Takashi uses the pattern *sumafo ja nakute, sumaho* 'not *sumafo,* but *sumaho.*' As you might have guessed, [Noun$_A$ *ja nakute*] is related to a pattern that you already know: [Noun$_A$ *ja nai desu*] 'it isn't Noun$_A$.' Below are some other examples.

エイミーじゃなくて、エミリーです。	*Eimii ja nakute, Emirii desu.*	Not Amy, (but) Emily.
今日じゃなくて、明日です。	*Kyoo ja nakute, ashita desu.*	Not today, tomorrow.
2時じゃなくて、2時半じゃないですか？	*Ni-ji ja nakute, ni-ji-han ja nai desu ka?*	Isn't it 2:30, not 2:00?

You can also use this pattern to correct what you yourself said when you realize you've made a mistake. We all make mistakes as we speak, and have to go back and do "repair." In English you might say, "Right, (sorry) I mean left." In Japanese, speakers correct themselves when naming things by using じゃなくて 'it's not.' Notice that this is one place where no apology is needed!

山田さんって、早稲田の学生ですか？ あ、山田さんじゃなくて、山本さん。	*Yamada-san tte, Waseda no gakusee desu ka? A, Yamada-san ja nakute Yamamoto-san.*	Is Yamada-san a student at Waseda? Oh, not Yamada-san, I mean Yamamoto-san.
A: 3時の授業ですね？ B: じゃなくて、3時の会議です。	*A: San-ji no jugyoo desu ne?* *B: Ja nakute, san-ji no kaigi desu.*	A: It's a 3:00 class, right? B: You mean (lit. 'it's not') it's a 3:00 meeting.

BTS 14 外来語 (がいらいご) *Gairaigo* Loanwords

You have already encountered many Japanese loanwords—words, and sometimes phrases, that are imported into Japanese from other languages. Overwhelmingly, contemporary Japanese loanwords come from English, but there are many loanwords from other languages, too. Keep in mind that when words are borrowed, they are "Japanized" to fit the Japanese sound system. That is, they change to fit the mora structure of Japanese, and their accent may change unpredictably. Thus 'McDonald's' becomes マクドナルド (まくどなるど) *ma⌐kudona¬rudo*, 'apple pie' becomes アップルパイ (あっぷるぱい) *a⌐ppu¬ru-pai*, etc. Do not try to predict what will happen to the pronunciation of words when they enter Japanese; there are patterns that we can observe, but there are also many exceptions. Note, for example, that ハンバーグ (はんばあぐ) *hanbaagu* refers to a cooked patty of ground beef eaten as a main course while a meat patty in a bun is called ハンバーガー (はんばあがあ) *hanbaagaa*. Similarly, the meaning of words can change dramatically when they go from another language into Japanese. English 'smart,' borrowed as スマート (すまあと) *sumaato* means 'slim and good-looking'; 'claim,' borrowed as クレーム (くれえむ) *kureemu* means 'complaint'; コンセント (こんせんと) *konsento* means 'electrical outlet' (from 'concentric plug'). Even phrases are borrowed into Japanese as single units. For example, ノープロブレム (のおぷろぶれむ) *noopuroburemu* 'no problem,' オンデマンド (おんでまんど) *ondemando* 'on demand,' and ドンマイ (どんまい) *donmai* 'don't worry about it' (from 'don't mind'). Remember, too, that simply because a Japanese speaker uses loanwords, it doesn't mean that he or she speaks English. It is best not to switch to English unless your host encourages you to do so.

Now go to the Activity Book for 練習 (れんしゅう) *Renshuu* **Practice and** 腕試し (うでだめし) *Udedameshi* **Tryout.**

Scene 3-4 一緒にしませんか？ *Issho ni shimasen ka?*
Would you like to do it together?

Yagi-bucho, invites Sasha to join her and Kanda-san for tennis.

 ## The script

八木	サーシャ
あさって、時間ありますか？	はい。
神田さんと一緒にテニスしませんか？	いいですねえ。ありがとうございます！朝ですか？
そう。朝の7時15分だけど……。	午前7時15分！
早いですか？	あ、いえ、あさってですね？ (Checking calendar) オッケーです。
じゃあ7時15分に。現地で。	よろしくお願いします。

Yagi	Saasha
A⌐sa¹tte, ji⌐kan arima¹su ka?	Ha¹i.
Ka⌐nda-san to issho ni te¹nisu shi⌐mase¹n ka?	I¹i desu nee. A⌐ri¹gatoo go⌐zaima¹su! A¹sa desu ka?
So¹o. A¹sa no shi⌐chi¹-ji ⌐ju¹u⌐go¹-fun da kedo . . .	Go⌐zen shi⌐chi¹-ji ⌐ju¹u⌐go¹-fun!
Ha⌐ya¹i desu ka?	A, i⌐e, a⌐sa¹tte desu ne. (Checking calendar) ⌐O¹kkee desu.
Ja¹, shi⌐chi¹-ji ⌐ju¹u⌐go¹-fun ni. Ge¹nchi de.	Yo⌐roshiku onegai-shima¹su.

Yagi	Sasha
Do you have time the day after tomorrow?	Yes.
Do you want to play tennis with Kanda-san?	Great. Thanks! In the morning?

106

Yagi	Sasha
Right. It's at 7:15 in the morning, but . . .	7:15 in the morning!
Is that early?	Oh, no, that's the day after tomorrow, right? (Checking calendar) Okay.
So then, at 7:15. On the court.	I look forward to it.

単語と表現 *Tango to hyoogen* Vocabulary and expressions

Nouns

時間	jikan	time
あさって	asatte	day after tomorrow
今度	kondo	next (upcoming) time
次	tsugi	next, following
週末	shuumatsu	weekend
午前	gozen	morning, a.m.
午後	gogo	afternoon, p.m.
朝	asa	morning
晩	ban	evening
だめ(な)	dame (na)	bad, useless, problematic
一緒	issho	together
みんな	minna	everyone, all
テニス	tenisu	tennis
ゴルフ	gorufu	golf
サッカー	sakkaa	soccer
現地	genchi	the place (we agree on)
図書館	toshokan	library

Verbs

話します(話さない)	hanash-imasu (hanas-anai)	talk
会います(会わない)	a-imasu (aw-anai)	meet, see
見ます(見ない)	mi-masu (mi-nai)	look, watch

107

Adjectives

早い	*hayai*	early
遅い	*osoi*	late

Phrase particles

PLACE で	PLACE *de*	[location of activity]
TIME に	TIME *ni*	[point of time]

Classifiers (time expressions)

～分	*-fun/pun*	classifier for naming and counting minute(s) (after the hour)			
1分	*ip-pun*	21分	*nijuu ip-pun*	41分	*yonjuu ip-pun*
2分	*ni-fun*	22分	*nijuu ni-fun*	42分	*yonjuu ni-fun*
3分	*san-pun*	23分	*nijuu san-pun*	43分	*yonjuu san-pun*
4分	*yon-pun/yon-*	24分	*nijuu yon-pun/*	44分	*yonjuu yon-pun/*
4分	*fun*	24分	*nijuu yon-fun*	44分	*yonjuu yon-fun*
5分	*go-fun*	25分	*nijuu go-fun*	45分	*yonjuu go-fun*
6分	*rop-pun*	26分	*nijuu rop-pun*	46分	*yonjuu rop-pun*
7分 7分	*shichi-fun/ nana-fun*	27分	*nijuu nana-fun*	47分	*yonjuu nana-fun*
8分	*hap-pun*	28分	*nijuu hap-pun*	48分	*yonjuu hap-pun*
9分	*kyuu-fun*	29分	*nijuu kyuu-fun*	49分	*yonjuu kyuu-fun*
10分	*jup-pun*	30分	*sanjup-pun*	50分	*gojup-pun*
11分	*juu ip-pun*	31分	*sanjuu ip-pun*	51分	*gojuu ip-pun*
12分	*juu ni-fun*	32分	*sanjuu ni-fun*	52分	*gojuu ni-fun*
13分	*juu san-pun*	33分	*sanjuu san-pun*	53分	*gojuu san-pun*
14分	*juu yon-pun/*	34分	*sanjuu yon-pun/*	54分	*gojuu yon-pun/*
14分	*juu yon-fun*	34分	*sanjuu yon-fun*	54分	*gojuu yon-fun*
15分	*juu go-fun*	35分	*sanjuu go-fun*	55分	*gojuu go-fun*

<ruby>１６<rt>じゅうろっぷん</rt></ruby>分	*juu rop-pun*	<ruby>３６<rt>さんじゅうろっ ぷん</rt></ruby>分	*sanjuu rop-pun*	<ruby>５６<rt>ごじゅうろっ ぷん</rt></ruby>分	*gojuu rop-pun*
<ruby>１７<rt>じゅうなな ふん</rt></ruby>分	*juu nana-fun*	<ruby>３７<rt>さんじゅうなな ふん</rt></ruby>分	*sanjuu nana-fun*	<ruby>５７<rt>ごじゅうなな ふん</rt></ruby>分	*gojuu nana-fun*
<ruby>１８<rt>じゅうはっ ぷん</rt></ruby>分	*juu hap-pun*	<ruby>３８<rt>さんじゅうはっぷん</rt></ruby>分	*sanjuu hap-pun*	<ruby>５８<rt>ごじゅうはっ ぷん</rt></ruby>分	*gojuu hap-pun*
<ruby>１９<rt>じゅうきゅう ふん</rt></ruby>分	*juu kyuu-fun*	<ruby>３９<rt>さんじゅうきゅう ふん</rt></ruby>分	*sanjuu kyuu-fun*	<ruby>５９<rt>ごじゅうきゅう ふん</rt></ruby>分	*gojuu kyuu-fun*
<ruby>２０<rt>にじゅっぷん</rt></ruby>分	*nijup-pun*	<ruby>４０<rt>よんじゅっぷん</rt></ruby>分	*yonjup-pun*	<ruby>６０<rt>ろくじゅっぷん</rt></ruby>分	*rokujup-pun*
<ruby>何分<rt>なんぷん</rt></ruby> <ruby>何分<rt>なんふん</rt></ruby>	*nan-pun/nan-fun*	what minute (of the hour)			

Special expressions

みんなで	*minna de*	all together
またあとで	*mata ato de*	again later
<ruby>オッケー<rt>おっけえ</rt></ruby>	*okkee*	okay

<ruby>拡張<rt>かくちょう</rt></ruby> *Kakuchoo* Expansion

1 What are common sport activities that people around you do on weekends? Find out, using the appropriate Japanese strategy, what you would call them in Japanese.
2 Think of one or two recreational activities you do frequently. Find out from a Japanese associate or friend what they are called and practice their pronunciation.

Behind the Scenes

BTS 15 PLACE + で PLACE + *de*

A place Noun followed by Particle *de* designates the location where some activity takes place:

<ruby>図書館<rt>としょかん</rt></ruby>で<ruby>読<rt>よ</rt></ruby>みました。	*Toshokan de yomimashita.*	I read it in the library.
<ruby>小<rt>ちい</rt></ruby>さい<ruby>コンビニ<rt>こんびに</rt></ruby>で<ruby>買<rt>か</rt></ruby>いました。	*Chiisai konbini de kaimashita.*	We bought it at a small convenience store
<ruby>ミーティング<rt>みいてぃんぐ</rt></ruby>は<ruby>田中<rt>たなか</rt></ruby>さんのお<ruby>宅<rt>たく</rt></ruby>であります。	*Miitingu wa Tanaka-san no otaku de arimasu.*	The meeting will take place at Tanaka-san's residence.

BTS 16 思いやり *Omoiyari:* negotiating a time for an activity

In this Scene, Ms. Yagi and Sasha are negotiating a time to meet. Each is careful not to insist on a particular time, listening to the needs and convenience of the other person. Once they settle on a date, they reconfirm the details of when and where they will meet. This concern for the other person is part of *omoiyari* 'consideration,' a highly valued trait in Japan. It refers to understanding, respect, acceptance, and attentiveness to others. The word *omoiyari* is used in public safety campaigns, volunteer efforts, environment and sustainability drives, and even marketing. According to research, it is one of the characteristics of a well socialized person.

BTS 17 X と一緒に Noun$_x$ *to issho ni*

Noun$_x$ *to issho ni* means 'together with X.' X might be a person, as you see in this conversation: *watashi to issho ni* 'together with me.'

It might also be a thing:

このお茶、クッキーと一緒にいただきます。	*Kono ocha, kukkii to issho ni itadakimasu.*	We'll drink this tea with the cookies.
このシャーペン、ペンと一緒に買います。	*Kono shaapen, pen to issho ni kaimasu.*	I'll by this mechanical pencil along with a pen.

BTS 18 Noun だ Noun *da*

There is an informal form of *desu* that can appear after a Noun: *da*.

A: それ、日本語?	*Sore, nihongo?*	Is that Japanese?
B: 日本語だよ。	*Nihongo da yo.*	It is (Japanese)!
or	*Nihongo yo.*	It is (Japanese)!
B: 日本語よ。		

Recall from the previous Act that it is not unusual for *desu* to drop completely in informal speech at the end of a sentence (but not before *kedo*). In fact, as you see in the foregoing example *da* does not occur in questions. The response above without *da* sounds a bit softer—and therefore more feminine—than the corresponding sentence with *da*; sentence-final *da* sounds direct and sometimes abrupt.

The negative informal equivalent of [Noun *da*] is [Noun *ja nai*].

A: これ、<ruby>何<rt>なに</rt></ruby>?   *Kore, nani?*   What's this?

B: <ruby>携帯<rt>けいたい</rt></ruby>じゃない?   *Keitai ja nai?*   Isn't it a cell phone?

BTS 19 Time expressions with classifier 〜<ruby>分<rt>ふん</rt></ruby>・〜<ruby>分<rt>ぶん</rt></ruby> *-fun/-pun*

The classifier for minutes in telling time is *-fun/-pun*. In telling time, the hour directly precedes minutes: *shichiji go-fun* '7:05.' Here you see the numbers through 60 as used on the clock for naming minutes. Note the following sound changes:

* 4 with this classifier is *yon* (*yon-pun*);
* *-fun* changes to *-pun* in combination with 1, 3, 4, 6, 8, and 10 (although this distinction is becoming blurred recently);
* the consonant morae *-ku* and *-chi* change to /p/ with 1, 6, and 8 (*ip-pun, rop-pun, hap-pun*);
* the number 10 changes to a double consonant: *jup-pun/jip-pun.*

BTS 20 Time + に *ni*

The Particle *ni* in combination with a time expression tells the point at which something will happen or happened. Clock time and calendar time expressions (which name a specific point) take *ni*:

<ruby>5時前<rt>ご じ まえ</rt></ruby>に<ruby>行<rt>い</rt></ruby>きましょう。   *Go-ji mae ni ikimashoo.*   Let's go before 5:00.

<ruby>何時<rt>なんじ</rt></ruby>にできますか。   *Nanji ni dekimasu ka.*   At what time will you be able to finish it?

12<ruby>時<rt>じ</rt></ruby>ごろに<ruby>会<rt>あ</rt></ruby>います。   *Juuni-ji goro ni aimasu.*   I'll meet them at about 12:00.

A number of Nouns (*kyoo, kinoo, ashita*) have come up that are used to refer to "relative time"—that is, words that derive their meaning from their relationship to the present (now or today), as opposed to words that refer to dates or days of the week. These words do not take the time Particle に.

BTS 21 Incomplete Sentences: <ruby>7時 1 5分<rt>しち じ じゅうご ふん</rt></ruby>に。 *Shichi-ji juugo-fun ni.* At 7:15.

It is common in spoken language to leave sentences unfinished, especially when the missing information is understood from the context. In this Scene, Yagi-san sums up their discussion by repeating the important details: *Jaa, shichi-ji juugo-fun ni. Genchi de.* 'So then, at 7:00. At the place.' *Genchi* is the agreed-upon destination. There is no Verb in either sentence, and it would sound quite artificial if there were.

Now go to the Activity Book for 練習 *Renshuu* **Practice and** 腕試し *Udedameshi* **Tryout.**

Scene 3-5 高くないですか？ *Takaku nai desu ka?*
Isn't it expensive?

Sasha and Kanda-san are looking at the handwritten prices for displayed items at a craft shop.

The script

サーシャ	神田
これ、１９０円ですか？ ７９０円ですか？	これですか？これは７じゃないですかねえ。
へえ、一個 ７９０円ですか。高くないですか？	そうですねえ。じゃあ、この赤いのは？
あ、かわいいですね。いくらですか？	３５０円です。

Saasha	*Kanda*
Ko⌐re, hyaˡku kyuuju⌐u-en desu ka? naˡnaˡ hyaku kyu⌐uju⌐u -en desu ka?	*Ko⌐re deˡsu ka? Ko⌐re wa naˡna ja ⌐naˡi desu ka ⌐neˡe.*
Heˡe, ˡiˡk-ko naˡnaˡhyaku kyu⌐uju⌐u-en desu ka. Taˡkaku ⌐naˡi desu ka?	*Soˡo desu nee. Jaˡa, ko⌐no aˡkaˡi no wa?*
A, ka⌐waiˡi desu ⌐neˡ. Iˡkura desu ka?	*⌐Saˡnbyaku go⌐ju⌐u-en desu.*

Sasha	Kanda
Is this 190 yen or 790 yen?	This? Isn't this a 7?
Really? 790 yen for one. Isn't that expensive?	It is, isn't it. So then, how about this red one?
Oh, it's cute, isn't it. How much is it?	¥350.

113

単語と表現 (たんごひょうげん) *Tango to hyoogen* Vocabulary and expressions

Numbers

0 (ぜろ・まる・れい)	zero, maru, *rei*

Tens (adding 60 through 90)

10 (じゅう)	*juu*	40 (よんじゅう)	*yonjuu*	70 (ななじゅう)	*nanajuu*
20 (にじゅう)	*nijuu*	50 (ごじゅう)	*gojuu*	80 (はちじゅう)	*hachijuu*
30 (さんじゅう)	*sanjuu*	60 (ろくじゅう)	*rokujuu*	90 (きゅうじゅう)	*kyuujuu*
何十 (なんじゅう)	*nan-juu*	how many tens			

Hundreds

100 (ひゃく)	*hyaku*	400 (よんひゃく)	*yon-hyaku*	700 (ななひゃく)	*nana-hyaku*
200 (にひゃく)	*ni-hyaku*	500 (ごひゃく)	*go-hyaku*	800 (はっぴゃく)	*hap-pyaku*
300 (さんびゃく)	*san-byaku*	600 (ろっぴゃっく)	*rop-pyaku*	900 (きゅうひゃく)	*kyuu-hyaku*
何百 (なんびゃく)	*nan-byaku*	how many hundreds			

Two- and three-digit numbers (samples)

13 (じゅうさん)	*juu san*	88 (はちじゅうはち)	*hachijuu hachi*	97 (きゅうじゅうなな)	*kyuujuu nana*
123 (ひゃくにじゅうさん)	*hyaku nijuu san*	694 (ろっぴゃくきゅうじゅうよん)	*roppyaku kyuujuu yon*	957 (きゅうひゃくごじゅうなな)	*kyuuhyaku gojuu nana*

Nouns

の	*no*	one(s)
サイフ・財布 (さいふ・さいふ)	*saifu*	wallet
チケット (ちけっと)	*chiketto*	ticket
ティーシャツ (てぃいしゃつ)	*tii-shatsu*	T-shirt
本 (ほん)	*hon*	book
ノート (のおと)	*nooto*	notebook
いくら	*ikura*	how much
たくさん	*takusan*	a lot

Adjectives

赤い	*akai*	red
青い	*aoi*	blue
黒い	*kuroi*	black
白い	*shiroi*	white
かわいい	*kawaii*	cute

Special expressions

へえ	*hee*	oh, yes? really?
全部でX	*zenbu de X*	X for everything; X all together
赤いの	*akai no*	the red one
このX	*kono* + Noun$_X$	this X
そのX	*sono* + Noun$_X$	that X
あのX	*ano* + Noun$_X$	that X over there
どのX	*dono* + Noun$_X$	which X

Classifiers

円	*en*	yen (Japanese currency)			
1円	*ichi-en*	1 yen	100円	*hyaku-en*	100 yen
2円	*ni-en*	2 yen	200円	*nihyaku-en*	200 yen
3円	*san-en*	3 yen	300円	*sanbyaku-en*	300 yen
4円	*yo-en*	4 yen	400円	*yonhyaku-en*	400 yen
5円	*go-en*	5 yen	500円	*gohyaku-en*	500 yen
6円	*roku-en*	6 yen	600円	*roppyaku-en*	600 yen
7円	*nana-en*	7 yen	700円	*nanahyaku-en*	700 yen
8円	*hachi-en*	8 yen	800円	*happyaku-en*	800 yen
9円	*kyuu-en*	9 yen	900円	*kyuuhyaku-en*	900 yen
10円	*juu-en*	10 yen	何円	*nan-en*	how many yen

ドル	*doru*	dollar(s) (U.S. currency)			
1ドル	*ichi-doru*	1 dollar	100ドル	*hyaku-doru*	100 dollars
2ドル	*ni-doru*	2 dollars	200ドル	*nihyaku-doru*	200 dollars
3ドル	*san-doru*	3 dollars	300ドル	*sanbyaku-doru*	300 dollars

４ドル	*yon-doru*	4 dollars	４００ドル	*yonhyaku-doru*	400 dollars
５ドル	*go-doru*	5 dollars	５００ドル	*gohyaku-doru*	500 dollars
６ドル	*roku-doru*	6 dollars	６００ドル	*roppyaku-doru*	600 dollars
７ドル	*nana-doru*	7 dollars	７００ドル	*nanahyaku-doru*	700 dollars
８ドル	*hachi-doru*	8 dollars	８００ドル	*happyaku-doru*	800 dollars
９ドル	*kyuu-doru*	9 dollars	９００ドル	*kyuuhyaku-doru*	900 dollars
１０ドル	*juu-doru*	10 dollars	何ドル	*nan-doru*	how many dollars

セント	*sento*	cent(s) (U.S. currency)			
１セント	*is-sento*	1 cent	６セント	*roku-sento*	6 cents
２セント	*ni-sento*	2 cents	７セント	*nana-sento*	7 cents
３セント	*san-sento*	3 cents	８セント	*has-sento*	8 cents
４セント	*yon-sento*	4 cents	９セント	*kyuu-sento*	9 cents
５セント	*go-sento*	5 cents	１０セント	*jus-sento*	10 cents
何セント	*nan-sento*	how many cents			

〜個	*ko*	classifier for counting small objects			
１個	*ik-ko*	1 item	６個	*rok-ko*	6 items
２個	*ni-ko*	2 items	７個	*nana-ko*	7 items
３個	*san-ko*	3 items	８個 ８個	*hachi-ko/hak-ko*	8 items
４個	*yon-ko*	4 items	９個	*kyuu-ko*	9 items
５個	*go-ko*	5 items	１０個	*juk-ko*	10 items
			何個	*nan-ko*	how many items

〜枚	*-mai*	classifier for counting thin, flat things			
１枚	*ichi-mai*	1 sheet	６枚	*roku-mai*	6 sheets
２枚	*ni-mai*	2 sheets	７枚	*nana-mai*	7 sheets
３枚	*san-mai*	3 sheets	８枚	*hachi-mai*	8 sheets
４枚	*yon-mai*	4 sheets	９枚	*kyuu-mai*	9 sheets
５枚	*go-mai*	5 sheets	１０枚	*juu-mai*	10 sheets
			何枚	*nan-mai*	how many sheets

〜本	*hon/bon/pon*	classifier for counting long objects			
１本	*ip-pon*	1 length	６本	*rop-pon*	6 lengths
２本	*ni-hon*	2 lengths	７本	*nana-hon*	7 lengths

さんぼん 3本	*san-bon*	3 lengths	はっぽん 8本	*hap-pon*	8 lengths
よんほん 4本	*yon-hon*	4 lengths	きゅうほん 9本	*kyuu-hon*	9 lengths
ごほん 5本	*go-hon*	5 lengths	じゅっぽん １０本	*jup-pon*	10 lengths
			なんぼん 何本	*nan-bon*	how many long objects

~冊	*-satsu*	classifier for counting bound volumes

いっさつ 1冊	*is-satsu*	1 bound volume	ろくさつ 6冊	*roku-satsu*	6 bound volumes
にさつ 2冊	*ni-satsu*	2 bound volumes	ななさつ 7冊	*nana-satsu*	7 bound volumes
さんさつ 3冊	*san-satsu*	3 bound volumes	はっさつ 8冊	*has-satsu*	8 bound volumes
よんさつ 4冊	*yon-satsu*	4 bound volumes	きゅうさつ 9冊	*kyuu-satsu*	9 bound volumes
ごさつ 5冊	*go-satsu*	5 bound volumes	じゅっさつ じっさつ １０冊・10冊	*jus-satsu, jis-satsu*	10 bound volumes
			なんさつ 何冊	*nan-satsu*	how many bound volumes

かくちょう 拡張 *Kakuchoo* Expansion

1 What currency is used where you grew up? Make an intelligent guess as to how it would be said in Japanese and see if you were right by checking with a Japanese associate or friend, then practice the pronunciation.

2 Find out the current exchange rate between dollars and yen. Where did you find the information? Keep track of how the exchange rate changes for five days.

3 Speak to someone who has lived in both Japan and the U.S. Find out if anything struck them as being relatively more or less expensive and what those things were.

Behind the Scenes

BTS 22 The この *kono* series

This new *ko-so-a-do* series is used before Nouns and Noun Phrases:

このうち	*kono uchi*	this house
どの山田さんですか?	*Dono Yamada-san desu ka?*	Which Yamada-san do you mean?
あの小さい図書館、きれいですねえ。	*Ano chiisai toshokan, kirei desu nee.*	That little library is beautiful, isn't it!

117

Note in the last example above that *ano* appears before an [Adjective + Noun] combination. This new series never appears directly before Noun *no* (see BTS note below), but it does occur before [Adjective + Noun] when the Noun is *no*:

その小さいの、きれいですねえ。　*Sono chiisai no, kirei desu nee.*　That small one is beautiful, isn't it!

BTS 23 X or Y?

When you want to ask which of two alternatives is the case, you use two questions in succession as a sentence.

Verbs

行きますか、行きませんか?　*Ikimasu ka, ikimasen ka?*　Are you going or not?

Adjectives

高いですか、安いですか?　*Takai desu ka, yasui desu ka?*　Is it expensive or cheap?

高いですか、高くないですか?　*Takai desu ka, takaku nai desu ka?*　Is it expensive or not?

Noun *desu*

１００円ですか、７００円ですか?　*Hyaku-en desu ka, nanahyaku-en desu ka?*　Is it ¥100 or ¥700?

エイミーですか?エミリーですか?　*Eimii desu ka? Emirii desu ka?*　'Is it Amy or Emily?' or 'Do you mean Amy or Emily?'

BTS 24 へ～ *Hee*

In Act 2 you saw an expression of surprise: *waa!* Here you see another expression of surprise: *hee.* These imply different reactions. *Waa* is used to indicate open cheerfulness or happiness in the face of something surprising. *Hee* is an indication of mild disbelief in response to new information. So in the foregoing conversation, Sasha is surprised (and not altogether happy) that the item under discussion is seven hundred yen.

BTS 25 Numbers through 999

Here you see the remaining numbers through 100 (*hyaku*) along with all hundreds. Note the following sound changes when 1 through 9 combine with *hyaku*: *sanbyaku* (300), *roppyaku* (600), *happyaku* (800).

The word for zero may be *zero, maru,* or *ree* depending on the context. You have seen that *rei* is used with classifiers *-ji* and *-fun. Maru* literally means 'circle' and you may hear it as a sign of approval ('no errors'). Your teacher may circle correct answers on your quizzes and exams. You may also hear *marumaru* as a substitute for a Noun that the speaker doesn't need to specify.

BTS 26 Classifiers 〜円 , 〜ドル , 〜セント , 〜個 , 〜枚 , 〜本 , 〜冊 -en, -doru, -sento, -ko, -mai, -hon, and -satsu

何時ですか?

The classifier for Japanese currency is *en*; the classifiers for American currency are *doru* and *sento*. It is possible to say *nan-en* 'how many yen?' '*nan-doru* 'how many dollars?' and *nan-sento* 'how many cents?' but a more general word for 'how much' is *ikura*.

一ドル、何円ですか?	*Ichi-doru, nan-en desu ka?*	How many yen to a dollar? (i.e. exchange rate)
これ、5ドル 5 9セントです。	*Kore, go-doru gojuu kyuu-sento desu.*	This is $5.59.

When counting things in Japanese, it is almost never possible to use a number plus a Noun as is done in English (two birds, four books, nine towels). Rather, numbers combine with "classifiers" that are determined by the size, shape, or other characteristics of the thing being counted. This has a parallel in English with words like *paper* ("two sheets of paper," not "two papers"), "bread" ("I ate two slices/pieces," not "two breads"). You have already seen the classifiers *-ji* and *-fun* for hours on the clock, *-en* and *-oru* for currency. In this Scene you see another classifier: *-ko*. The classifier *-ko* is one of the most general and is used for small items such as pieces of fruit, cookies, paper clips, golf balls, eggs, etc.

ケーキ、何個ですか?	*Keeki, nan-ko desu ka?*	How many pieces of cake?

Another classifier is *-mai,* which is used for thin, flat objects (paper, shirts, towels, and the like).

チケット、5枚ですね?	*Chiketto, go-mai desu ne?*	Five tickets, right?

A classifier for long, narrow objects, such as pens, pencils, bottles, knives, forks, and spoons is *-hon*. Note the sound changes in *ippon, sanbon, roppon, happon, jippon/juppon,* and *nanbon*.

ビール、一本飲みませんか？   *Biiru, ippon nomimasen ka?*   Shall we drink one bottle of beer?

A classifier for bound volumes, such as books, notebooks, and dictionaries is *-satsu,* which is used even if the book is electronic. Note the sound changes in *issatsu, hassatsu,* and *jissatsu*.

おもしろい本、一冊読みましょう。 | *Omoshiroi hon, is-satsu yomimashoo.* | Let's read one interesting book.

BTS 27 Quantity$_X$ + quantity$_Y$

English is flexible in telling how much a quantity costs. Tutoring might be 'thirty dollars an hour' or 'an hour for thirty dollars.' Apples at the market might be 'two dollars for three' or 'three for two dollars.' Japanese, in contrast, is very strict about the order of the Nouns: the quantity comes first and the cost comes second.

三枚５００円 | *San-mai go-hyaku-en* | ¥500 for three sheets (e.g., art paper)
1個３０ドル | *Ik-ko san-juu-doru* | $30 per item (e.g., an electronic part)
２冊１００円です。 | *Ni-satsu hyaku-en desu.* | ¥100 for two volumes. Or two volumes for ¥100.
１０枚９００円ですね？ | *Juu-mai kyuuhyaku-en desu ne?* | It's ¥900 for ten sheets, right? Or ten sheets are ¥900, right?

BTS 28 The Noun の *no*

The Noun *no* occurs as a substitute for something that is already known in the context. Once we know that we are talking about cars, I can tell you *Ii no desu* 'It's a good one.' This *no* is not used to refer to people. It can appear directly after an Adjective as in the previous conversation. Here are some examples:

おいしいケーキ *oishii keeki*   delicious cake(s)   >   おいしいの *oishii no* delicious one(s)

すごいスマホ *sugoi sumaho*   the awesome smart phone   >   すごいの *sugoi no*   the awesome one

120

おもしろそうな本　　　　　　a book that looks　　>　おもしろそうなの　　one that looks
omoshirosoo na hon　　　　 interesting　　　　　　　 *omoshirosoo na no*　 interesting

It is possible to have multiple modifiers combined with Nouns.

あのおもしろいのと一緒　　　*ano omoshiroi*　　　　　 together with that interesting one
　　　　　　　　　　　　　　no to issho

Now go to the Activity Book for 練習 *Renshuu* Practice and 腕試し *Udedameshi* Tryout.

Scene 3-6 それは私(わたし)のです。
Sore wa watashi no desu. That's mine.

Takashi is trying to pick out the umbrella that belongs to the faculty advisor to the club.

The script

孝(たかし)	エイミー(えいみい)
生(せん)の傘(かさ)、ここにありますか?これかな?	いや、それは私(わたし)のです。
え、じゃこれですかねえ。	いや、それも違(ちが)いますよ。先生(せんせい)のって青(あお)いのだよね?
そうですけど……。	ないですねえ、やっぱり。雨(あめ)ですか?
いや、そうじゃないけど……	

Takashi	***Eimii***
Se⌈nse⌉e no ⌈ka⌉sa, koko ni arimasu ka? ko⌈re ka na.	*I⌈ya⌉, so⌈re wa⌉ wa⌈tashi no⌉ desu.*
E, ja⌉ ko⌈re de⌉su ka ⌈ne⌉e.	*I⌈ya⌉, so⌈re mo chigaima⌉su yo. Se⌈nse⌉e no tte a⌈o⌉i no da yo ne.*
So⌉o desu kedo . . .	*Na⌉i desu ⌈ne⌉e, ya⌈ppa⌉ri. A⌉me desu ka?*
I⌈ya⌉, ⌈so⌉o ja nai kedo . . .	

Takashi	**Amy**
The professor's umbrella, is it here? Is it this one?	No, that one is mine.
What, then is it this one?	No, that's also not it! The professor's is a blue one, you know, right?
That's so, but . . .	It's not here after all. Is it raining?
No, it's not but . . .	

単語と表現 <ruby>単<rt>たん</rt></ruby><ruby>語<rt>ご</rt></ruby>と<ruby>表<rt>ひょう</rt></ruby><ruby>現<rt>げん</rt></ruby> *Tango to hyoogen* Vocabulary and expressions

Nouns

<ruby>傘<rt>かさ</rt></ruby>	*kasa*	umbrella
かばん	*kaban*	bag, briefcase
<ruby>消<rt>け</rt></ruby>し<ruby>ゴ<rt>ご</rt></ruby><ruby>ム<rt>む</rt></ruby>	*keshigomu*	(pencil) eraser
<ruby>パ<rt>ぱ</rt></ruby><ruby>ソ<rt>そ</rt></ruby><ruby>コン<rt>こん</rt></ruby>	*pasokon*	personal computer, laptop
<ruby>紙<rt>かみ</rt></ruby>	*kami*	paper
ともだち	*tomodachi*	friend
<ruby>部<rt>ぶ</rt></ruby><ruby>長<rt>ちょう</rt></ruby>	*buchoo*	division chief
<ruby>同<rt>どう</rt></ruby><ruby>僚<rt>りょう</rt></ruby>	*dooryoo*	co-worker, colleague
<ruby>ク<rt>く</rt></ruby><ruby>ラ<rt>ら</rt></ruby><ruby>ス<rt>す</rt></ruby><ruby>メ<rt>め</rt></ruby><ruby>ー<rt>え</rt></ruby><ruby>ト<rt>と</rt></ruby>	*kurasumeeto*	classmate
<ruby>ル<rt>る</rt></ruby><ruby>ー<rt>う</rt></ruby><ruby>ム<rt>む</rt></ruby><ruby>メ<rt>め</rt></ruby><ruby>ー<rt>え</rt></ruby><ruby>ト<rt>と</rt></ruby>	*ruumumeeto*	roommate
<ruby>雨<rt>あめ</rt></ruby>	*ame*	rain
<ruby>雪<rt>ゆき</rt></ruby>	*yuki*	snow
<ruby>同<rt>おな</rt></ruby>じ	*onaji*	same

Verbs

| <ruby>違<rt>ちが</rt></ruby>います（<ruby>違<rt>ちが</rt></ruby>わない） | *chigaimasu (chigaw-anai)* | different (not different) |

Phrase particles

| に | *ni* | [inanimate location particle] |
| も | *mo* | also, too |

Sentence particles

| よね | *yo ne* | [sentence particle indicating shared certainty] |

Special expressions

| よくわかりませんけど | *yoku wakarimasen kedo* | I'm not sure, but . . . |
| （Xと）<ruby>違<rt>ちが</rt></ruby>います・<ruby>同<rt>おな</rt></ruby>じです | *(X to) chigaimasu/onaji desu* | different from/same as X |

BTS 29 More on Particle の *no*:
私_{わたし}のです。 vs 新_{あたら}しいの<u>の</u>のどこですか。
Watashi no desu. vs *Atarashii <u>no</u> no doko desu ka?*

Recall that when one Noun modifies another the two Nouns are connected by Particle *no*: *sensee no kasa* 'the teacher's umbrella,' *watashi no pasokon* 'my laptop.' What happens when the second Noun is *no* meaning 'one(s)'? In that case, connecting Particle *no* plus Noun *no* collapses to a single *no*: *Sensee no* 'the teacher's (one),' *watashi no* 'mine.'

The reverse is <u>not</u> true. When Noun *no* precedes connecting *no* the two do not collapse. When we know that we are talking about various companies, *Atarashii <u>kaisha</u> no doko desu ka?* 'Where in the new company?' becomes *Atarashii <u>no</u> no doko desu ka?* 'Where in the new one?'

The connector *na* remains unchanged before *no*: *omoshirosoo na hon* 'an interesting looking book' becomes *omoshirosoo na no* 'an interesting looking one.'

BTS 30 Location にあります・います
Location *ni arimasu/imasu*

In this Scene you see Particle *ni* used for the location where something or someone exists.

チケット_{ちけっと}、どこにありますか?	*Chiketto, doko ni arimasu ka.*	Where are the tickets?
かばん、ないですよね。	*Kaban, nai desu yo ne.*	You don't have a briefcase, right?
神田_{かんだ}さん、いませんよね。	*Kanda-san, imasen yo ne.*	Kanda-san isn't here, right?

BTS 31 Noun + も *mo*

A Noun plus Particle *mo* indicates that the Noun is in addition to something or someone else. The English equivalent is 'too' or 'also' (with an affirmative) or 'either' (with a negative).

今日_{きょう}も行_いかないです。	*Kyoo mo ikanai desu.*	I won't go today either.
八木_{やぎ}さんも来_きませんねえ。	*Yagi-san mo kimasen nee.*	Yagi-san isn't coming either, is she?
これも高_{たか}いですよ。	*Kore mo takai desu yo.*	This is also expensive, you know.

Note that in English the word 'too' can apply to any element in a sentence. 'I will buy books tomorrow, too' might mean 'I also (in addition to other people) will buy books tomorrow,' 'I bought books also (in addition to other things) yesterday,' or 'I will buy books tomorrow also (in addition to other days).' In Japanese, *mo* must follow the Noun that is additional and the meaning is always clear.

When two Nouns in a sentence occur with *mo* (X *mo* Y *mo*) the meaning is 'both X and Y' (with an affirmative) or 'not/neither X or/nor Y' (with a negative).

これもそれも高いですよ。	*Kore mo sore mo takai desu yo.*	Both this and that are expensive, you know.
今日もあしたもないです。	*Kyoo mo ashita mo nai desu.*	It isn't here today or tomorrow.
八木さんも神田さんも来ませんよ。	*Yagi-san mo Kanda-san mo kimasen yo.*	Neither Yagi-san nor Kanda-san is coming, you know.

When two (or more) things in combination are exceptional in some way—for example, it is unusual for two professors to come to a class, or to eat both ramen and sushi—the Nouns occur in the combination X *mo* Y *mo* rather than X *to* Y.

BTS 32 Inverted Sentences

Japanese word order is very flexible in spoken style. So far you have seen that the basic Core Sentence (Verb, Adjective, or Noun +*desu*) typically comes last in a sentence, with other elements preceding it.

やっぱりないです。	*Yappari nai desu.*	Wouldn't you know it's not here.
今日会います。	*Kyoo aimasu.*	I will see her today.
これ、高いですねえ!	*Kore, takai desu nee!*	This is expensive, isn't it!

But Nouns can also be added as afterthoughts, clarifications, or elaborations to Core Sentences. Note that this includes Nouns in combination with their Particles.

ないです、ここに。	*Nai desu, koko ni.*	There aren't any—in here.
買います、今日。	*Kaimasu, kyoo.*	I will buy it—today.
高いですねえ、これ。	*Takai desu nee, kore.*	It's expensive, isn't it—this thing!
高くないですねえ、これ。	*Takaku nai desu nee, kore.*	It's not expensive, is it—this thing!

The Core Sentence has its usual final intonation, while the additional word or phrase is slightly lower pitched.

BTS 33 Multiple Sentence Particles: よね *yo ne*

You saw the Sentence Particles *yo* (assertion or certainty) and *ne* (assumed agreement) in Act 2. Here you see the two used together, with a combined meaning of 'I'm sure of this and I think you'll agree.' You will see other Particles coming together at the end of a Sentence in successive Acts.

ここのラーメン、おいしいですよね。	*Koko no raamen, oishii desu yo ne.*	The ramen here is good, isn't it.
明日は、宿題ないですよね。	*Ashita wa shukudai nai desu yo ne.*	There's no homework tomorrow, right?
今日のミーティングはそちらですよね。	*Kyoo no miitingu wa sochira desu yo ne.*	Today's meeting is there, isn't it.

Now go to the Activity Book for 練習 *Renshuu* Practice and 腕試し *Udedameshi* Tryout.

Then do 評価 *Hyooka* Assessment activities.

3-6

何時ですか?

126

◆ 読み書き *Yomi-kaki* Reading and writing

よ か

This lesson introduces the remaining 22 hiragana symbols. Remember when you practice to imitate the version that you see on the far right.

Scene 3-7R 何時ですか？ What time is it?

なん じ

Sasha's colleague Kuno-san sent an email using an app that provides furigana for kanji and katakana. What does Kuno-san want to know?

テキスト Text

Subject: あしたの会議

かい ぎ

サーシャさん

さ あ しゃ

すみません、あしたの会議は何時ですか? 朝の１０時半ですか?

かい ぎ なん じ　　　　あさ　じゅうじはん

久野

く の

Subject: Tomorrow's meeting

Sasha-san

Excuse me, what time is tomorrow's conference? Is it 10:30 in the morning?

Kuno

文字と例 Symbols with examples

も じ れい

#25. *no*

Examples

1. 会議の時間 — time for the meeting; the meeting time
2. 高校の先生 — high school teacher
3. ＪＬＣの坂田です。 — I am Sakata of JLC.
4. その傘ですね。 — That umbrella (near you), right?
5. あれ、高いのですか。 — Is that an expensive one?
6. こちらの先生ですが‥‥‥。 — (I mean) the teacher (near me), but . . .
7. あれ、だれの傘ですか。 — Whose umbrella is that?
8. あの傘、だれのですか。 — That umbrella–whose is it?
9. あ、あの、須田さんですか。 — Oh, um, are you Ms. Suda?
10. あの、あしたの会議のことですが‥‥‥。 — It's about tomorrow's meeting, but . . .

#26. な* na   な

* This is a 4-stroke symbol.

Examples

1. 名前 — names
2. お名前 — names (polite)
3. ないです。 — There aren't any. I don't have any.
4. 田中さん — Tanaka-san
5. 何ですか。 — What is it?
6. 何語ですか。 — What language is it?
7. さようなら。 — Goodbye.
8. そうかなあ。 — I wonder if it is so.
9. どなたですか。 — Who is it? (polite)
10. お帰りなさい。 — Welcome home.
11. 何と言いますか。 — What do you call it? How do you say it?
12. 今何時ですか。 — What time is it now?
13. 田中さん、遅いな。 — Tanaka-san is late/slow, isn't he.
14. これとそれ、同じですか。 — Are this and that the same?

#27. く   ku   く

Examples

1. 大学（だいがく） — university, college
2. 学生（がくせい） — student(s)
3. 韓国語（かんこくご） — Korean (language)
4. 大学院（だいがくいん） — graduate school
5. たかし君（くん） — Takashi-kun
6. いくらですか。 — How much is it?
7. よくないです。 — It is not good.
8. よくありません。 — It is not good.
9. すごくいいですね。 — It's really good, isn't it!
10. これ、高（たか）くないですか。 — Isn't this expensive?
11. 英語（えいご）と韓国語（かんこくご）、できますか。 — Can you handle English and Korean?
12. ここ、すごくおいしくないですか。 — Isn't this place really tasty?
13. 今（いま）ですか。忙（いそが）しくないです。 — Right now? I'm not very busy.

#28. **み** *mi*   **み**

Examples

1. 見（み）ます。 — I'll look. I'll watch/see it.
2. みんな — everyone
3. みなさん#¹ #² — everyone, ladies and gentlemen
4. 飲（の）みます。 — I'll drink it.
5. 読（よ）みます。 — I'll read it.
6. すみません。 — Pardon me. Excuse me.
7. どうもすみません。 — Pardon me. My apologies.
8. みんなで飲（の）みませんか。 — Why don't we drink it together?
9. これ、見（み）ませんか。 — Why don't we watch this?
10. これとあれ、読（よ）みませんか。 — Why don't we read this and that?

Now go to the Activity Book for 練習（れんしゅう） *Renshuu* **Practice.**

Notes

1 Expressions marked by # are not previously introduced in the Speaking/Listening sections.
2 Do not use みなさん when referring to groups of people that include yourself or people in your in-group (when talking to outsiders). It is like attaching -さん to your own name.

Scene 3-8R　よろしくお願<ruby>願<rt>ねが</rt></ruby>いします！　See you then!

Sasha is checking an email she sent out to her colleague, using an app that provides furigana for kanji. What important information does Sasha provide?

テキスト Text

Subject: Re: あしたの<ruby>会議<rt>かいぎ</rt></ruby>

<ruby>久野<rt>くの</rt></ruby>さん

どうもすみません。

あしたの<ruby>会議<rt>かいぎ</rt></ruby>は <ruby>１１<rt>じゅういち</rt></ruby> <ruby>時<rt>じ</rt></ruby>にあります。

よろしくお<ruby>願<rt>ねが</rt></ruby>いします！

<ruby>サーシャ・モリス<rt>さ あ しゃ　も り す</rt></ruby>

Subject: Re: Tomorrow's meeting

Kuno-san

My apologies (for not telling you sooner).

Tomorrow's conference is at 11:00.

See you then!

Sasha Morris

文字と例 Symbol with examples

#29. ろ　　*ro*　　　　　　　　ろ

Examples

1. <ruby>黒<rt>くろ</rt></ruby>いです。　　　　　　　It is black.
2. <ruby>１時<rt>いち じ</rt></ruby>ごろ　　　　　　　approximately 1:00
3. よろしく。　　　　　　　Nice to meet you (lit. 'please treat me favorably').

131

4.	どうぞよろしく。	Nice to meet you (lit. 'please treat me favorably').
5.	どうぞよろしくお願いします。	Nice to meet you (lit. 'please treat me favorably').

#30. も　*mo*　も

Examples

1.	どうも。	(Thanks) very much.
2.	坂本	[family name]
3.	坂本先生	Professor Sakamoto
4.	おもしろいです。	It is interesting/funny/intriguing/entertaining.

#31. は　*ha, wa* (as particle)　 *ba*　は

BTL 1 Particle *wa* は

The particle *wa* is written with は **not** わ. This is left over from a historical change in the pronunciation of this particle. Note that the greetings こんにちは。 and こんばんは。 also use は.

Examples

1.	はい。	Yes. Got it.
2.	かばん	bag(s), briefcase(s)
3.	頑張ります。	I will do my best.
4.	3時半です。	It's 3:30.
5.	おはよう。	Good morning. (informal)
6.	おはようございます。	Good morning. (formal)
7.	あの、お名前は?	Um, your name is . . .?
8.	田中さんは?	How about Mr. Tanaka?
9.	これ、いいですね。あれは?	This is good. What about that one?
10.	明日は忙しくないです。	I'm not very busy tomorrow (at least).

#32. け　*ke*　げ　*ge*　け

何時ですか?　3-8R

Examples

1. 試験{しけん}   examination, test

2. そうですけど......[1]。   It is so, but . . .

3. あの、あしたの会議{かいぎ}ですけど、何時{なんじ}ですか。   Um, the meeting tomorrow—what time is it?

Now go to the Activity Book for 練習{れんしゅう} *Renshuu* Practice.

Note

1 Recall that けど is more common in spoken language. In the written language you will more often find が as well as other versions of けど: けれど, けども, けれども.

Scene 3-9R お先に失礼します。
Excuse me (for leaving ahead of you)

Brian is reading an email he received from his senior colleague in the Japanese Club, using an app that provides furigana for kanji and katakana.

 テキスト Text

Subject: 明日の練習

日本語クラブのみなさん

お疲れ様です。

今日と明日の練習はやっぱりお休みです。

次の練習はあさってですが、2時じゃなくて3時に始めます。

今度のテストも難しいですけど、勉強頑張りましょう!

では、お先に失礼します。

古田

Subject: Tomorrow's practice

Everyone in the Japanese Club

Hello.

Practice for today and tomorrow will be cancelled as expected.

Next practice will be on the day after tomorrow and it will start at 3, not 2.

The upcoming test will be difficult (just like the previous ones), so let's study hard!

See you later. (lit. 'Sorry for leaving ahead of you.')

Furuta

 文字と例 Symbol with examples

#33. *tsu* *du* つ

Examples

1. 別^{べっ}に   not particularly
2. つまらない。   is boring, uninteresting
3. 失礼^{しつれい}します。   Excuse me.
4. お疲^{つか}れ様^{さま}でした。   Good job. (lit. 'You must be tired.')

BTL 2 *Soku-on* (small っ)

You have seen that ああ、いい、うう、えい、おう represent long vowels in hiragana. Long consonants are represented by a reduced (half size) っ placed right before the symbol for the consonant being lengthened. The smaller symbol is written slightly lower than surrounding symbols in horizontal writing, and slightly to the right in vertical writing.

Hiragana	Romanization
〜っこ	*-kko*
〜っし	*-sshi*
〜って	*-tte*

Examples

1. 学校^{がっこう}   school(s)
2. あさって   the day after tomorrow
3. よかったら   if you would like (lit. 'if it is good')
4. 行^いってきます。   I'm off; see you later. (lit. 'I'll go and come back.')
5. 言^いってください。   Please say it.
6. ＪＬＣって、何^{なん}ですか。   What is "JLC"?
7. もう一度^{いちど}言^いってください。 Please say it one more time.
8. みんなで言^いってください。 Please say it all together.
9. 行^いって(い)らっしゃい。   Bye; see you later
10. これ、よかったらどうぞ。 This—please (have some), if you'd like.
11. 会議^{かいぎ}って、あさってですか。 The meeting, is it the day after tomorrow?
12. どっちですか。こっちですか。 Where—this way?

13. 先生のって、大きいのですよね。　　　The teacher's (house) is a large one, isn't it.

14. あの学生って、たかし君のことですね。　(By) "that student," you mean Takashi-kun, right?

#34. や　*ya*　　　　　　や

#35. ゆ　*yu*　　　　　　ゆ

Examples

1. 安いです。　　　　　　　It's cheap.

2. 休みます。　　　　　　　She will go to rest/take a break.

3. 田中さんはお休みです。　Ms. Tanaka is off/absent.

4. あ、雪ですよ。　　　　　Look, it's snow(ing).

5. 易しいですね。[2]　　　It's easy, isn't it.

6. これ、安くないですか。　Isn't this cheap?

7. あさって、休みませんよね。You won't be absent the day after tomorrow, right?

BTL 3 *Yoo-on* (small や , ゆ , よ)

Compare *kiya* and *kya*. The first is represented in hiragana by two equal size symbols: きや. The second is represented by *ki* followed by a reduced *ya*: きゃ. Thus morae that contain a glide (see the chart below) are represented by the hiragana symbol [consonant + -*i*] followed immediately by a reduced *ya*, *yu*, or *yo*. Like the small っ, the small や is written slightly lower than surrounding symbols in horizontal writing, and slightly to the right in vertical writing.

r	m	(h)	n	t	s	k
りゃ *rya*	みゃ *mya*	(ひゃ *hya*)	にゃ *nya*	ちゃ *cha*	しゃ *sha*	きゃ *kya*
りゅ *ryu*	みゅ *myu*	(ひゅ *fyu*)	にゅ *nyu*	ちゅ *chu*	しゅ *shu*	きゅ *kyu*
りょ *ryo*	みょ *myo*	(ひょ *hyo*)	にょ *nyo*	ちょ *cho*	しょ *sho*	きょ *kyo*

(p)	(b)	z	g
(ぴゃ *pya*)	(びゃ *bya*)	じゃ *ja*	ぎゃ *gya*
(ぴゅ *pyu*)	(びゅ *byu*)	じゅ *ju*	ぎゅ *gyu*
(ぴょ *pyo*)	(びょ *byo*)	じょ *jo*	ぎょ *gyo*

Note: The *ja* じゃ that you have seen in negatives (*Kore ja arimasen.* これじゃありませ
ん 'It's not this.' or *Ja, mata ato de* じゃ、またあとで 'So then, see you later.') is actually a
contraction of *de wa* では. The full form with *de wa* では is much more typical of formal
writing (letters, newspapers, academic writing). Thus, in representing spoken style (for
example, novels or stories that reflect speech) you see これじゃないです and これじゃあ
りません. But in formal writing you see これではないです and これではありません. It is
fine to use the contracted form in texts and emails to your friends.

Examples

1.	今日	today
2.	寮	dormitory
3.	お茶	green tea; Japanese tea; tea (in general)
4.	予習	study in advance
5.	会社	company, office
6.	宿題	homework, assignment
7.	授業	class
8.	練習	practice
9.	週末	weekend
10.	図書館	library
11.	ちょっと⋯⋯	It is a little bit (difficult/inconvenient) . . .
12.	大丈夫です。	I am fine/okay.
13.	じゃ、また。	Well then, see you again.
14.	じゃ、あとで。	So then, see you later.
15.	じゃ、またあとで。	Well then, see you again later.
16.	今、会社ですか。	Are you at the office now?
17.	これじゃないです。	It is not this one.
18.	これじゃありません。	It is not this one.
19.	じゃ、そうしましょう。	Okay, let's do so.
20.	ちょっと高いですね。	It is a little expensive, isn't it.
21.	あした、寮で会いませんか。	Won't we meet at the dormitory tomorrow?
22.	あしたじゃなくて、あさってです。	It's not tomorrow, but the day after tomorrow.

#36.	わ	*wa*	
#37.	に	*ni*	
#38.	ほ	*ho*	

Examples

1.	わあ。	Wow!
2.	私 (わたし・わたくし)	I, me
3.	電話ですか。 (でん わ)	Is it a telephone/telephone call?
4.	早稲田大学 (わ せ だ だいがく)	Waseda University
5.	かわいいですね。	It's cute, isn't it.
6.	それ、わかりますね。	That—(you) understand it, right?
7.	よくわかりませんけど‥‥‥	I'm not sure I understand, but . . .
8.	お先に。 (さき)	(I'll leave) ahead of you.
9.	じゃ、3時に。 (さん じ)	Well then, (I'll see you) at 3:00.
10.	お先に失礼します。 (さき) (しつれい)	Excuse me (for leaving ahead of you).
11.	4時に帰りましょう。 (よ じ) (かえ)	Let's go home at 4:00.
12.	何時に会いましょうか。 (なん じ) (あ)	At what time shall we meet?
13.	何³か仕事ありますか。 (なに) (し ごと)	Is (there) any work to be done?
14.	日本語 (に ほん ご)	Japanese (language)
15.	ＪＬＣって日本語で何と言いますか。 (に ほん ご) (なん い)	"JLC" is what in Japanese?

#39.	ひ	*hi*	び	*bi*	
#40.	ふ*	*fu*	ぶ	*bu*	ひふへむ
#41.	へ	*he, e* (as particle)⁴	べ	*be*	
#42.	む	*mu*			

* Note that this is a 4-stroke symbol when it is handwritten.

何時ですか?

Examples

1.	昼ご飯	lunch
2.	ロビー	lobby
3.	コピー	copy
4.	平気です。	It's fine/cool/calm.
5.	食べます。	I'll eat it.
6.	難しいです。	It's difficult.
7.	勉強します。	I'll study.
8.	うちで勉強します。	I'll study at home.
9.	これ、よかったら食べませんか。	If you would like—won't you eat some of this?
10.	この宿題、ちょっと難しくないですか。	Isn't this homework a bit difficult?

#43.	め	*me*	
#44.	ぬ	*nu*	
#45.	る	*ru*	

Examples

1.	雨	rain
2.	だめ	is no good/not working
3.	始めます。	I'll start/begin.
4.	だめですね。	It's no good, is it.
5.	じゃ、始めましょうか。	Okay, then, shall we begin/start?
6.	上沼さん	[family name]-*san*
7.	布川さん	[family name]-*san*
8.	古田さん	[family name]-*san*
9.	なるほど。	That makes sense. Of course.

BTL 4 *Handakuon: Maru* (ぱ , ぴ , ぷ , ぺ , ぽ)

Adding a small circle (or *maru*) to any /*h*/ mora changes the /*h*/ to a /*p*/.

は	*ha*	ば	*ba*	ぱ	*pa*
ひ	*hi*	び	*be*	ぴ	*pi*
ふ	*fu*	ぶ	*bu*	ぷ	*pu*
へ	*he*	べ	*be*	ぺ	*pe*
ほ	*ho*	ぼ	*bo*	ぽ	*po*

Handakuon occur much more frequently with katakana words. See Act 6 for details.

Example

1. やっぱり   as expected, after all

BTL 5 Fonts

Just as alphabetic languages use a variety of fonts, Japanese has a variety of styles to choose from. Below you see six possible ways that you might see the word *hiragana* represented. In advertising, symbols can get even more distorted. And just as in English, handwriting style in Japanese is very distinctive. You may struggle at first, but the more you read the more easily you will become familiar with these different styles of writing.

ひらがな　ひらがな

ひらがな　ひらがな

ひらがな　ひらがな

BTL 6 Japanese names

It is estimated that there are over 100,000 surnames in use in Japan. Almost all are written in kanji, and most use the *kunyomi* of the characters. Here are the twenty most common Japanese family names. Can you arrange them in *gojuuon* order?

何時ですか？ 3-9R

Summary of symbols in Act 3

n	w	r	y	m	h	n	t	s	k	
ん n	わ wa	ら ra	や ya	ま ma	は ha	な na	た ta	さ sa	か ka	あ a
		り ri		み mi	ひ hi	に ni	ち chi	し shi	き ki	い i
		る ru	ゆ yu	む mu	ふ fu	ぬ nu	つ tsu	す su	く ku	う u
		れ re		め me	へ he	ね ne	て te	せ se	け ke	え e
		ろ ro	よ yo	も mo	ほ ho	の no	と to	そ so	こ ko	お o

p	b	d	z	g
ぱ pa	ば ba	だ da	ざ za	が ga
ぴ pi	び bi	（ぢ）ji	じ ji	ぎ gi
ぷ pu	ぶ bu	（づ）du	ず zu	ぐ gu
ぺ pe	べ be	で de	ぜ ze	げ ge
ぽ po	ぼ bo	ど do	ぞ zo	ご go

ry	my	hy	ny	ch	sh	ky
りゃ rya	みゃ mya	ひゃ hya	にゃ nya	ちゃ cha	しゃ sha	きゃ kya
りゅ ryu	みゅ myu	ひゅ fyu	にゅ nyu	ちゅ chu	しゅ shu	きゅ kyu
りょ ryo	みょ myo	ひょ hyo	にょ nyo	ちょ cho	しょ sho	きょ kyo

py	by	j	gy
ぴゃ *pya*	びゃ *bya*	じゃ *ja*	ぎゃ *gya*
ぴゅ *pyu*	びゅ *byu*	じゅ *ju*	ぎゅ *gyu*
ぴょ *pyo*	びょ *byo*	じょ *jo*	ぎょ *gyo*

Now go to the Activity Book for 練習 *Renshuu* Practice. Then do 評価 *Hyooka* Assessment activities, including 読んでみよう *Yonde miyoo* Contextualized reading, 書き取り *Kakitori* Dictation, and 書いてみよう *Kaite miyoo* Contextualized writing.

Notes

1 Note that ず and づ have the same pronunciation. The symbol づ is used only in a few places in modern Japanese; ず is used otherwise.
2 やさしい has two different meanings, each of which is represented by a different kanji: 易しい 'it's easy,' and 優しい 'he's kind, he's gentle.' However, both are often written in hiragana.
3 Remember that the pronunciation of なん・なに depends on what follows. See Scene 3 in Act 2.
4 See Act 5, Scene 5-4 for details on this particle.

第4幕
Act 4

れんらくき
連絡来ました？

Renraku kimashita?

Did they get in touch?

とき かね
時は金なり *Toki wa kane nari*
Time is money.

143

◆ 話す・聞く *Hanasu/kiku* Speaking and listening

Scene 4-1 大きくしました。*Ookiku shimashita.* I enlarged it.

Sasha shows Kanda-san a poster that she enlarged for a meeting.

 The script

(This is the last Act in which you will see romanization for the Japanese. Try using the Japanese script with furigana this time. Remember to work with the audio files!)

サーシャ	神田
ちょっと大きくしました。	すごくいいポスターですね。高かったでしょう。
いや、それほどじゃなかったですよ！3000円ぐらいでした。	まあまあでしたね。

Saasha	*Kanda*
Cho⌐tto⌐ o⌐okiku shi⌐ma⌐shita.	*Su⌐go⌐ku ⌐i⌐i⌐ po⌐sutaa desu ⌐ne⌐. Ta⌐kakatta deshoo.*
I⌐ya, so⌐re hodo⌐ ja ⌐na⌐katta desu yo! Sa⌐n-zen-en gu⌐rai deshita.	*Ma⌐ama⌐a deshita ne.*

Sasha	Kanda
I made it a bit bigger.	Really nice poster! It must have been expensive.
No, it wasn't that much! It was about ¥3000.	Not so much, was it. ('It was so-so.')

145

単語と表現 *Tango to hyoogen* Vocabulary and expressions

Nouns

ポスター	*posutaa*	poster

Number: 1000s

千・一千	*sen/issen*	1000	六千	*rokusen*	6000
二千	*nisen*	2000	七千	*nanasen*	7000
三千	*sanzen*	3000	八千	*hassen*	8000
四千	*yonsen*	4000	九千	*kyuusen*	9000
五千	*gosen*	5000	何千	*nanzen*	how many thousands

Number: 10,000s

万・一万	*man/ichiman*	10,000	六万	*rokuman*	60,000
二万	*niman*	20,000	七万	*nanaman*	70,000
三万	*sanman*	30,000	八万	*hachiman*	80,000
四万	*yonman*	40,000	九万	*kyuuman*	90,000
五万	*goman*	50,000	何万	*nanman*	how many ten thousands

Verbs

作ります(作らない)	*tsukurimasu (tsukur-anai)*	make
作りました(作らなかった)	*tsukurimashita (tsukuranakatta)*	made
買います(買わない)	*kaimasu (kaw-anai)*	buy
買いました(買わなかった)	*kaimashita (kawanakatta)*	bought

Adjectives

高かった	*takakatta*	was expensive
新しい	*atarashii*	new
新しかった	*atarashikatta*	was new
古い	*furui*	old
古かった	*furukatta*	was old

Special expressions

それほど	*sore hodo*	that much; to that extent
まあまあ	*maamaa*	so-so
Xぐらい・くらい	X *gurai/kurai*	about X, approximately X

Behind the Scenes

BTS 1 Past forms: Verbs, Adjectives, and Noun *desu*

In the previous Acts, you learned how to express your thoughts in the non-past:

Verb	買います。	*Kaimasu.*	I will buy it. I do buy it.
	買わないです。	*Kawanai desu.*	I won't buy it.
	買いません。	*Kaimasen.*	I don't buy it.
Adjective	高いです。	*Takai desu.*	It will be expensive. It is expensive.
	高くないです。	*Takaku nai desu.*	It isn't expensive.
	高くありません。	*Takaku arimasen.*	It won't be expensive.
Noun *desu*	大学です。	*Daigaku desu.*	It's a university.
	大学じゃないです。	*Daigaku ja nai desu.*	It isn't a university.
	大学じゃありません。	*Daigaku ja arimasen.*	

All of these Core Sentences have a past form, in both affirmative and negative, formal and informal. All of these come up in this Scene.

a. Verbs

To change a non-past affirmative Verb into the past affirmative, change *-masu* to *-mashita*. (Recall *wakarimashita* 'got it' from Act 2.) Since there are two alternative non-past negatives for a Verb (*kawanai desu* and *kaimasen*), there are two corresponding past negatives. To form the past negative, change *-nai desu* to *-nakatta desu* or *-masen* to *-masen deshita*.

買いました。	*Kaimashita.*	I bought it.
買わなかったです。	*Kawanakatta desu.*	I didn't buy it.
買いませんでした。	*Kaimasen deshita.*	I didn't buy it.

147

Note that both *kawanai desu* and *kawanakatta desu* forms can be made informal by dropping です.

b. Adjectives

To make a non-past Adjective past, change *-i desu* to *-katta desu*. Since there are two alternative non-past negatives for an Adjective (*takaku nai desu* and *takaku arimasen*), there are two corresponding past negatives. To form the past negative, change *-nai desu* to *-nakatta desu* or *-masen* to *-masen deshita*.

高かったです。	*Takakatta desu.*	It was expensive.
高くなかったです。	*Takaku nakatta desu.*	It wasn't expensive.
高くありませんでした。	*Takaku arimasen deshita.*	

As with the affirmative forms, past forms of the Adjective can be made informal by dropping です。

c. Noun です Noun *desu*

To make a non-past [Noun *desu*] past, change *-desu* to *-deshita*. Since there are two alternative non-past negatives for a [Noun *desu*] combination (*daigaku ja nai desu* and *daigaku ja arimasen*), there are two corresponding past negatives. *Daigaku ja nai desu* changes just as any Adjective would for the past: drop *-i* and add *-katta* (*daigaku ja nakatta desu*). *Daigaku ja arimasen* changes just as any verb would: add *deshita* to the negative form (*daigaku ja arimasen deshita*).

大学でした。	*Daigaku deshita.*	It was a university.
大学じゃなかったです。	*Daigaku ja nakatta desu.*	It wasn't a university.
大学じゃありませんでした。	*Daigaku ja arimasen deshita.*	It wasn't a university.

You have now seen a number of informal equivalents of the Core Sentences. Here is a table to remind you of what has come up so far. You will learn the missing forms later.

Informal	Non-past, affirmative	Non-past, negative	Past, affirmative	Past, negative
Verb		*kawanai*		*kawanakatta*
Adjective	*takai*	*takaku nai*	*takakatta*	*takaku nakatta*
Noun *desu*	*daigaku (da)*	*daigaku ja nai*		*daigaku ja nakatta*

Here are some more examples.

作ります。	*Tsukurimasu.*	I will make it.
作りました。	*Tsukurimashita.*	I made it.
作りませんでした。	*Tsukurimasen deshita.*	I didn't make it.

148

早いです。	*Hayai desu.*	It's early.
早かったです。	*Hayakatta desu.*	It was early.
早くなかったです。	*Hayaku nakatta desu.*	It wasn't early.
早くありませんでした。	*Hayaku arimasen deshita.*	It wasn't early.
今日です。	*Kyoo desu.*	It's today.
今日でした。	*Kyoo deshita.*	It was today.
今日じゃなかったです。	*Kyoo ja nakatta desu.*	It wasn't today.
今日じゃありませんでした。	*Kyoo ja arimasen deshita.*	It wasn't today.

BTS 2 Sentence でしょう（か）*deshoo (ka)*

Deshoo (with falling intonation) is a tentative form of *desu*, meaning 'probably.' Because it is tentative, it is a little more polite. For now, you will see *deshoo* with Adjectives or Nouns in non-past, past, affirmative, and negative. Nouns that combine with *deshoo* include question words (such as *nan, dare*), even though there is no Sentence Particle *ka* at the end of the Sentence. Here are some examples.

遅いでしょう。	*Osoi deshoo.*	They'll probably be late.
高かったでしょう。	*Takakatta deshoo.*	It was probably expensive.
高くないでしょう。	*Takaku nai deshoo.*	It probably isn't expensive.
私でしょう。	*Watashi deshoo.*	It's probably me.
部長ってだれでしょう。	*Buchoo tte dare deshoo.*	I wonder who the division chief might be.

The addition of *ka* after *deshoo* (again with falling intonation) makes it even less certain: 'do you suppose that . . .?' or 'would it be that . . .?'

田中さんでしょうか。	*Tanaka-san deshoo ka.*	Would it be Ms. Tanaka?
高かったでしょうか。	*Takakatta deshoo ka.*	Do you suppose it was expensive?
高くないでしょうか。	*Takaku nai deshoo ka.*	Do you suppose it isn't expensive?
いつでしょうか。	*Itsu deshoo ka.*	When do you suppose it is?

Compare:

高いですね？	*Takai desu ne?*	It's expensive, isn't it?
高いでしょう。	*Takai deshoo.*	It's probably expensive.
高いでしょうか。	*Takai deshoo ka.*	Would it be expensive?

All of these show uncertainty. In the first, it sounds like the speaker is reasonably sure that the item is expensive, and is seeking agreement. The second sounds less certain about whether the item is expensive: 'I suspect it is, but I will give you the final say.' The third is the least certain and is relying on the listener to provide assurance.

BTS 3 Manner expressions: Adjective *-ku* form + Sentence

The *-ku* form of an Adjective links to a following Sentence to qualify or affect its meaning. This use of the *-ku* form is one kind of manner expression. Other manner expressions are introduced in Scenes below.

早く行きました。	*Hayaku ikimashita.*	I went early.
遅く帰ります。	*Osoku kaerimasu.*	I go home late.
大きく作ります。	*Ookiku tsukurimasu.*	We'll make it big.
新しく買います。	*Atarashiku kaimasu.*	I'll buy it again (lit. 'newly').

Note that the *-ku* form of *ii* 'good' is *yoku*. This can mean either 'well' (*Yoku wakarimasu nee!* 'You understand well, don't you!'), 'often' (*Yoku ikimasu nee!* 'You go often, don't you!'), or 'a lot' (*Yoku tabemasu nee* 'He eats a lot, doesn't he!'). Special mention should also be made of the Adjective *sugoi* which means 'amazing, wonderful.' In its *-ku* form it intensifies the Sentence that follows, meaning something like 'awfully, really, amazingly.'

すごく安いです。	*Sugoku yasui desu.*	It is really inexpensive.
すごくおいしいクッキー	*sugoku oishii kukkii*	amazingly delicious cookies

These days, in informal settings, *sugoi* is used as a manner expression:

すごい安いです。	*Sugoi yasui desu.*	It is really inexpensive.
すごいおいしいクッキー	*sugoi oishii kukkii*	amazingly delicious cookies

BTS 4 Large numbers 千・万 *sen/man*

Thousands are counted in Japanese using *-sen*. When a number starts with 1000 (for example, 1200) *sen* (not *issen*) is preferred (*sen-nihyaku*). Note the sound change of /s/ to /z/ with 3000 (*sanzen*), 8000 (*hassen*) and 'how many thousand (*nanzen*).'

Numbers of five places or more are grouped by ten-thousands (*-man*). 10,000 is *ichiman;* 100,000 is *juuman;* 1,000,000 is *hyakuman;* 10,000,000 is *senman*. Terms beyond this (*oku* and *choo*) are not often used in daily conversation, but are used for real estate, governmental budgets, and the like. One hundred million is *ichioku* and trillions are designated in *choo*.

| さんまんいっせんえん
¥ 3 1,0 0 0 | *sanman-issen-en* | ¥31,000 |
| ごじゅうななまんはっせんどる
$ 5 7 8,0 0 0 | *gojuunanaman-hassen-doru* | $578,000 |

BTS 5 Quantity + ぐらい *-gurai*

Recall from the previous Act that *-goro* combines with time expressions to indicate approximation (8:00-*goro* 'about 8:00'). Here you see *-gurai* combining with quantity expressions (*-en, -hon, -satsu*, etc.) to indicate approximation.

| せんえん
¥1000ぐらいの らーめんラーメンです。 | *Sen-en-gurai no raamen desu.* | It's ramen that's about ¥1000. |
| じゅう まい
1 0 枚ぐらいあります。 | *Juu-mai-gurai arimasu.* | I have about ten sheets. |

The general question word for this pattern is *dono gurai* 'about how much.'

| どのぐらい 作つくりましょうか。 | *Dono gurai tsukurimashoo ka.* | About how much shall I make? |

Note that you will hear both *-gurai* and *-goro* in naming approximate time.

| じゅうにじ
12:00 ごろ・ぐらいに 来きま
しょう。 | *Juuni-ji-goro/gurai ni kimashoo.* | Why don't I come at about 12:00. |

But the reverse is not true—for counting, only -gurai can be used.

Now go to the Activity Book for れんしゅう **練 習** *Renshuu* **Practice and** うでだめし **腕試し** *Udedameshi* **Tryout.**

Scene 4-2 専攻は日本学でした。

Senkoo wa nihongaku deshita. My major was Japanese.

Sasha and Kanda-san are talking during a break.

The script

サーシャ	神田
神田さん、大学の専攻は?	数学でした。
へえ、数学!	今は全然使わないですけどね。サーシャさんは?
専攻は日本学でした。あとビジネスのコースもけっこう取りました。	ふうん、日本学って日本語だけじゃないですよね。
ええ、歴史とか文学とかも。	宗教も?
私は取りませんでしたけど……。	

Saasha	Kanda
Kaⁿnda-san, daⁿigaku no gosenkoo wa?	Suⁿugaku deⁿshita.
Heⁿe, suⁿugaku!	Iⁿma wa zeⁿnzen tsukawanaⁿi desu kedo ne. Saⁿasha-san wa?

Se⌐nkoo wa ni⌐ho⌐ngaku deshita. A⌐to ⌐bi⌐ jinesu no ko⌐osu mo ⌐ke⌐kkoo to⌐rima⌐shita.	Fu⌐un. Ni⌐ho⌐ngaku tte ni⌐hongo dake⌐ ja ⌐na⌐i desu yo ne.
E⌐e, re⌐kishi to⌐ka ⌐bu⌐ngaku to ka mo.	Shu⌐ukyoo mo?
Wa⌐tashi wa torimase⌐n deshita kedo . . .	

Sasha	Kanda
Kanda-san, what was your major in college?	It was mathematics.
Wow! Mathematics!	I don't use math at all now though. How about you, Sasha?
My major was Japanese studies. And then I also took a fair amount of business courses.	Hmm. "Japanese studies" is not just Japanese (language), is it.
Yes, it's also fields like history and literature.	Religion too?
I didn't take it, but . . .	

 単語と 表現 *Tango to hyoogen* Vocabulary and expressions

たんご　ひょうげん

Nouns

(ご) 専攻 せんこう	(go)senkoo	major field of study
(ご)専門 せんもん	(go)senmon	specialization, major
数学 すうがく	suugaku	mathematics
歴史 れきし	rekishi	history
日本学 にほんがく	nihongaku	Japanese studies
宗 教(学) しゅうきょうがく	shuukyo (gaku)	religion (religious studies)
社会学 しゃかいがく	shakaigaku	sociology
経済(学) けいざいがく	keizai(gaku)	economics
文学 ぶんがく	bungaku	literature
言語学 げんごがく	gengogaku	linguistics
工学 こうがく	koogaku	engineering
物理(学) ぶつりがく	butsur(gaku)	physics
全然 ぜんぜん	zenzen	not at all, entirely

4-2

連絡来ました?

153

Verbs

使(つか)います(使わない)	*tsukaimasu (tsukaw-anai)*	use
取(と)ります(取らない)	*torimasu (tor-anai)*	take (a class)

Phrase particles

とか	*to ka*	(things) like, such as
とかも	*to ka mo*	also (things) like, such as
だけ	*dake*	just, only

Special expressions

ふうん	*fuun* (w/ rising intonation)	hmm
けっこう	*kekkoo*	quite, nice, wonderful, enough, sufficient (often by implication 'no thank you')
あまり	*amari*	not very much (plus negative)
あと	*ato*	lastly, remaining, and then

拡張(かくちょう) *Kakuchoo* Expansion

Find out the Japanese equivalent for your academic major or specialization and learn to say it.

Behind the Scenes

BTS 6 Academic majors and areas of specialization 大学(だいがく)の専攻(せんこう)

A major or field of study at university is called *senkoo*. A few sample majors are introduced above. A more general term is *senmon* which refers to specialization within a field of study but also areas of expertise in the day-to-day world or something that a person is simply interested in or good at. For instance, *Burajiru-koohii no senmon* 'a specialist on Brazilian coffee.'

BTS 7 [Noun + Phrase Particle] as a question

You have seen [Noun *wa?*] used to contrast an item with other items in the discussion. In this Scene we find Kanda-san asking Sasha about her major, using two Sentence fragments consisting of a [Noun plus Phrase Particle]:

サーシャさんは？	*Saasha-san wa?*	How about you, Sasha?
宗教も？	*Shuukyoo mo?*	Religion, too?

Sentence fragments are typical of casual conversation, but may occur in formal conversations, especially to follow up on what the other person just said. Kanda-san's first question (*Saasha-san wa?*) follows Sasha's question about his major, while the second (*Shuukyoo mo?*) follows Sasha's listing of what is included in a Japanese major.

BTS 8 Noun$_x$ + とか Noun$_x$ + *to ka*

[Noun + *to ka*] is used in relatively casual settings to mean 'things like.' There may be just one thing mentioned:

クッキーとか食べますか？	*Kukkii to ka tabemasu ka?*	Do you eat things like cookies?

Or there may be multiple examples listed:

お茶とかコーヒーとかあります よ。	*Ocha to ka koohii to ka arimasu yo.*	We have things like tea and coffee, you know.

BTS 9 Noun だけ Noun *dake*

a. Noun だけ Noun *dake*

The word *dake* means 'only, just.' Kanda-san asks Sasha about what is included in a Japanese major: *Nihongaku tte, nihongo dake ja nai desu ne.* 'Japanese studies isn't only Japanese language, right?'

ラーメンだけ食べました。	*Raamen dake tabemashita.*	I ate only ramen.
神田さんだけ使いました。	*Kanda-san dake tsukaimashita.*	Only Kanda-san used it.

b. Category は・って X だけ Category *wa/tte* X *dake*

In the pattern [Noun$_X$ *wa/tte* Noun$_Y$ *dake desu*], Noun$_Y$ designates some limitation on Noun$_X$. Compare:

<table>
<tr><td>日本学って、日本語だけじゃないですよね?</td><td>*Nihongaku tte, Nihongo dake ja nai desu yo ne?*</td></tr>
<tr><td>日本学は、日本語だけじゃないですよね?</td><td>*Nihongaku wa, Nihongo dake ja nai desu yo ne?*</td></tr>
</table>

Both of these are roughly equivalent to 'Japanese studies isn't only Japanese language, right?'

<table>
<tr><td>今日は神田さんだけです。</td><td>*Kyoo wa Kanda-san dake desu.*</td><td>Today it's only Kanda-san (who's coming).</td></tr>
<tr><td>図書館ってここだけですか。</td><td>*Toshokan tte koko dake desu ka.*</td><td>Is this the only library?</td></tr>
</table>

BTS 10 Multiple Phrase Particles: Phrase Particle + も・は *mo/wa*

You have seen Phrase Particles *wa* and *mo* following Nouns. Here you see that both of these Particles may also follow other Phrase Particles with the same function. Here are some examples:

<table>
<tr><td>A: コーヒー、飲みますか?</td><td>*Koohii, nomimasu ka?*</td><td>Do you drink coffee?</td></tr>
<tr><td>B: ええ、お茶とかも飲みますよ。</td><td>*Ee, ocha to ka mo nomimasu yo.*</td><td>Yes, I drink Japanese tea and that sort of thing, too, you know.</td></tr>
<tr><td>A: 紙、ここにはないですよ。</td><td>*Kami, koko ni wa nai desu yo.*</td><td>There's no paper in here, is there.</td></tr>
<tr><td>B: あそこには?</td><td>*Asoko ni wa?*</td><td>How about over there?</td></tr>
<tr><td>A: あそこにもないですが。</td><td>*Asoko ni mo nai desu ga.*</td><td>There's not any in there either, but . . .</td></tr>
</table>

BTS 11 あと + Noun

In a series of Nouns, the last one mentioned may be preceded by *ato*. This indicates that Noun following *ato* is somehow different from what precedes, or that the list is complete with the final Noun. The list then might be followed by a Phrase Particle, as with any other Noun.

<table>
<tr><td>社会学、歴史、あと宗教も勉強しました。</td><td>*Shakaigaku, rekishi, ato shuukyoo mo benkyoo-shimashita.*</td><td>I studied sociology . . . history . . . oh, and also religion.</td></tr>
</table>

| おすし、やきとり、あと
ラーメンも好きです。 | *Osushi, yakitori, ato raamen mo suki desu.* | I like sushi, yakitori, and oh, also ramen. |

When *ato* precedes a quantity Noun, it indicates how much or how many remain or are left.

| あと5分です。 | *Ato go-fun desu.* | There are five minutes left. |
| あと10個作ってください。 | *Ato juk-ko tukutte kudasai.* | Please make ten more. |

BTS 12 曖昧 Ambiguity

Conventionally in Japan, it is considered to be easier on listeners if you indicate some uncertainty when talking about circumstances. Even when you ask your Japanese friend if she is going to the party on Saturday, she is likely to say "probably" when asked. If your friend saw Tanaka at the library and you ask if Tanaka is on campus, your friend might say, "I think so." Dividing the world into black and white is not a Japanese trait. In fact, ambiguity can be a virtue, especially if it preserves interpersonal harmony.

You have now seen multiple examples of vagueness and/or indirect speech in Japan. In this Act you find two additional ways of showing uncertainty:

a   Tentative でしょう *desyoo* 'probably'
b   Noun$_X$ +って *tte* (in contrast to Noun$_X$ + *wa*)

In previous Acts, you have seen other patterns that are associated with indirectness or uncertainty:

c   Negative questions to indicate uncertainty

| 高くないですか？ | *Takaku nai desu ka?* | Isn't it expensive? |

d   The use of ちょっと *chotto* as a polite refusal or to show difficulty
e   Leaving sentences unfinished with けど *kedo* or が *ga*
f   Hesitating with そうですねぇ。 *Soo desu nee.*

Listen for these strategies when you talk to your Japanese teacher and/or friends. Try to include them in your own speech.

Now go to the Activity Book for 練習 *Renshuu* Practice and 腕試し Tryout.

Note

1   The prefix *go-* makes a word more polite. You will learn more about this in Act 6.

Scene 4-3 私がしました。 *Watashi ga shimashita.*
I'm the one who did it.

Sasha surprises Kanda-san by telling him that she was responsible for finishing a task.

 The script

神田	サーシャ
これは、山下さんですね?	あ、いや、私がしました。
本当ですか?	はい。
いつ?	先週しました。
すごいな。大変だった?	いえ、別に。
お疲れ様。	

Kanda	*Saasha*
Ko⌐re wa Ya⌐ma¬shita-san desu ne?	*A, i⌐ya, wa⌐tashi ga shima¬shita.*
Ho⌐ntoo de¬su ka?	*Ha¬i.*
I¬tsu?	*Se⌐nshuu shima¬shita.*
Su⌐go¬i ⌐na¬. Ta⌐ihen da¬tta?	*I⌐e, be⌐tsu ni.*
O⌐tsukaresama.	

Kanda	Sasha
This (job) is Yamashita-san's (doing), right?	Oh, no, I'm the one who did it.
Really?	Yes.
When?	I did it last week.
Amazing! Was it tough?	No, not especially.
You worked hard.	

158

単語と表現 *Tango to hyoogen* Vocabulary and expressions

Nouns

いつ	*itsu*	when?
先週	*senshuu*	last week
きのう	*kinoo*	yesterday
おととい	*ototoi*	day before yesterday
先月	*sengetsu*	last month
先学期	*sengakki*	last semester
先日	*senjitsu*	thc other day
去年	*kyonen*	last year
(お)先	*(o)saki*	ahead, previous
本当	*hontoo*	true
大変(な)	*taihen (na)*	tough (to do), awful, terrible
山下さん	*Yamashita-san*	Yamashita-san

Verbs

しました	*shimashita*	did
考えます (考えない)	*kangaemasu (kangae-nai)*	think about, consider
考えました (考えなかった)	*kangaemashita (kangae-nakatta)*	thought
手伝います (手伝わない)	*tetsudaimasu (tetsudaw-anai)*	help
手伝いました (手伝わなかった)	*tetsudaimashita (tetsudaw-anakatta)*	helped

Phrase particle

が	*ga*	[subject particle]

Behind the Scenes

BTS 13 Phrase Particle が *ga*

You have seen that Nouns can hook up to Core Sentences in a number of ways. When a Noun is the subject of a Sentence, it connects directly to the Core Sentence:

私、神田です。	*Watashi, Kanda desu.*	I'm Kanda.
これ、おいしいですよ。	*Kore, oishii desu yo.*	This is tasty, you know.

You have also seen that the Phrase Particle *wa* might mark this Noun when there is a sense of contrast with other Nouns:

<ruby>私<rt>わたし</rt></ruby>は<ruby>神田<rt>かんだ</rt></ruby>です。 *Watashi wa Kanda desu.* I (in contrast to others) am Kanda.

これはおいしいですよ。 *Kore wa oishii desu yo.* This (compared to other things) is tasty, you know.

Yet another possibility is that the Noun is in addition to something or someone else, in which case it is marked by *mo*:

<ruby>私<rt>わたし</rt></ruby>も<ruby>神田<rt>かんだ</rt></ruby>です。 *Watashi mo Kanda desu.* I am also Kanda.

これもおいしいですよ。 *Kore mo oishii desu yo.* This is also tasty, you know.

In this Scene you see another possible subject marker: *ga*. Phrase Particle *ga* marks a subject when the Noun provides new information or information that the speaker believes the other person is looking for. Another way to look at this is that *ga* puts a spotlight on its Noun.

<ruby>私<rt>わたし</rt></ruby>が<ruby>神田<rt>かんだ</rt></ruby>です。 *Watashi ga Kanda desu.* <u>I</u> am the one who is Kanda.

これがおいしいですよ。 *Kore ga oishii desu yo.* <u>This</u> is delicious, you know. (i.e. This is what is good [is what we want].)

そばが<ruby>好<rt>す</rt></ruby>きです。 *Soba ga suki desu.* (What) I like (is) <u>soba noodles</u>.

<ruby>山下<rt>やました</rt></ruby>さんが<ruby>来<rt>き</rt></ruby>ますよ。 *Yamashita-san ga kimasu yo.* <u>Yamashita-san</u> is the one who's coming, you know.

It is no accident that question words in the subject position are more likely than other Nouns to be marked by *ga*:

だれが<ruby>作<rt>つく</rt></ruby>りますか？ *Dare ga tsukurimasu ka.* Who's going to make it?

どれが<ruby>高<rt>たか</rt></ruby>いですか？ *Dore ga takai desu ka.* Which one is expensive?

BTS 14 Past informal [Noun だった] [Noun *datta*] It was X

The past form of *da* is *datta*. Here Kanda-san mixes formal and informal forms in finding out who did a task. His use of informal when he asks *Itsu?* and *Taihen datta?* sounds friendlier and more sympathetic than *Itsu deshita ka?* and *Taihen deshita ka?* Keep in mind that he is Sasha's *senpai* at the company, and it is part of his job to encourage her.

あの<ruby>会議<rt>かいぎ</rt></ruby>、<ruby>去年<rt>きょねん</rt></ruby>だった。 *Ano kaigi, kyonen datta.* That meeting was last year.

<ruby>坂本先生<rt>さかもとせんせい</rt></ruby>の<ruby>授業<rt>じゅぎょう</rt></ruby>が<ruby>好<rt>す</rt></ruby>きだった。 *Sakamoto-sensei no jugyoo ga suki datta.* (What) I liked was Sakamoto-sensei's class.

160

It should not come as a surprise that the negative form of [Noun *datta*] is [Noun *ja nakatta*] (drop *desu* from the formal [Noun *ja nakatta desu*]).

あの会議、先月じゃなかった?	*Ano kaigi, sengetsu ja nakatta?*	Wasn't that meeting last month?
神田さんの専攻は、歴史じゃなかったよ。文学だった。	*Kanda-san no senkoo wa, rekishi ja nakatta yo. Bungaku datta.*	Kanda-san's major wasn't history! It was literature.

Now go to the Activity Book for 練習 *Renshuu* Practice and 腕試し *Udedameshi* Tryout.

Scene 4-4 会議の時間 *Kaigi no jikan*
かい ぎ   じ かん
The time of the meeting

Kanda-san wants to confirm the particulars about an upcoming meeting.

The script

神田 かん だ	サーシャ さ あ しゃ
連絡、来ました? れんらく き	え?何ですか? なん
来月の会議の時間。 らいげつ かい ぎ じ かん	ああ、そのことですか。今朝 聞きました。 け さ き ２０日の１０時ですよね? はつ か じゅうじ
半からじゃなかったですか? はん	いや、１０時から１１時半までですけど……。 じゅうじ じゅういち じ はん
そうか。えっと、場所は?いつものところですね? ば しょ	はい、２０１番の会議室です。 にひゃくいちばん かい ぎ しつ

Kanda	*Saasha*
Reˈnraku, kiˈmaˈshita?	E? Naˈn desu ka?
Raˈigetsu no ˈkaˈigi no jiˈkan.	Aˈa, soˈno kotoˈ desu ka. Keˈsa kiˈkimaˈshita. Haˈtsuka no ˈjuˈu-ji desu yo ne.
Haˈn kara ja ˈnaˈkatta desu ka?	Iyˈa, juˈu-ji kara juˈu-ichi-ji-haˈn made desu kedo …
Soˈo ka. Eˈeto, baˈsho wa? Iˈtsu mo no toˈkoroˈ desu ne?	Haˈi, niˈ-hyaku-ichiˈ ban no kaˈigiˈshitsu desu.

Kanda	Sasha
Did they get in touch with you?	Eh? About what?
The time of the meeting next month.	Oh, about that. I heard this morning. It's at 10:00 on the twentieth, right?
Wasn't it from half past (ten)?	No, it'll be from 10:00 to 11:30.
Is that so. Uhh, what about the place? Where we always meet, right?	Yes, in meeting room 201.

たんご ひょうげん

Nouns

連絡（します）	*renraku (shimasu)*	contact, communication
イベント	*ibento*	event
コンサート	*konsaato*	concert
こと	*koto*	matter
場所	*basho*	place
ところ	*tokoro*	place
いつも	*itsu mo*	always
会議室	*kaigishitsu*	meeting room
教室	*kyooshitsu*	classroom
レストラン	*resutoran*	restaurant
カフェ	*kafe*	café
ホテル	*hoteru*	hotel
公園	*kooen*	park
来月	*raigetsu*	next month
今月	*kongetsu*	this month
今週	*konshuu*	this week
来週	*raishuu*	next week
今年	*kotoshi*	this year
来年	*rainen*	next year
来学期	*raigakki*	next term/semester
明治	*Meiji*	Meiji era (1868–1912)
大正	*Taishoo*	Taisho era (1912–1926)
昭和	*Shoowa*	Showa era (1926–1989)
平成	*Heisei*	Heisei era (1989–2019)
令和	*Reiwa*	Reiwa era (2019–present)
今朝	*kesa*	this morning
今晩	*konban*	this evening
さっき	*sakki*	a while ago
２０日	*hatsuka*	the twentieth day of the month

4-4

連絡来ました？

163

Verbs

聞きます (聞かない)	*kikimasu (kik-anai)*	hear; listen
聞きました (聞かなかった)	*kikimashita (kik-anakatta)*	heard; listened

Phrase particles

から	*kara*	from (starting point)
まで	*made*	up to, until

Classifiers

〜日	*-nichi/-ka*	classifier for naming the day of the month				
1日	*tsuitachi*	the 1st	17日	*juu-shichi-nichi*		the 17th
2日	*futsuka*	the 2nd	18日	*juu-hachi-nichi*		the 18th
3日	*mikka*	the 3rd	19日	*juu-ku-nichi*		the 19th
4日	*yokka*	the 4th	20日	*hatuka*		the 20th
5日	*itsuka*	the 5th	21日	*ni-juu-ichi-nichi*		the 21st
6日	*muika*	the 6th	22日	*ni-juu-ni-nichi*		the 22nd
7日	*nanoka*	the 7th	23日	*ni-juu-san-nichi*		the 23rd
8日	*yooka*	the 8th	24日	*ni-juu-yokka*		the 24th
9日	*kokonoka*	the 9th	25日	*ni-juu-go-nichi*		the 25th
10日	*tooka*	the 10th	26日	*ni-juu-roku-nichi*		the 26th
11日	*juu-ichi-nichi*	the 11th	27日	*ni-juu-shichi-nichi*		the 27th
12日	*juu-ni-nichi*	the 12th	28日	*ni-juu-hachi-nichi*		the 28th
13日	*juu-san-nichi*	the 13th	29日	*ni-juu-ku-nichi*		the 29th
14日	*juu-yokka*	the 14th	30日	*san-juu-nichi*		the 30th
15日	*juu-go-nichi*	the 15th	31日	*san-juu-ichi-nichi*		the 31st
16日	*juu-roku-nichi*	the 16th	何日	*nan-nichi*		what date?
-月	*-gatsu*	classifier for naming the months of the year				
一月	*ichi-gatsu*	January	七月	*shichi-gatsu*		July
二月	*ni-gatsu*	February	八月	*hachi-gatsu*		August
三月	*san-gatsu*	March	九月	*ku-gatsu*		September
四月	*shi-gatsu*	April	十月	*juu-gatsu*		October
五月	*go-gatsu*	May	十一月	*juuichi-gatsu*		November
六月	*roku-gatsu*	June	十二月	*juuni-gatsu*		December
			何月	*nan-gatsu*		what month

連絡来ました？ 4-4

番 (ばん)	*ban*	classifier for naming a numbers in a series
年 (ねん)	*nen*	classifier for naming the years
２０１８年 (にせんじゅうはちねん)	*ni-sen-juu-hachi-nen*	the year 2018

Special expressions

そうか。	*Soo ka.*	Is that so. (expression of awareness)
いつものX	*itsu mo no X*	the usual X (e.g., 場所 (ばしょ) *basho* place, 時間 (じかん) *jikan* time, ところ *tokoro* place)

拡張 (かくちょう) *Kakuchoo* Expansion

1 Find out the Japanese equivalent for the next major holiday where you live and learn how to say it.
2 Pick some of your favorite restaurant or fast food chains and find out if they are in Japan. If they are, find out how to say the name in Japanese.

Behind the Scenes

BTS 15 Questions without か

Here you find that Kanda-san asks Sasha if someone has been in touch, using a question without a final Sentence Particle か. This is typical of speech that is a bit less formal but not yet informal or casual. Listen carefully for the pitch profile of questions like this.

昼 (ひる)ごはん、食 (た)べました？	*Hiru-gohan, tabemashita?*	Did you eat lunch?
この漢字 (かんじ)、わかります？	*Kono kanji, wakarimasu?*	Do you know this kanji?
今日 (きょう)の 宿題 (しゅくだい)しました？	*Kyoo no shukudai shimashita?*	Did you do today's homework?

BTS 16 そのこと　*Sono koto* That matter, that thing

You have seen *koto* in previous Acts in the pattern [Noun + *no koto*] meaning 'matters having to do with N.' Here you see it in combination with *sono*. Remember that *sono* N refers to 'that N near you' but also, as is the case here, 'that N you just mentioned.' Compare *sono koto* to *ano koto* 'that matter/experience that we both know (but that will remain unmentioned here).'

165

BTS 17 Classifier 〜番 *-ban*

When you want to name numbers in a series or sequence, the classifier is *-ban*.

１５番、何ページですか。	*Juugo-ban, nan-peeji desu ka.*	What page is number fifteen?
あしたのクラス、 ３１０番教室です。	*Ashita no kurasu, sanbyakujuu-ban kyooshitsu desu.*	Tomorrow's class is in classroom 310.

There is a good deal of flexibility in naming room numbers. So *kyooshitsu sanbyakujuu-ban, sanbyakujuu-ban no kyooshitsu,* and *san-maru-ichi no kyooshitsu* are all correct. Japanese does <u>not</u> break room numbers into two-digit chunks as English does (2138, for example, becomes twenty-one thirty-eight in English).

You may also be surprised to find that the numbers 4 (*shi*) and 42 (*shini*) are often skipped in room and floor numbers in Japan. The pronunciations of these are the same as 'death' and they are considered to be unlucky.

BTS 18 Calendar and holidays

In addition to being fully aware of the Western calendar, Japan maintains its own calendar in which years are counted by era. An era ends when one emperor dies or abdicates (as in the case of the Heisei emperor) and a new emperor ascends to the throne. The emperor is never referred to by any given name (even though he has one). Rather, when an emperor takes the throne, he chooses (in close collaboration with advisors) a name for his era which is the name by which he himself will be known thereafter. In common parlance the current emperor is known as 天皇陛下 *Tennoo-heika* (the Emperor). The first year of an era is called 元年 *gan-nen.* Thereafter the years are counted with the Chinese numeral plus 年 *-nen.* The most recent eras are Meiji, Taisho, Showa, Heisei, and Reiwa.

Japan recognizes fifteen national holidays:

1. New Year's Day (元日): January 1. The New Year's season is more commonly called お正月. Most offices are closed January 1–3.
2. Coming of Age Day (成人の日): second Monday in January. This holiday acknowledges those who have reached the age of maturity (20) during the year.
3. Foundation Day (建国記念日): February 11. On this day citizens are encouraged to reflect on the establishment of Japan as a nation.
4. Emperor's Birthday (天皇誕生日): February 23.

166

5. Vernal Equinox (春分の日): usually around March 20.
6. Showa Day (昭和の日): April 29. Celebrates the Showa Emperor who died in 1989.
7. Constitution Day (憲法記念日): May 3. Commemorates the day (in 1948) on which Japan's postwar constitution took effect.
8. Green Day (緑の日): May 4. Celebrated as a day to appreciate nature.
9. Children's Day (こどもの日): May 5.
10. Marine Day (海の日): third Monday of July. Celebrated as a day to appreciate the sea and the maritime nation that is Japan.
11. Respect for the Aged Day (敬老の日): third Monday of September.
12. Autumnal Equinox (秋分の日): usually around September 23.
13. Sports Day (スポーツの日): second Monday of October.
14. Culture Day (文化の日): November 3.
15. Labor/Thanksgiving Day (勤労感謝の日): November 23.

Note that Showa Day, Constitution Day, Green Day, and Children's Day all fall within a week of each other (April 29–May 5). This string of holidays is known as "Golden Week" and is a time when many Japanese people travel or take a special holiday.

BTS 19 Japanese numerals and naming dates in a month

Use of the Japanese series is limited in the sense that it remains for only numerals 1 through 10 (with a few exceptions). Above, you see the dates of the month. The classifier for days is [Japanese numeral + -ka] for 2 through 10, then [Chinese numeral + -nichi] after 10. Note the exceptions for the first, fourteenth, twentieth, and twenty-fourth.

１６日に行きましょう。	*Juu-roku-nichi ni ikimashoo.*	Let's go on the sixteenth.
５日に帰りましたよ。	*Itsuka ni kaerimashita yo.*	He went home on the fifth, you know.
２日に来ませんか?	*Futsuka ni kimasen ka?*	Won't you come on the second?

Like clock time (-ji), dates of the month take Phrase Particle *ni* in a Sentence.

BTS 20 Relative time

A number of Nouns have come up that are used to refer to "relative time"—that is, words that derive their meaning from their relationship to the present (now or today), as opposed to words that refer to dates or days of the week. These include all of the words in the list below, as well as *sakki, ima,* and *ato de.*

おととい	*ototoi*	day before yesterday	去年	*kyonen*	last year
きのう	*kinoo*	yesterday	今週	*konshuu*	this week
今日	*kyoo*	today	今月	*kongetsu*	this month
あした	*ashita*	tomorrow	今年	*kotoshi*	this year
先週	*senshuu*	last week	来週	*raishuu*	next week
先月	*sengetsu*	last month	来月	*raigetsu*	next month
先学期	*sengakki*	last term/semester	来学期	*raigakki*	next term/semester
			来年	*rainen*	next year

You do not need to know what day today is in order to understand 'Let's meet on June 26.' But you do need to know what day today is in order to understand 'Let's meet tomorrow.' For the most part, Nouns indicating relative time do <u>not</u> take Phrase Particle *ni* in a Sentence.

あした行きましょう。	*Ashita ikimashoo.*	Let's go tomorrow.
おととい帰りましたよ。	*Ototoi kaerimashita yo.*	He went home the day before yesterday, you know.
昨日 7時にできました。	*Kinoo 7:00 ni dekimashita.*	It was finished yesterday at 7:00.

BTS 21 The past used in recall

In this Scene, when Kanda-san asks Sasha about the time of next month's meeting, he says:

半からじゃなかったですか？	*Han kara ja nakatta desu ka?*	Wasn't it from half-past?

He is actually asking about the future, but uses the past *ja nakatta.* This use of the past typically indicates that the speaker knows this from some past experience, and is drawing on memory or has just realized that something is true. In English, too, we might say, "Wasn't her name Yamamoto?" We don't mean that it's changed—only that that's what we remember. This use of the past to recall things can also be a polite way of asking someone a question. Imagine that your co-worker assumes that you are covering tomorrow's assignment. You might politely disagree by using the past:

明日は鈴木さんじゃなかったですか？	*Ashita wa Suzuki-san ja nakatta desu ka?*	Wasn't tomorrow (supposed to be) Suzuki-san?

168

The use of the past (and the negative) here makes your contradiction of your co-worker more indirect and softer.

BTS 22 Noun + から・まで Noun + *kara/made*

Two new Phrase Particles are introduced here for designating the starting point and end point of a time sequence: *kara* 'from' and *made* 'until, up to (and including).'

<ruby>2<rt></rt></ruby>日から<ruby>1 0<rt></rt></ruby>日まで<ruby>行<rt>い</rt></ruby>きます。   *Futsuka kara tooka made*   We'll go from the second until
<ruby>ふつ<rt></rt></ruby>か <ruby>と<rt></rt></ruby>お<ruby>か<rt></rt></ruby>   *ikimasu.*   the tenth.

<ruby>今日<rt>きょう</rt></ruby>はここまで。   *Kyoo wa koko made.*   That's all for today. (lit. 'Up to here for today.' Teachers often say this to dismiss class)

Phrase Particles *wa* and *mo* can also combine with these two Particles, in their usual sense.

<ruby>1 9<rt></rt></ruby>日からは<ruby>行<rt>い</rt></ruby>きません。 *Juu-ku-nichi kara wa ikimasen.* I won't be going from the nineteenth.
<ruby>じゅうくにち<rt></rt></ruby>

<ruby>2 0<rt></rt></ruby>日までは？   *Hatsu-ka made wa?*   How about up until the twentieth?
<ruby>はつ<rt></rt></ruby>か   (i.e. Will you be available?)

In fact, these Particles can mark the start and end point for location, as well.

<ruby>東京<rt>とうきょう</rt></ruby>から<ruby>帰<rt>かえ</rt></ruby>りました。   *Tookyoo kara kaerimashita.*   I returned from Tokyo.

<ruby>2 0 0<rt></rt></ruby>ページまでしました。 *Ni-hyaku-peeji made shimashita.* I did up to page two hundred.
<ruby>にひゃく<rt></rt></ruby>   <ruby>ぺ<rt></rt></ruby>え<ruby>じ<rt></rt></ruby>

Now look again at the *kotowaza* that introduced Act 2, from the ancient Chinese scholar Lao Tzu (604-531 BC):

<ruby>千里<rt>せんり</rt></ruby>の<ruby>道<rt>みち</rt></ruby>も<ruby>一歩<rt>いっぽ</rt></ruby>から *Senri no michi mo ippo kara* A journey of a thousand miles begins with a single step

In this phrase *ippo kara* means 'from step one.' The entire phrase literally means, 'Even the road to a distant place starts from step one.'

BTS 23 Phrase Particle ＋です Phrase Particle + *desu*

Up until now, you have only seen the various forms of *desu* in combination with Nouns. Here you see the combination [Noun + Phrase Particle] acting as a Noun followed by *desu*:

<ruby>1 0<rt></rt></ruby>時から<ruby>1 1<rt></rt></ruby>時まで<ruby>です<rt></rt></ruby>。 *Juu-ji kara juu-ichi-ji made* It's from 10:00 until 11:00.
<ruby>じゅうじ<rt></rt></ruby>   <ruby>じゅういちじ<rt></rt></ruby>   *desu.*

クラスは今日からじゃないで すか?	*Kurasu wa kyoo kara ja nai* *desu ka?*	Don't classes start today? (Aren't classes from today?)
今日はここまでです。	*Kyoo wa koko made desu.*	That's all for today.

Not all Phrase Particles combine with *desu* in this way. Other combinations will be noted as they come up.

It follows that these [Noun + Phrase Particle] combinations can modify another Noun if they are connected with Particle の. This pattern only occurs with Phrase Particles such as まで, から, へ , and で.

誰からのレポートですか?	Who is it a report from? (lit. 'It's a report from whom?')
あ、今日までの宿題、忘れました!	Oh, I forgot about the homework (that was to be done) by today!

Now go to the Activity Book for 練習 *Renshuu* Practice and 腕試し *Udedameshi* Tryout.

Scene 4-5 使いやすかったですよ! *Tsukaiyasukatta desu yo!*
It was easy to use!

Amy asks Takashi for his opinion about which room to use for a project they are working on.

The script

エイミー	孝
何番の部屋を使いましょうか。	一階の１０７番教室はどうですか？
１０７番ですか？	はい、昨日も使いましたけど、わりと使いやすかったですよ!
そうですか。じゃあそうしましょう。	

Amy	*Takashi*
Na¹nban no he⌐ya¹ o tsu⌐kaimasho¹o ka.	*I⌐k-kai no hya⌐ku-nana-ban kyo¹oshitsu wa ⌐do¹o desu ka?*
I⌐chi-ma¹ru-na⌐na¹-ban desu ka?	*Ha¹i, ki⌐no¹o mo tsu⌐kaima¹shita kedo, wa⌐ri to tsukaiya¹ sukatta desu yo!*
So¹o desu ka. Ja¹a so⌐¹o shima¹shoo.	

Amy	Takashi
What number room should we use?	How about classroom 107?
107?	Yes, we used it yesterday too, and it was relatively easy to use!
Is that so. Well, then let's do that.	

単語と表現 *Tango to hyoogen* Vocabulary and expressions

Nouns

部屋	*heya*	room
オフィス	*oisu*	office
フォント	*fonto*	font
自転車	*jitensha*	bicycle
地下	*chika*	basement, underground

Adjectives

使いやすい	*tsukaiyasui*	easy to use
使いにくい	*tsukainikui*	hard to use

Classifiers

階	*kai*	classifier for naming and counting floors in a building				
1階	*ik-kai*	one floor/first floor	6階		*rok-kai*	six floors/sixth floor
2階	*ni-kai*	two floors/second floor	7階		*nana-kai*	seven floors/seventh floor
3階	*san-gai*	three floors/third floor	8階・8階		*hak-kai/hachi-kai*	eight floors/eighth floor
4階	*yon-kai*	four floors/fourth floor	9階		*kyuu-kai*	nine floors/ninth floor
5階	*go-kai*	five floors/fifth floor	10階・10階		*jik-kai/juk-kai*	ten floors/tenth floor
			何階		*nan-gai*	how many floors/which floor

〜番教室	*-ban kyooshitsu*	classifier for naming classroom numbers
〜号室	*-gooshitsu*	classifier for naming room numbers

Phrase particles

を	*o*	[object particle]

Special expressions

そうしましょう。	*Soo shimashoo*	Let's do that.
わりと	*wari to*	relatively
一番	*ichi-ban*	most

Behind the Scenes

BTS 24 Phrase Particle を *o*

You have seen that Nouns can hook up to Core Sentences in a number of ways. When a Noun is the object of a Sentence, it connects directly to the Core Sentence:

焼き鳥、食べますか。	*Yakitori, tabemasu ka.*	Do you eat yakitori?
これ、使いましたね?	*Kore, tsukaimashita ne.*	You used this, didn't you?

You have also seen that the Phrase Particle *wa* might mark this Noun when there is a sense of contrast with other Nouns:

焼き鳥は食べますか。	*Yakitori wa tabemasu ka.*	Do you eat yakitori? (It seems that you don't eat other things, but how about yakitori?)
これは使いましたね?	*Kore wa tsukaimashita ne.*	How about this, you used it, didn't you?

Yet another possibility is that the Noun is in addition to something or someone else, in which case it is marked by *mo*:

焼き鳥も食べますか。	*Yakitori mo, tabemasu ka.*	Do you eat yakitori too?
これも使いましたね?	*Kore mo tsukaimashita ne.*	You used this too, didn't you?

In this Scene you see another possible object marker: *o*. Phrase Particle *o* marks an object when the Noun is new information or is information that the speaker believes the other person is looking for. Another way to look at this is that *o* puts a spotlight on its Noun. It is no accident that question words are much more likely than other Nouns to be marked by *o*:

何を作りますか。	*Nani o tsukurimasu ka.*	What are you going to make?
どれを一番読みますか。	*Dore o ichiban yomimasu ka.*	Which one do you read most?

Other examples include (note the English translations):

この部屋を使いますか。	*Kono heya o tsukaimasu ka.*	Will you use this room? (Is this the room you will use?)
これをお願いします。	*Kore o onegai-shimasu.*	I'll take this. (This is what I request.)
昨日授業を始めました。	*Kinoo jugyoo o hajimemashita.*	We started class yesterday. (What we started yesterday was class.)
一番古いのを買いましたよ。	*Ichiban hurui no o kaimashita yo.*	I bought the oldest one, you know. (What I bought was the oldest one, you know.)

Note that *ga* (subject marker) and *o* (object marker) have a lot in common. Both put special emphasis on their Noun as important information that the listener may not know.

BTS 25 Compounds

a. Verb$_X$ stem 〜やすい・にくい Verb$_X$ stem -*yasui*/-*nikui*

The stem of a Verb (-*masu* form minus the -*masu*) combined with -*yasui* yields an Adjective that means 'easy to X':

読みやすい	*yomiyasui*	easy to read
しやすい	*shiyasui*	easy to do

Similarly, the stem of a Verb combined with -*nikui* yields an Adjective that means 'hard to X':

読みにくい	*yominikui*	hard to read
しにくい	*shinikui*	hard to do

Here are more examples:

この宿題は読みにくかったですねえ!	*Kono shukudai wa yominikukatta desu nee!*	This homework was hard to read, wasn't it!
すごい買いやすいですよ。	*Sugoi kaiyasui desu yo.*	It's really easy to buy, you know.

Note that *minikui* has two meanings. It can mean 'hard to see, obscure.' But it can also mean 'ugly, unattractive.' These two meanings are distinguished in writing with different kanji.

b. Compound words

You have seen numerous examples of compound words so far. Among Nouns these include *Fukuzawa-daigaku* 'Fukuzawa University' and *Nihongo-kurabu* 'Japanese Language Club.' These compounds all refer to a specific entity. The difference between *Tookyoo no daigaku* and *Tookyoo-daigaku* is that the former refers to 'universities in Tokyo' while the latter refers only to Tokyo University.

A Noun in combination with some form of *shimasu* is a compound Verb. *Shitsurei-shimasu* 'excuse me' is a compound made up of *shitsurei* 'rude' plus *shimasu* 'do.' *Onegai-shimasu* 'please give me a hand' is a combination of the Verb root *onegai* 'request' plus *shimasu* 'do.' Other combinations include:

勉強	*benkyoo*	study (Noun)	勉強します	*benkyoo-shimasu*	study (Verb)
電話	*denwa*	telephone (Noun)	電話します	*denwa-shimasu*	make a phone call (Verb)
仕事	*shigoto*	work (Noun)	仕事します	*shigoto-shimasu*	(do) work (Verb)

BTS 26 わりと *wari to*

Wari to is an expression that means 'relatively, rather, unusually, pretty.'

わりと高かったですけど……。 *Wari to takakatta desu kedo . . .* It was pretty expensive, but . . .

You have now seen a variety of expressions that can qualify the meaning of a Sentence. Compare:

わりと読みにくいですよ。	*Wari to yominikui desu yo.*	It's pretty hard to read, you know.
結構読みにくいですよ。	*Kekkoo yominikui desu yo.*	It's quite hard to read, you know.
すごく読みにくいですよ。	*Sugoku yominikui desu yo.*	It's awfully hard to read, you know.
あまり読みにくくないですよ。	*Amari yominikuku nai desu yo.*	It's not very hard to read, you know.
全然読みにくくないですよ。	*Zenzen yominikuku nai desu yo.*	It's not at all hard to read, you know.

Now go to the Activity Book for 練習 *Renshuu* Practice and 腕試し *Udedameshi* Tryout.

Scene 4-6 頑張ります。 *Ganbarimasu.* I'll do my best.

Kanda-san and Sasha just completed a task.

The script

神田	サーシャ
お疲れ様。時間、どのぐらいかかりましたか？すごくかかりませんでしたか？	そうですねえ。ほとんど３時間ぐらいですかねえ。
大変でしたね。明日もお願いしますね？	はい、頑張ります！

Kanda	Saasha
O⌐tsukaresama. Ji⌐kan⌐, do⌐no-gurai kakarima⌐shita ka? Su⌐go⌐ku ka⌐karimase⌐n deshita ka?	So⌐o desu ⌐ne⌐e. Ho⌐to⌐ndo sa⌐njikan gu⌐rai desu ka ⌐ne⌐e.
Ta⌐ihen de⌐shita ⌐ne⌐. A⌐shita⌐ mo o⌐negai shima⌐su ⌐ne⌐.	Hai, ga⌐nbarima⌐su!

Kanda	Sasha
You must be tired. How much time did it take? Didn't it take an awful lot?	Hmm . . . I guess it took almost about three hours.
That was tough, wasn't it. Please do it tomorrow too, okay?	Yes, I'll do my best!

単語と表現 *Tango to hyoogen* Vocabulary and expressions

Nouns

ほとんど	*hotondo*	almost; barely (plus negative)
３時間	*sanjikan*	three hours

176

月曜（日）	getsuyoo(bi)	Monday
火曜（日）	kayoo(bi)	Tuesday
水曜（日）	suiyoo(bi)	Wednesday
木曜（日）	mokuyoo(bi)	Thursday
金曜（日）	kin'yoo(bi)	Friday
土曜（日）	doyoo(bi)	Saturday
日曜（日）	nichiyoo(bi)	Sunday
何曜（日）	nan'yoo(bi)	what day (of the week)?
今学期	kongakki	this academic term

Verbs

かかります (かからない)	kakarimasu (kakar-anai)	take (time), cost (money)
かかりました (かからなかった)	kakarimashita (kakar-anakatta)	took (time), cost (money)
頑張ります (頑張らない)	ganbarimasu (ganbar-anai)	do one's best
頑張りました (頑張らなかった)	ganbarimashita (ganbar-anakatta)	did one's best
いります (いらない)	irimasu (ir-anai)	need
いりました (いらなかった)	irimashita (ir-anakatta)	needed

Classifiers

～日	-nichi/-ka	classifier for naming and counting days
1日	ichi-nichi	one day
曜（日）	yoo(bi)	days of the week

時間	jikan	classifier for counting hours			
1時間	ichi-jikan	1 hour	6時間	roku-jikan	6 hours
2時間	ni-jikan	2 hours	7時間	shichi-jikan / nana-jikan	7 hours
3時間	san-jikan	3 hours	8時間	hachi-jikan	8 hours
4時間	yo-jikan	4 hours	9時間	ku-jikan	9 hours
5時間	go-jikan	5 hours	10時間	juu-jikan	10 hours
			何時間	nan-jikan	how many hours?

しゅうかん
週間　　*shuukan*　　classifier for counting weeks

いっしゅうかん 1 週間	*is-shuukan*	1 week	ろくしゅうかん 6 週間	*roku-shuukan*	6 weeks
にしゅうかん 2 週間	*ni-shuukan*	2 weeks	ななしゅうかん 7 週間	*nana-shuukan*	7 weeks
さんしゅうかん 3 週間	*san-shuukan*	3 weeks	はっしゅうかん 8 週間	*has-shuukan*	8 weeks
よんしゅうかん 4 週間	*yon-shuukan*	4 weeks	きゅうしゅうかん 9 週間	*kyuu-shuukan*	9 weeks
ごしゅうかん 5 週間	*go-shuukan*	5 weeks	じっしゅうかん 10 週間 じゅっしゅうかん 10 週間	*jis-shuukan* *jus-shuukan*	10 weeks
			なんしゅうかん 何 週間	*nan-shuukan*	how many weeks?

かげつ
か月　　*kagetsu*　　classifier for counting months

いっ げつ 1 か月	*ik-kagetsu*	1 month	なな げつ 7 か月	*nana-kagetsu*	7 months
に げつ 2 か月	*ni-kagetsu*	2 months	はち げつ 8 か月	*hachi-kagetsu*	8 months
さん げつ 3 か月	*san-kagetsu*	3 months	きゅう げつ 9 か月	*kyuu/ku-kagetsu*	9 months
よん げつ 4 か月	*yon-kagetsu*	4 months	じっ げつ 10 か月	*jik-kagetsu*	10 months
ご げつ 5 か月	*go-kagetsu*	5 months	じゅういっ げつ 1 1 か月	*juu-ik-kagetsu*	11 months
ろっ げつ 6 か月	*rok-kagetsu*	6 months	じゅうに げつ 1 2 か月	*juu-ni-kagetsu*	12 months
			なん げつ 何か月	*nan-kagetsu*	how many months?

ねん
年　　*nen*　　classifier for naming and counting years

いちねん 1 年	*ichi-nen*	1 year, first year	ろくねん 6 年	*roku-nen*	6 years, sixth year
にねん 2 年	*ni-nen*	2 years, second year	ななねん 7 年	*nana-nen*	7 years, seventh year
さんねん 3 年	*san-nen*	3 years, third year	はちねん 8 年	*hachi-nen*	8 years, eighth year
よねん 4 年	*yo-nen*	4 years, fourth year	きゅうねん 9 年	*kyuu-nen*	9 years, ninth year
ごねん 5 年	*go-nen*	5 years, fifth year	じゅうねん 1 0 年	*juu-nen*	10 years, tenth year
			なんねん 何年	*nan-nen*	how many years, which year?

がっき
学期　　*gakki*　　academic term

いちがっき 1 学期	*ichi-gakki*	1 term/first term	さんがっき 3 学期	*san-gakki*	3 terms/third term
にがっき 2 学期	*ni-gakki*	2 terms/second term	なんがっき 何学期	*nan-gakki*	how many terms; which term

4-6

連絡来ました？

178

Behind the Scenes

BTS 27 Double-*ga* Sentences: 時間<small>じかん</small>がかかります。
Jikan ga kakarimasu. It takes time.

Accomplishing the actions described by some Verbs, such as *wakarimasu* 'understand,' *dekimasu* 'can do, become finished,' *irimasu* 'need,' *kakarimasu* 'take (time, money)' and *arimasu* 'have, exist' is not under human control. You cannot decide to understand or that you can do something. These Verbs do not take a Noun marked by *o*. There might be two Nouns associated with any of these Core Sentences, and either or both can be marked by *ga*.

英語<small>えいご</small>が分<small>わ</small>かります。	*Eigo ga wakarimasu.*	He understands English. (It's English that he understands.)
田中<small>たなか</small>さんが分<small>わ</small>かります。	*Tanaka-san ga wakarimasu.*	Tanaka-san understands it. (It's Tanaka-san who understands.)
田中<small>たなか</small>さんが英語<small>えいご</small>が分<small>わ</small>かります。	*Tanaka-san ga eigo ga wakarimasu.*	It's Tanaka-san who understands English.

Kakarimasu, which comes up in this Act, is a Verb that means 'take/require some resource (such as time, money, etc.).' *Irimasu* is a Verb that means 'need/require' in a general sense.

In addition to the above-mentioned Verbs, all Adjectives and [Noun *desu*] are often labeled "double-*ga*" for the very reason that you might see two *ga*-phrases in a single Sentence.

その宿題<small>しゅくだい</small>、時間<small>じかん</small>がかかりましたねえ。	*Sono shukudai, jikan ga kakarimashita nee.*	That homework took time, didn't it!
日本語<small>にほんご</small>のクラス<small>くらす</small>で紙<small>かみ</small>がいります。	*Nihongo no kurasu de kami ga irimasu.*	In the Japanese class we need some paper.
田中<small>たなか</small>さんが英語<small>えいご</small>が上手<small>じょうず</small>です。	*Tanaka-san ga eigo ga joozu desu.*	Tanaka-san is good at English. (It's Tanaka who is good at English.)
どれが使<small>つか</small>いやすいですか?	*Dore ga tsukaiyasui desu ka?*	Which one is easy to use?
どの店<small>みせ</small>がカレーライス<small>かれえらいす</small>がおいしいですか?	*Dono mise ga kareeraisu ga oishii desu ka?*	Which store has good curry rice?

(tab) 4-6 連絡来<small>れんらくき</small>ました?

179

BTS 28 Word order

Now that you have seen sentences with multiple [Noun + Particle] combinations, you may also notice that word order is quite flexible in Japanese. All of the following are fine.

神田さんが月曜日から金曜日まで行きます。	*Kanda-san ga getsuyoobi kara kinyoobi made ikimasu.*	Kanda-san will go from Monday until Friday.
月曜日から金曜日まで神田さんが来ます。	*Getsuyoobi kara kinyoobi made Kanda-san ga kimasu.*	From Monday until Friday Kanda-san will come.
日本語のクラスで紙がいります。	*Nihongo no kurasu de kami ga irimasu.*	In the Japanese class we need some paper.
紙が日本語のクラスでいります。	*Kami ga Nihongo no kurasu de irimasu.*	We need some paper in the Japanese class.
紙はあしたの日本語のクラスでいります。	*Kami wa ashita no Nihongo no kurasu de irimasu.*	As for paper, we need some in the Japanese class tomorrow.

In general, word order in a Sentence follows the pattern [Time + Place + Subject + Object + Verb/Adjective/Noun *desu*]. But depending on the context and focus of attention, this can change. Notice also that [Noun *wa*] phrases tend to go first.

BTS 29 Naming vs. counting classifiers

You have seen the following classifiers so far:

> *-ji* for naming (o'clock) hours, *-fun* for counting minutes, *-mai* for counting thin flat objects, *-en* 'yen,' *-doru* 'dollars,' *-sento* 'cents.'

We can divide these classifiers into two kinds:

a   Naming classifiers, or those that name an element in a sequence (*-ji,* TIME-*mae,* TIME-*sugi*)
b   Counting classifiers, or those that indicate an amount *(-mai, -en, -doru, -sento)*

In this Scene we see six new classifiers. Make special note of the use of Phrase Particle *ni* with naming classifiers in the examples that follow. Notice also that *dono gurai* and *dore gurai* can be used interchangeably to mean 'about how much.'

a *-yoobi*: a classifier for naming the seven days of the week

水曜日に使います。   *Suiyoobi ni tsukaimasu.*   We will use it on Wednesday.
(*suiyoobi* is a naming classifier)

b *-jikan*: a classifier for counting the number of hours

2時に帰りました。   *Ni-ji ni kaerimashita.*   We went home at 2:00. (*-ji* is a naming classifier)

2時間かかりました。   *Ni-jikan kakarimashita.*   It took two hours. (*-jikan* is a counting classifier)

c *ichi-nichi*: the use of *-nichi* to count one day. Compare *tsuitachi* for naming the first of the month. For all other dates, the naming classifier is the same as the counting classifier.

1日に帰りました。   *Tsuitachi ni kaerimashita.*   We went home on the first. (*tsuitachi* is a naming classifier)

1日いましたよ。   *Ichi-nichi imashita yo.*   We were there for a day, you know. (*-nichi* is a counting classifier)

d *-shuukan*: a classifier for counting weeks

2 週 間ぐらい かかりましたね。   *Ni-shuukan gurai kakarimashita ne.*   It took about two weeks, didn't it. (*-shuukan* is a counting classifier)

e *-kagetsu*: a classifier for counting months

一か月ぐらい かかりましたね。   *Ikkagetsu gurai kakarimashita ne.*   It took about one month, didn't it. (*-kagetsu* is a counting classifier)

f *-nen*: a classifier for both naming and counting years.

3 年ぐらいいました。   *San-nen gurai imashita.*   I was there for about three years. (*-nen* is a counting classifier)

2010年に行きました。   *Nisenjuu-nen ni ikimashita.*   We went in 2010. (*-nen* is a naming classifier)

g *-gakki*: a classifier for both naming and counting academic terms (such as semesters or quarters).

二学期に行きました。   *Ni-gakki ni ikimashita.*   I went in the second term. (*-gakki* is a naming classifier)

一学期しました。   *Ichi-gakki shimashita.*   I did it for one semester. (*-gakki* is also a counting classifier)

Now go to the Activity Book for 練習 *Renshuu* Practice and 腕試し *Udedameshi* Tryout. Then do 評価 *Hyooka* Assessment activities.

◆ 読(よ)み書(か)き *Yomi-kaki* Reading and writing

Now you should be familiar with all the hiragana symbols. This act introduces additional conventions for hiragana, along with reading practice.

BTL 1 About the written language じゃ vs では

All languages, including English, distinguish between spoken and written style. But in Japanese the difference between spoken and written style is more pronounced than in English. This is a result of the history of the development of the written language in Japan. So far you have seen that:

> けど is more common in spoken language. In the written language you are more likely to find が as well as けれど、けども、けれども.
> The particle *wa* is written using は.
> In the written language, 〜ません forms are more common than 〜ないです.

In what follows, you will also see that じゃ is a contraction of では, which is much more typical of written style. So although you may hear 大学(だいがく)じゃないです。 'It's not a university,' you are likely to see in print 大学(だいがく)ではないです。 or 大学(だいがく)ではありません。 Similarly, you often hear じゃ 'well then' in spoken language, but in writing or on formal occasions you will see or hear では.

You should expect to see more differences as you progress in Japanese. These will be pointed out here as they come up.

Scene 4-7R どこがよろしいですか。 Where would be good?

Sasha is reading an email she received from Yagi-san-bucho, using an app that provides furigana for kanji.

 テキスト Text

From: Yagi Reiko <ryagi@ogaki.co.jp>
Date: Tuesday, June 27, 2019 at 10:32 AM
To: Sasha Morris <smorris@ogaki.co.jp >
Subject: RE: 303 on Wednesday?

モリスさん
いいですね。では、そこを使^{つか}いましょう。
あしたは神田^{かんだ}さんと午後^{ごご}２：１５分^{にじゅうごふん}に３０３番^{さんびゃくさんばん}で会^あいましょう。
八木^{やぎ}

On Monday, June 26 at 3:45 PM, Sasha Morris wrote:

八木部 長^{やぎぶちょう}

あさっての会議^{かいぎ}はどこがよろしいですか。
３Ｆ^{さんがい}の３０３^{さんまるさん}はどうでしょうか。
モリス

From: Yagi Reiko <ryagi@ogaki.co.jp>
Date: Tuesday, June 27, 2019 at 10:32 AM
To: Sasha Morris <smorris@ogaki.co.jp >
Subject: RE: 303 on Wednesday?

Morris-san,
Sounds good. Let's use that (room), then.
Let's meet in #303 with Kanda-san at 2:15 p.m. tomorrow.
On Monday, June 26 at 3:45 PM, Sasha Morris wrote:
Division Chief Yagi,
Where would be good for the conference the day after tomorrow?
How about 303 on the third floor?
Morris

BTL 2 Particle を

#46.　　を　　*o* (particle)　　を

While お and を are pronounced the same, を is used only to represent the particle *o*. This is a remnant of historical changes in Japanese.

Examples

1.　どれをしましたか。　　Which one did you do?
2.　どれを見ましたか。　　Which did you watch/see/look at?
3.　どの傘を買いましたか。　　Which umbrella did you buy?
4.　白井先生の歴史を取ります。　　I'm going to take Professor Shirai's history (class).

Recall from Act 3 that the particle *wa* is written withは not わ. This, too, is left over from a historical change in the pronunciation of this particle. For example,

1.　私は学生です。　　I am a student.
2.　田中さんは？　　How about Tanaka-san?

Note that the greetings こんにちは and こんばんは also use は.

Examples

1.　あちらは？　　What about that direction?
2.　八木さんは？　　What about Yagi-san?
3.　４時ごろは (どうですか)？　　How about around 4:00?
4.　それは田中さんのです。　　That is Tanaka-san's.
5.　それは先生のとは違います。　　That is different from the teacher's.

Here is a summary of the phrase particles introduced so far:

は　が　を　も　と　で　から　まで　とか

Examples

1.　田中さんのは？　　What about Tanaka-san's?
2.　坂本さんがしました。　　Sakamoto-san did it. It's Sakamoto-san who did it.

3.	これをしました。	I did this one.
4.	これとそれをしました。	I did this and that.
5.	これもそれもしました。	I did both this and that.
6.	これをしました。あ、あれもしました。	I did this. Oh, I did that also.
7.	これはしましたが、あれはしませんでした。	I did this one (at least) but didn't do that one.
8.	会議は４時からです。	The meeting starts at 4:00.
9.	会議は４時から５時までです。	The meeting is from 4:00 to 5:00.
10.	歴史とか数学とかですね。	History, mathematics, things like that.
11.	じゃ、またあとで。	See you later.
12.	みんなで行きませんか。	Why don't we all go together?
13.	ここからあそこまで、どのぐらいかかりますか。	How much (time/money) does it take from here to there?

Go back to Scenes in the earlier lessons to see what is written in hiragana only, etc.

BTL 3 Keyboard Input

Now you are ready to begin Japanese input on your computer. If you have never done this before, do the following:

1 Make sure that your computer is Japanese enabled. There are videos online that can lead you through this.
2 Practice toggling back and forth on your operating system between Japanese and English input.

Ready to input Japanese? The romanization that you see in the table at the end of Act 3 will take care of most morae. Here are the exceptions:

1 For ん type /n/ twice.
2 For Particle を type /wo/.
3 Remember that Particle は is pronounced *wa* but written /ha/.
4 Remember that Particle へ is pronounced *e* but written /he/.
5 For small つ (as it まって *matte*) hit the consonant key twice then the vowel.
6 For small あ, い, う, え, お type /x/ followed by the vowel.

As you type, hiragana will appear lightly underlined. If you want just hiragana, hit the 'Return' key. When you begin to use kanji, you will choose among the options that appear as you input text, using either the arrow keys or the space bar. If you find that you have entered kanji, but wanted hiragana, the escape (esc) key will change what you've written back to hiragana.

185

There is also a Japanese keyboard available, but for word processing most Japanese people use the romanization input method described above. Japanese keyboard input is far more popular on smart phones. If you want to use this option, check online for instructions that match your smartphone.

Summary of hiragana

n	w	r	y	m	h	n	t	s	k	
ん *n*	わ *wa*	ら *ra*	や *ya*	ま *ma*	は *ha*	な *na*	た *ta*	さ *sa*	か *ka*	あ *a*
		り *ri*		み *mi*	ひ *hi*	に *ni*	ち *chi*	し *shi*	き *ki*	い *i*
		る *ru*	ゆ *yu*	む *mu*	ふ *fu*	ぬ *nu*	つ *tsu*	す *su*	く *ku*	う *u*
		れ *re*		め *me*	へ *he*	ね *ne*	て *te*	せ *se*	け *ke*	え *e*
	を *o*	ろ *ro*	よ *yo*	も *mo*	ほ *ho*	の *no*	と *to*	そ *so*	こ *ko*	お *o*

p	b	d	z	g
ぱ *pa*	ば *ba*	だ *da*	ざ *za*	が *ga*
ぴ *pi*	び *bi*	(ぢ) *ji*	じ *ji*	ぎ *gi*
ぷ *pu*	ぶ *bu*	(づ) *zu*	ず *zu*	ぐ *gu*
ぺ *pe*	べ *be*	で *de*	ぜ *ze*	げ *ge*
ぽ *po*	ぼ *bo*	ど *do*	ぞ *zo*	ご *go*

Now go to the Activity Book for 練習 *Renshuu* Practice.

Then do 評価 *Hyooka* Assessment activities, including 読んでみよう *Yonde miyoo* Contextualized reading, 書き取り *Kakitori* Dictation, and 書いてみよう *Kaite miyoo* Contextualized writing.

お願^{ねが}いしてもいいですか。

May I ask a favor of you?

聞^きくは一時^{いっとき}の恥^{はじ}、聞^きかぬは一生^{いっしょう}の恥^{はじ}
To ask may lead to shame for a moment,
but not to ask leads to shame for a lifetime.

◆ 話す・聞く Speaking and listening

Scene 5-1 私が決めていいですか？
Is it all right if I make the decision on this?

Sasha checks with Kanda-san to see if it's all right for her to proceed with the decisions (which room to reserve, who to invite) on an upcoming meeting at their company.

The script

サーシャ	神田
これ、私が決めていいですか？	もちろん、そうしてください。なるべく早くお願いします。
わかりました。でも今すぐじゃなくてもいいですか？	全然平気です。あすでもあさってでも構いませんよ。
了解です！	よろしく。

Sasha	Kanda
Is it okay if I make the decision on this?	Of course, please do that. As soon as possible, please.
Understood. But is it okay if it's not right this minute?	No problem at all. Tomorrow or the next day will be no problem.
Got it!	Thanks for taking care of it.

お願いしてもいいですか。

単語と表現 Vocabulary and expressions

Nouns

すぐ	soon, immediately, right away
あす	tomorrow (slightly more formal than あした)
少し	a little, a few
了解(する)	understanding, consent, agreement

Verbs (including 〜て form)

決めます(決めない;決めて)	decide (something)
急ぎます(急がない;急いで)	hurry
構います(構わない;構って)	mind, care, be concerned about (most commonly occurs in the negative)

Special expressions

もちろん	of course
なるべく	As . . . as possible
でも	but, however, and yet
X でも Y でも	whether it's X or Y
X でも X じゃなくても	whether it's X or not X

Behind the Scenes

BTS 1 〜て Forms

All three Core Sentences (Verb, Adjective, Noun です) have a 〜て form. Multiple uses of the 〜て form come up in this Act.

a. Verbs in the 〜て form

The 〜て form of an affirmative Verb depends on which of four classes it fits into. (The 〜ない form of the Verb is actually an Adjective. See Adjectives in (b) below.)

-*NAI* Verbs: You have seen Verbs such as たべます, できます etc. that change to the negative by dropping -*masu* and adding -*nai desu*. In the 〜て form these Verbs also drop -*masu* and add -*te*. These will be explained in more detail in Act 7.

190

食_たべます	eat	食_たべて
できます	can do	できて
見_みます	see	見_みて
決_きめます	decide	決_きめて

-*ANAI* Verbs: The 〜て form depends on the consonant that appears before -*imasu*. Below is an example of all possible combinations. These will be analyzed in more detail in Act 7.

分_わかります	understand	分_わかって
使_{つか}います	use	使_{つか}って
待_まちます	wait	待_まって
飲_のみます	drink	飲_のんで
死_しにます	die	死_しんで
呼_よびます	call	呼_よんで
話_{はな}します	talk	話_{はな}して
書_かきます	write	書_かいて
急_{いそ}ぎます	hurry	急_{いそ}いで

The Verb 行_いきます is slightly different from other Verbs like 書_かきます since its 〜て form is 行_いって.

Irregular Verbs: These Verbs are irregular for reasons that will be explained in Act 7. They are 来ます and します.

来_きてす	come	きて
します	do	して

A fourth group will be introduced in Act 7. In the meantime, get to know as many of these Verbs as possible in both their 〜ます and their 〜て forms.

b. Adjectives in the 〜て form

The ~て form of the affirmative Adjective is formed by adding ~て to the ~く form, while the negative is formed by adding ~て to the ~なく form. Notice that the 〜ない form of the Verb is, in this sense, an Adjective!

高_{たか}い > 高_{たか}くて	expensive
新_{あたら}しい > 新_{あたら}しくて	new
赤_{あか}くない > 赤_{あか}くなくて	isn't red
早_{はや}くない > 早_{はや}くなくて	isn't early

191

食た べない > 食た べなくて	doesn't eat
飲の まない > 飲の まなくて	doesn't drink
しない > しなくて	doesn't do

c. Noun です in the 〜て form

The 〜て form of the affirmative です is 〜で. The 〜て form of the negative じゃないです is じゃなくて, which you saw in Act 3 (スマフォじゃなくて、スマホ 'not *sumafo,* (but) *sumaho.*')

ここです > ここで	is here
だめです >だめで	is problematic
私わたし じゃない >私わたし じゃなくて	isn't I/me
だめじゃない >だめじゃなくて	isn't problematic

BTS 2 Uses of the 〜て form

a. Request patterns

The 〜て form has quite a number of uses, one of which came up in "Instructional Expressions" where you saw it combined with ください to ask for things or encourage someone to do something.

PERSON に言い ってください。	Please say it to PERSON.
PERSON に聞き いてください。	Please ask PERSON.
PERSON にもう一度いちど き聞いてください。	Please ask PERSON again.
PERSON に答こた えてください。	Please answer PERSON.
どうぞ使つか ってください。	Please go ahead and use it.
急いそ いでください。	Please hurry.

b. Permission: 〜て form + いいですか

Another use of the 〜て form is for asking or giving permission or to find out whether something is acceptable. In this pattern, the 〜て form is followed by a phrase such as いいですか or 大丈夫だいじょうぶ ですか.

これ、私わたし が決き めていいですか?	Is it okay if I make the decision on this?
早はや く帰かえ って大丈夫だいじょうぶ でしょうか?	Would it be all right if I go home early?

ひらがなで大丈夫ですか?	Is (writing it in) hiragana acceptable?
来週でよろしいですか?	Is next week all right?
部長じゃなくて結構です。	It will do if it isn't the division chief.
漢字、使わなくていいですか。	Is it all right if I don't use kanji?
ブライアンに言わなくて大丈夫でしょうか。	Do you suppose it's all right if we don't tell Brian?
使いやすくなくていいですか?	Is it all right if it's not easy to use?

c. 〜て Form + も

A 〜て form in combination with Phrase Particle も means something like 'even if.' Thus Noun でも means 'even if it's Noun.' (literally, 'even being Noun')

千円でも買いません。	Even if it's ¥1000 I won't buy it.

A question word (いつ、どこ、だれ、何) plus でも means 'no matter X.' Thus いつでも 'no matter when, any time,' どこでも 'no matter where,' だれでも 'no matter who,' 何でも 'no matter what.'

何でもいいですよ。	Anything is fine. (No matter what it is, it's fine.)

Similarly, Adjectives in the 〜くても form mean 'even if it's Adjective.'

新しくても買いません。	Even if it's fresh (i.e. fish), I won't buy it.

Verbs behave in the same way.

勉強してもわからないです。	Even if I study, I don't understand.
勉強しなくてもできました。	I was able to do it even without studying.

When either of two options is possible or acceptable, they are set up in parallel with each other using 〜ても・でも. The second option may be the negative of the first, the opposite of the first, or some alternative to the first.

1000円でも9000円でも買いません。	Whether it's ¥1000 or ¥9000, I won't buy it.
安くても安くなくても買わないです。	Whether it's cheap or not, I won't buy it.
今日しても明日しても同じでしょう?	It's the same whether you do it today or tomorrow, right?

In this Scene you hear Kanda-san tell Sasha when an assignment is due:

あすでもあさってでも。 Either tomorrow or the day after.

d. 〜て Forms and "manner expressions"

Sometimes Verbs in the 〜て form can be manner expressions—elements that qualify Sentences or tell how something occurs. This pattern is very important in expressing movement because the manner of motion (walking, running, swimming, in a hurry, etc.) is regularly used in the 〜て form in combination with a directional verb like 行きます or 来ます. The most reasonable Japanese equivalents of "I walked here" would be 歩いて来ました not 歩きました.

頑張ってやりました。	I did my best.
急いできました。	They came in a hurry.

As you saw with 全部で and みんなで in Act 3, Noun plus で can also be a manner expression. Essentially, the combination of Noun + で (〜て form of です) establishes the existence of something ('being X') that is relevant to what follows in the Sentence.

全部で7000円でした。	It was ¥7000 in total.
全部で8枚じゃないですか。	Isn't it eight sheets all together?
1時間でできます。	I can do it in an hour.
3枚で1500円	¥1500 for three.
明日で一ヶ月です。	As of tomorrow it's one month.

These join other manner expressions that have come up so far. In this Scene you find なるべく and 全然. なるべく combines with another expression to mean 'as . . . as possible.'

なるべく早く帰りましょう。 Let's go home as early as possible.

全然 combines with both affirmative and negative Sentences as an intensifier.

全然大丈夫です。	It's absolutely fine.
部長の日本語って全然わかりません。	I don't understand the division chief's Japanese at all.

Other manner expressions that you have seen include:

すぐ	すぐ分かりました。	They understood right away.	すぐ tells how they understood—right away.

194

あまり	あまりできないです。	I can't do it much.	あまり tells how much I can do—not much.
わりと	わりと安く買いました。	They bought it pretty cheaply.	わりと tells how they bought it—cheaply.
一緒に	コーヒーと一緒に食べます。	We'll eat it with coffee.	一緒に tells how we will eat something (such as cake)—with coffee.
すごく	すごくきれいでした。	It was amazingly clean.	すごく tells how clean it was—amazingly.
早く	早く帰りました。	I went home early.	早く qualifies my return home—early.

Remember that Adjectives in the 〜く form (すごく and 早く above) are common manner expressions. Note also that Noun+に is often a manner expression.

きれいに書いてください。　　　　　　　Please write neatly.

Now go to the Activity Book for 練習 Practice and 腕試し Tryout.

Scene 5-2 質問してもいいですか？
Is it all right if I ask a question?

Brian asks Professor Sakamoto when a homework assignment is due.

 The script

坂本先生	ブライアン
はい、じゃあ４７ページを見てください。	すみません。質問してもいいですか?
はい、どうぞ。	この宿題はあしたまでですね?
いや、今日までだったでしょう?	あ、そうでしたか。すみません。
じゃあ、今日やって、あす出してください。	分かりました。どうもすみませんでした。

Prof. Sakamoto	Brian
All right then, please look at page forty-seven.	Excuse me. May I ask a question?
Yes, go ahead.	We have until tomorrow for this homework, right?
No, it was until today wasn't it?	Oh, was that it. Sorry.
So, do it today and turn it in tomorrow.	Understood. I'm really sorry.

単語と表現 Vocabulary and expressions

Nouns

質問(しゃっもん)(します)　　　　　　　　(ask a) question

Verbs

やります(やらない;やって)　　　　do (less formal than する)
出(だ)します(出(だ)さない;出(だ)して)　　submit (an assignment); take out (of a container);
　　　　　　　　　　　　　　　　　send out (mail)

Classifiers

ページ(ぺ え じ)　　　　　　　　　　　pages

Special expressions

今日(きょう)までだったでしょう?　　　It was until today, wasn't it?

Behind the Scenes

BTS 3 Sentence でしょう?

In Act 4 you saw でしょう with falling intonation meaning 'probably.' In this Scene, you see でしょう? with rising intonation meaning 'right? don't you think? wouldn't it be the case?'

神田(かんだ)さん、背(せ)が高(たか)いでしょう?　　Kanda-san is tall, don't you think?
今日(きょう)は病院(びょういん)でしょう?　　　　Today is (you're going to) the hospital, right?
あとで休(やす)むでしょう?　　　　　We'll take a break later, won't we?

A special use of でしょう? alone with question intonation is a response to something that the speaker feels to be self-evident: 'Didn't I tell you?' 'Don't you think?'

A: ああ、おいしい!　　　　　　　Oh, it's delicious!
B: でしょう?　　　　　　　　　Don't you think?

197

BTS 4 More uses of the 〜て form

e. Permission: Verb 〜てもいいですか

In Scene 1 you saw Sasha ask permission using the 〜ていいですか pattern: 私が決めていいですか? 'Is it all right if I decide it?'

When other alternatives are clearly acceptable, the 〜て form is followed by も. For example, when you find a small flower decorating the sushi on your plate, you might ask:

これ、食べてもいいですか?　　　　　Is it all right to eat this too?

When you know that a meeting starts at 10:00 but your bus will arrive at 9:00, you might ask to get into the conference room early by saying:

9時に来ても大丈夫ですか?　　　　　Is it also okay to come at 9:00?

In some situations, other alternatives may not be obvious from the context, but it sounds more polite to imply that they exist by using the 〜てもいいです pattern.

見なくてもいいですよ。　　　　　　It's all right if you don't look!
あした来なくてもよろしいですか?　　Would it be all right if I don't come tomorrow?

f. 〜て forms for sequences

Another use of 〜て forms is introduced here, and that is to link Sentences together to show a sequence of activities or states. Here are two Sentences:

今日やります。　　　　　　　　　　I'll do it today.
あした出します。　　　　　　　　　I'll turn it in tomorrow.

These can be combined into a single Sentence by changing the first Sentence into its 〜て form:

今日やって明日出します。　　　　　I'll do it today and turn it in tomorrow.

Two <u>or more</u> Sentences can be combined:

ラーメンを食べて、すぐ帰って、勉強しました。I had ramen, went home right away, and studied.

Note that the 〜て form gives no indication as to whether the Sentence will be past, non-past, a request, or something else. It is only the final Verb, Adjective, or Noun です (or context) that tells us how to interpret the 〜て form.

今日やって明日出してください。	Do it today and turn it in tomorrow.
今日やって明日出しましょう。	Let's do it today and turn it in tomorrow.
きのうやって今日出しました。	I did it yesterday and turned it in today.

Similarly, the 〜て form can be used for sequences that involve Noun です and Adjectives.

真ん中でいいです	is nice and central
きれいでよかった	was nice and clean
難しくてわかりません	is difficult and I don't understand
寒くて大変	is cold and dreadful

Notice that there is very often a sense that there is a causal connection between the first and the second member of the combination. Something is nice because it is convenient, or dreadful because it is cold.

Now go to the Activity Book for 練習 Practice and 腕試し Tryout.

Scene 5-3 持ってきていただけますか？
Can I have you bring it?

Kanda-san is in charge of promotional materials for meetings with clients. Sasha wants him to bring what she needs for another meeting tomorrow.

お願いしてもいいですか。

The script

サーシャ	神田
すみません。一つだけお願いしてもいいですか？	どうぞ。何でしょう。
申し訳ありませんが、これあしたも持ってきていただけますか？	いいですよ。全部ですか？
そうですねえ。すみませんが、一応全部お願いできますか？	わかりました。
すみません。	平気、平気。任せてください。

Sasha	Kanda
I'm sorry. May I ask just one favor?	Go ahead. What could it be?
I'm really sorry, but can I have you bring these again tomorrow?	Of course, it's fine. Everything?
Let's see. Sorry, but tentatively everything please.	Understood.
Thank you.	Not a problem, not a problem. Leave it to me.

単語と表現 Vocabulary and expressions

Nouns

ぜん ぶ 全部	all, everything
いちおう 一応	for the time being, tentatively, more or less

Verbs

も も も 持ちます(持たない;持って)	hold, have, carry
も も も 持ってきます(持ってこない;持ってきて)	bring (a thing)
も も 持っていきます(持っていかない;持 っていって)	take (a thing) along
か か か 借ります(借りない;借りて)	borrow
ねが ねが お願いできます(お願いできない;お願 いできて)	can request
いただけます(いただけない;いただけて)	can receive; can have
まか まか まか 任せます(任せない;任せて)	leave it to someone else; let someone else do it

Classifiers

~つ

ひと 一つ	one thing/item	むっ 六つ	six things/items
ふた 二つ	two things/items	なな 七つ	seven things/items
みっ 三つ	three things/items	やっ 八つ	eight things/items
よっ 四つ	four things/items	ここの 九つ	nine things/items
いつ 五つ	five things/items	とお 十	ten things/items
		いくつ・おいくつ	how many things/items

Special expressions

申^{もう}し訳^{わけ}ありません・ないです。	I'm sorry. (polite)
申^{もう}し訳^{わけ}ありませんでした・なかったです。	I'm sorry for what happened. (polite)
そうですねえ	(to express consideration) let's see
何^{なん}でしょう。	What? What could it be?
持^もってきていただけますか?	Can I have you bring it?
任^{まか}せてください。	Please leave it to me. Let someone do it.
お願^{ねが}いできますか?	Can I ask a favor of you?

Behind the Scenes

BTS 5 Polite requests

You have seen two options to make a request in past Acts:

Verb 〜て plus ください	待^まってください。	Please wait.
Noun (を)お願^{ねが}いします	ご紹介^{しょうかい}をお願^{ねが}いします。	Please introduce us.

In situations where the request is more serious, a more polite way to make a request is to substitute いただけますか for ください. This form means something like 'Can I have you do X?' Note the difference between いただきます 'I'll have some' from Act 1 and いただけますか 'Can I have you . . .' This is an example of how a single vowel can change meaning.

待^まっていただけますか?	Can I have you wait?
急^{いそ}いでいただけますか?	Can I have you hurry?

In this Scene you hear Sasha ask Kanda-san:

これあしたも持^もってきていただけますか?	Can I have you bring these again tomorrow?

If you are asking someone to do something out of the ordinary, an even more polite way to ask is to use the negative:

待^まっていただけませんか?	Can't we have you wait?
急^{いそ}いでいただけませんか?	Can't I have you hurry?

202

BTS 6 〜つ Japanese numeral series and multiple classifiers in a sentence

The classifier 〜つ is used when there is no special classifier for an object and for intangible things such as ideas, arguments, and the like.

When counting items
(a) the Noun usually comes before the amount;
(b) when you want to mention more than one item, the Nouns can be connected by と;
(c) when Phrase Particles が and を occur, they usually follow the Noun, not the classifier.

名刺3枚	three business cards
教室三つ	three classrooms
ペン(を)2本と紙(を)4枚お願いします。	Please give me two pens and four sheets of paper.

You may hear other combinations of [Noun (Phrase Particle) + Quantity (Phrase Particle)], depending largely on the speaker's focus and the surrounding discourse.

Now go to the Activity Book for 練習 Practice and 腕試し Tryout.

Scene 5-4 連れていっていただけませんか？
Can I have you take me with you?

Kanda-san is going out on an errand and, since Sasha is still getting used to her new environment, she asks him to take her along.

The script

神田	サーシャ
ちょっと銀行に行ってきますけど、何かありますか？	あ、じゃあすみませんが、私も一緒に連れていっていただけませんか？
いいですよ。	助かります。銀行まで歩いていきますか？
いや、車で行きましょう。	

Kanda	Sasha
I'm just going to the bank, but is there anything (you need)?	Oh, well, if it's all right, can I have you take me along?
Of course, it's fine.	That's a big help. Will we walk to the bank?
No, let's go by car.	

単語と表現 Vocabulary and expressions

Nouns

銀行	bank
本屋	book store
スーパー	supermarket
郵便局	post office
病院	hospital
工場	factory, workshop

買い物 (か い物)	shopping
車 (くるま)	car
バス (ば す)	bus
地下鉄 (ち か てつ)	subway
電車 (でんしゃ)	train

Verbs

連れていきます (つ)	take (a person) along
連れてきます (つ)	bring (a person) along
出ます(出ない;出て) (で)(で)(で)	go out, leave, attend (an event), appear
助かります(助からない;助かって) (たす)(たす)(たす)	be helped, be saved, be rescued
歩きます(歩かない;歩いて) (ある)(ある)(ある)	walk
乗ります(乗らない;乗って) (の)(の)(の)	ride

Phrase particles

Xに	to, towards X
Xへ	to, towards X
Xで	by means of X

Special expressions

歩いて (ある)	on foot

拡張 Expansion

What kinds of stores do you go to on a regular basis? If you don't know how to say the name of one of these kinds of stores in Japanese, find out how to say it in Japanese.

Behind the Scenes

BTS 7 Verb ～ていきます・きます

A notable use of ～て form plus a Sentence is in combination with the Verbs of coming and going such as きます and いきます. You first saw this in Scene 8 of the Act 1: 行ってきま (い) す This is a ritual phrase that is translated as 'See you later,' but it literally means something like 'I'll go and come back' or 'be right back.' In English we might say, "I'll go and have lunch now" or "I'll just go and make coffee." The going is mentioned and the coming back is assumed. In contrast, in Japanese the going is assumed, but the coming back is included:

食べてきます。 I'll go and have lunch now. (I'll have lunch and come back.)

ちょっとコーヒー、買ってきます。 I'll just go and buy coffee. (I'll buy coffee and come back.)

A 〜て form in combination with いきます, on the other hand, means that the 〜て form will happen in combination with going somewhere.

ラーメンを食べていきました。 I had ramen and then went.

コーヒーを買っていきましょう。 Let's buy coffee and then go.

Compare the following.

買ってきます。 I'll go and buy it. (I'll buy it and come back.)

買っていきます。 I'll buy it and then go.

Note that the combinations 持っていく・くる and 連れていく・くる are special. 持っていく・くる means 'take/bring a thing' while 連れていく・くる means 'take/bring a person.'

ノートパソコンを持っていきます。 I'll take my laptop.

ノートパソコンを持ってきます。 I'll bring my laptop.

神田さんを連れていきます。 I'll take Kanda-san.

神田さんを連れてきます。 I'll bring Kanda-san.

Finally, note that in this pattern, these "helping" Verbs are more often than not written in hiragana, not kanji. There is a good deal of variation and no hard and fast rule for this, so be prepared to see both.

BTS 8 Place/goal に・へ

A place Noun followed by Phrase Particle に or へindicates the goal of a motion Verb (such as 行く, 来る, 帰る, etc.). (Remember that まで can also indicate the final goal of a motion Verb.) Note that the Phrase Particle へ is pronounced *e*, not *he*.

大阪へ・に行きます。 I'll go to Osaka.

うちへ・に帰りました。 I returned home.

銀行へ・に行ってきますけど……。 I'll go to the bank and be right back, but . . .

206

The difference between へ and に is subtle. Most native speakers will say that へ indicates movement <u>towards</u> a place while に assumes arrival <u>at</u> the goal. But the two can be used interchangeably with Verbs of motion.

With other types of (non-motion) Verbs, only に is acceptable for marking the goal or end point of a process:

自転車に乗 って行きましょう。	Let's go by bicycle.
私に任せてください。	Please leave it to me.
神田さんに言っていただけませんか?	Can (literally 'can't') I have you tell Kanda-san?
この仕事に時間がかかります。	It will take time for (to finish) this work.

Remember that は and も combine with these Phrase Particles in their usual sense.

大阪に・へは行かないです。	I won't go to Osaka (though I may get as far as Kyoto).
神田さんには言いませんでした。	I didn't tell Kanda-san (though I may have told others).

BTS 9 Means で

A Noun followed by Phrase Particle で tells the means by which something is done. Notice in the examples below that there are a number of ways in which this might be translated into English.

車で来ました。	I came by car.
カタカナで書いてください。	Please write with/using katakana.
ドルで買いましょう。	Let's buy it with/using dollars.

Compare Phrase Particle で with the で form of です that is introduced above. They look alike but mean different things!

ここでよろしいですか?	Is this area all right? (で form of です)
車で来ました。	I came by car. ('by means of' Particle で)

Now go to the Activity Book for 練習 Practice and 腕試し Tryout.

207

Scene 5-5 呼んでくださってありがとうございます。
Thank you for inviting me.

Yamamoto-san of Aoi Publishing has invited people from Sasha's office. He mentions the invitation again at the end of a meeting a few days before the reception.

The script

Pay attention to how Sasha accepts the invitation from Yamamoto-san. Both speakers use strategies to be polite.

山本	サーシャ
金曜日のうちのレセプションには、いらっしゃいますね?	はい。呼んでくださってありがとうございます。
あ、レセプションの前に短いプレゼンがございますから、よろしければそちらへもいらしてください。	あ、そうですか。はい、喜んで伺います。
では、レセプションの20分ぐらい前までにいらしていただけますか?	わかりました。では、6時過ぎまでに参ります。ありがとうございます。

Yamamoto	Sasha
Friday's company reception, you're coming, right?	Yes, I'll attend. Thank you for inviting me.
Oh, before the reception there's a short presentation, so if you'd like to, please come to that as well.	Oh, really. Yes, certainly.
Can we have you come about twenty minutes before the reception?	Understood. So then I'll show up by a little after 6:00. Thank you.

単語と表現 Vocabulary and expressions

Nouns

レセプション	reception
プレゼン	presentation
発表 (はっぴょう)	presentation, announcement, breaking news
うち	our company

Verbs

呼びます(呼ばない;呼んで)	call, invite
伺います↓(伺わない;伺って)	visit (humble)
喜びます(喜ばない;喜んで)	be delighted, be pleased
ございます+	have, exist (polite)
教えます(教えない;教えて)	tell, teach
見せます(見せない;見せて)	show
参ります↓(参らない・参って)	go, come (humble)
いらっしゃいます↑ (いらっしゃらない; いらっしゃって↑ or いらして↑)	go, come (honorific)

Adjectives

短い	short
長い	long

Phrase particles

TIME までに	by TIME X

Sentence particles

REASON から	because of REASON X

Special expressions

うちのX	our company's X
喜んで	delighted
よろしければ	if you would like, if it pleases you
是非	certainly, without fail
X くださって↑ありがとう（ございます）。	Thank you for doing X.

Behind the Scenes

BTS 10 敬語 Politeness

You will often hear "TPO" when Japanese people talk about appropriate language and behavior. TPO stands for 'time, place, and occasion,' and is a reminder that language changes depending on who is talking to whom, who or what speakers are talking about, who is listening, as well as where and when speakers are talking. Japanese people calibrate their language very carefully to reflect their attitudes and feelings about TPO. This system of language as a whole in Japanese is called 敬語。

a. 丁寧語 Formality

You have already learned about ~ます and です as markers of formality (Act 2) (called 丁寧語 in Japanese). The expression さよなら 'goodbye' is also formal, compared to バイバイ 'bye bye.' Formal forms put distance between the speaker and the listener. This could be because they don't know each other well, the relationship is formal by convention (doctor-patient), or the context feels formal (friends might speak formally to one another in front of outsiders). In some cases, only one side of the equation uses formality—for example, the lower-ranking 後輩 uses formal forms while the higher-ranking 先輩 does not.

b. 尊敬語 and 謙譲語 Honorific and humble forms

In addition to formality, Japanese has an elaborate system of Verbs and Verb endings that convey politeness. Unlike formality (which depends on the relationship between speaker and listener), politeness is a matter of the relationship between the speaker and those who s/he is talking about, which could include the listener. Thus いらっしゃいますか is polite to the subject of the sentence, whether it means 'Is he going?' or 'Are you going?' Politeness is also more typical of the language of working adults, as opposed to students who tend not to stand on ceremony.

210

Politeness can be communicated in two different ways. One way of being polite is to raise the status of the other person, in which case the speaker uses an honorific Verb (尊敬語) (marked here by an upward arrow ↑). Notice that by using an honorific form, you are identifying the other person as そと—you would never use an honorific in talking about うち.

いらっしゃいます↑ (honorific form of 行きます and 来ます)	何時にいらっしゃいます↑か?	When will you go/come↑?

Another way to indicate politeness is to lower your own status or that of someone in your うち, in which case the speaker uses a humble Verb (謙譲語) (marked here by a downward arrow ↓).

参ります↓ (humble form of 行きます and 来ます)	あした早く参りましょう↓か?	Shall I go/come↓ early tomorrow?
伺います↓ (another humble form of 行きますand 来ます)	7時に伺います↓。	I'll go/come/visit↓ at 7:00.

Plain	Polite-honorific↑	Polite-humble↓
来ます	いらっしゃいます↑	参ります↓
		伺います↓

Note that humble forms are used only when the speaker's behavior impinges somehow on the other person, not simply to diminish their own behavior.

c. Other politeness markers

You have seen polite Verbs: honorifics such as いらっしゃいます↑ and humble forms such as 参ります↓. In this Scene, Yamamoto-san wishes to be very polite to a representative of his client company. He therefore uses the Verb ございます rather than あります in telling Sasha that there will be a presentation. ございます is neither honorific nor humble. Rather, it is simply more polite than あります. Such polite forms are typical of the speech of service personnel (salespeople, waiters, etc.) and very formal occasions.

Customer: すみません。これ、赤いのありますか?	Excuse me. Do you have any red ones of these?

Salesperson: あ、赤いのはございませ んねえ。	Ah, red ones, we don't have.
Hotel Receptionist: お忘れ物、ござい ませんか。	You didn't forget anything?
Customer: はい、どうも。	No, thanks.

You have also seen the prefixes お~ and ご~ attached to Nouns to indicate politeness (お願い 'request,' お疲れ様 'good work,' お先に 'excuse me for going ahead of you,' お茶 'tea,' お好き 'like,' 'love,' ごちそうさま 'thanks for the meal,' ご専攻 'university major,' ご主人 'husband').

Formality and politeness are not simply a matter of 'on' or 'off.' You have seen Sentence fragments in conversations that are otherwise formal. In Scene 3, Kanda-san says 平気、平気 (without です) in an otherwise formal exchange to reassure Sasha that he will bring what she needs the next day. Thus formality and politeness can increase and recede depending on what is at stake.

Finally, be assured that 敬語 as a whole is not just about rank. Not all users of 敬語 are showing respect to the people they are talking to or about, and not all 敬語 expressions are designed to show formality and politeness in the way you might understand these in your own culture. 敬語 is used as an agent to build harmony, gauge distance, and assert or refute membership (who is うち and who is そと) in various social groups. 敬語 is one important way in which you will find your way in the Japanese cultural landscape.

BTS 11 Thanking

a. Noun ありがとうございます

When you want to express your gratitude for what someone has given you, a straightforward pattern is Noun + ありがとう(ございます). Note there is no Phrase Particle in this construction:

| お茶、ありがとうございます。 | Thank you for the tea. |
| プレゼント、ありがとう。 | Thanks for the present. |

Some action-like Nouns, such as 連絡, 発表, and 買い物 also can occur in this pattern:

| ご連絡、ありがとうございました。 | Thank you for contacting me. |
| ご質問、ありがとうございます。 | Thank you for inviting me. |

212

b. Verb 〜てくださってありがとうございます Thank you for X

You have seen a number of ways to ask others to do things, including 〜てください:

お名前を教えてください。	Please tell me her name.
本を持ってきてください。	Please bring the books.
バスまで連れていってください。	Please take me as far as the bus.

くださいis a command form of an honorific Verb くださいます↑ meaning 'give (from そと to うち).' When you want to thank someone for doing X for you, it is common to use the Verb X in its 〜て form plus くださって (the 〜て form of くださいます↑) plus ありがとうございます:

お名前を教えてくださってありがとうございます。	Thank you for telling me her name.
本を持ってきてくださってありがとうございます。	Thank you for bringing the books.
バスまで連れていってくださってありがとうございます。	Thank you for taking me as far as the bus.

BTS 12 Sentence + から : reasons

A Sentence plus から indicates the reason for something. The Sentence before から may be past or non-past, affirmative or negative, formal or informal. (It is usually informal, but in extremely serious settings such as public speaking or a job interview it may also be formal.) If the Sentence before から is formal, the final Sentence will also be formal. If the Sentence before から is informal, the final Sentence may be formal or informal. This is another example of the potential for making your communication more or less formal. The final form determines formality, but formality can be "turned up" in other parts of the Sentence.

鞄を持って行きませんでしたから、ノートもありませんでした。	I didn't take my bag so I didn't even have a notebook.
新しいから、おいしいでしょう。	It's fresh (i.e. fish), so it's probably delicious.
試験、あしたから、頑張って勉強しましょう。	Our test is tomorrow, so let's do our best and study.

In this Scene you hear Yamamoto-san say:

レセプションの前に短いプレゼンがございますから、よろしければそちらへもいらしてください。	There's a presentation before the reception, so if you'd like to, please go to that as well.

213

When the result is already mentioned or known, the Sentence may simply end in から.

A: 行きませんか？   You are not going?

B: ええ、ぜんぜんわからないですから……。   Yes, I won't understand anything so . . .

A: 買いませんね？   You won't buy it, right?

B: ええ、使わないですから。   Yes, because we won't use it.

BTS 13 Time までに

A time expression plus までに means 'by' a given time:

明日までにできます。   I can do it by tomorrow.

６時１０分ごろまでに参ります。   I'll come by about 6:10.

Now go to the Activity Book for 練習 Practice and 腕試し Tryout.

5-5

お願いしてもいいですか。

Scene 5-6 お時間いただけませんか？
Can I have some of your time?

Brian approaches Professor Sakamoto to request an appointment.

 The script

ブライアン	坂本先生
先生、今日ちょっと お時間、いただけませんか？	はい、何でしょう。
僕、読み書きが弱くて ……。	そうか ……。難しくなりましたか。
はい。	じゃあ、3時間目の授業のあとで練習しましょうか。
お願いできますか？	いいですよ。じゃあ、研究室へ来てください。
すみません。よろしくお願いします。	

Brian	Professor Sakamoto
Professor, can I have some of your time today?	Yes, what would it be?
My reading and writing are weak . . .	I see . . . Has it gotten harder?
Yes.	Well, shall we practice after the third hour's class.
Can I ask you do that?	Of course, it's fine. So then, come to my office.
Thank you for helping me.	

5-6

お願いしてもいいですか。

215

単語と表現 Vocabulary and expressions

Nouns

お時間	your time
アドバイス	advice
読み書き	reading and writing
読み	reading
書き	writing
会話	conversation
文法	grammar
語彙	vocabulary
聞き取り	listening
書き取り	dictation
あと・後	time after, later
練習(します)	practice, rehearse
予習(します)	prepare for a lesson
復習(します)	review

Verbs

なります(ならない;なって)	become

Adjectives

弱い	weak
強い	strong

Classifiers

～目	classifier for naming numbers in a series

Special expressions

難しくなりました。	It became difficult.
あとで	later, X のあとで = 'after X'
そうしていただけますか?	Can I have you do that?

お願いしてもいいですか。

5-6

Behind the Scenes

BTS 14 Change of state: Adjective ～くなります・なりました

You have already seen Adjectives in their く form in a number of places: to form the negative (新しくないです), in combination with Sentences (Act 4, Scene 1 新しく買いました。), and in this lesson in their ～て form (新しくて). Here you see the く form in combination with the verb なります 'become, get.'

ここからは少し難しくなりますよ。	From here it gets a little difficult.
遅くなってすみません。	Sorry to be late. (I'm sorry I became late.)
会議の時間が早くなりましたよ。	The time for the meeting changed to (became) earlier.

Note that ～ない forms have a ～く form, and therefore pattern like Adjectives.

食べない　　　食べなくなりました。	I stopped eating. (lit. 'I became not eating.')
きのうの会議で、神田さんの話がわからなくなりました。	At yesterday's conference, I stopped understanding what Kanda-san said.
授業に出なくなりました。	I stopped going to class.

BTS 15 甘え Dependence

Many visitors to Japan are surprised at how much underlings rely on their superiors (teachers, supervisors, *senpai*) for help and support. This reliance is called *amae,* often translated as 'dependence.' Much has been written about 甘え[1] but you see an example of it in this Scene when Brian asks his teacher for help. Subordinates ask supervisors for all kinds of help—personal as well as professional—in Japanese organizations. It is, of course, the higher-up's responsibility to take these requests seriously and try to solve the problem.

BTS 16 Classifier ～目

Adding the classifier 目 to a number changes it to an ordinal (a form that describes the numerical position of an object in a series, e.g., first, second, third, etc.). Thus 3 時間 means 'three hours,' while 3 時間目 means 'the third hour.'

217

5-6 お願いしてもいいですか。

スペイン語のクラスは3時間目です。　　　　Spanish class is the third hour.

試験って5週間目じゃないですか?　　　　Isn't the test in the fifth week?

Now go to the Activity Book for 練習 Practice and 腕試し Tryout.

Then do 評価 Assessment activities.

Note

1　If you want to know more about 甘え try these sources:

Doi, T. (1978). *The Anatomy of Dependence*. (J. Bester, Trans.) (1st edition). Tokyo, New York: Kodansha America, Inc.

Johnson, F. (1995). *Dependency and Japanese Socialization: Psychoanalytic and Anthropological Investigations into Amae*. NYU Press.

Smith, H., and Nomi, T. (2000). Is Amae the Key to Understanding Japanese Culture? Retrieved February 20, 2017, from http://www.sociology.org/content/vol005.001/smith-nomi.html

The Anatomy of Dependence. (2016, March 19). In *Wikipedia*. Retrieved from https://en.wikipedia.org/w/index.php?title=The_Anatomy_of_Dependence&oldid=710815020

お願いしてもいいですか。

BTL 1 Katakana

The next three lessons introduce katakana. This is the kana system that is used for writing loanwords from foreign languages (such as ビール 'beer'), onomatopoeic expressions (such as those you see in *manga*), as well as words that the writer wants to emphasize (ダメです。'It's no good.'). Katakana was developed in the 9th century by taking parts of kanji as a form of shorthand. Below is a chart that illustrates where each character came from. The left character in each block is the katakana symbol, while the right is the kanji source of the character.

ア	阿	イ	伊	ウ	宇	エ	江	オ	於
カ	加	キ	機	ク	久	ケ	介	コ	己
サ	散	シ	之	ス	須	セ	世	ソ	曽
タ	多	チ	千	ツ	川	テ	天	ト	止
ナ	奈	ニ	仁	ヌ	奴	ネ	祢	ノ	乃
ハ	八	ヒ	比	フ	不	ヘ	部	ホ	保
マ	末	ミ	三	ム	牟	メ	女	モ	毛
ヤ	也			ユ	由			ヨ	與
ラ	良	リ	利	ル	流	レ	礼	ロ	呂
ワ	和	ヰ	井			ヱ	恵	ヲ	乎
ン	尒								

Figure 5.2.1 Origin of *katakana* characters

Source: https://en.wikipedia.org/wiki/Katakana#/media/File:Katakana_origine.svg

As with hiragana, there are 46 katakana symbols. Katakana in this and subsequent lessons are introduced in the order of 五十音, along with conventions and tips for reading.[1]

Note

1 The symbols ヰ (*wi*) and ヱ (*we*) in the w-row are no longer used in modern Japanese.

Scene 5-7R タクシーでいらしてください。
Please come by taxi.

Sasha is helping Oscar-san, her coworker at Ogaki Trading, who is reading an email he received from Yamamoto-san of Aoi Publishing.

 テキスト Text

From: M. Yamamoto <myamamoto@ogaki.co.jp>
Date: Tuesday, May 15, 2020 at 13:32
To: John Oscar <joscar@ogaki.co.jp >
Subject: RE: Reception

オスカーさん

メールしてくださってありがとうございます。
わたしは１６：００ごろになりますからウッドさんとタクシーでいらしてください。
１７：００にはケーシーさんのプレゼン*もございますから、よろしければそちら
にもどうぞ。

ガイドもおります。よろしくおねがいいたします。

山本

* *purezen*, a common abberiviation for *purezenteeshon*. You will learn these symbols soon.

From: M. Yamamoto <myamamoto@ogaki.co.jp>
Date: Tuesday, May 15, 2020 at 13:32
To: John Oscar <joscar@ogaki.co.jp >
Subject: RE: Reception

Oscar-san,

Thank you for emailing me

I will be (there) around 16:00, so please come by taxi with Wood-san. There will be a presentation by Casey-san at 17:00, so please (come to that) as well if time permits.

We will have a guide, so please (make use of that).

Yamamoto

 ## 文字と例 Symbols with examples

	Common Font	Reading in *hiragana*	Handwritten version
#1.	ア	あ	ア
#2.	イ	い	イ
#3.	ウ	う	ウ
#4.	エ	え	エ
#5.	オ	お	オ
#6.	カ	か	カ
#7.	キ	き	キ
#8.	ク	く	ク
#9.	ケ	け	ケ
#10.	コ	こ	コ
#11.	サ	さ	サ
#12.	シ	し	シ

#13.	ス	す
#14.	セ	せ
#15.	ソ	そ

ス
セ
ソ

Examples

Names

1.	キアさん	Kia-san
2.	ケイさん	Kay-san
3.	カイさん	Kai-san

Others

4.	エコでしょうか。	Is it eco(-friendly)?
5.	タイでしょうか。	Is it Thailand?
6.	ココアでしょうか。	Is it cocoa?
7.	カカオ７０％でしょうか。	Is it 70% cacao?

Between the lines

BTL 2 Long vowels (ちょうおん 長音)

Katakana indicates long vowels with this symbol:——(called ぼうせん 棒線 in Japanese). On your computer, this should appear when you hit the dash or hyphen key within Japanese input.[1] Study the difference between hiragana and katakana below.

hiragana	katakana
ああ	アー
いい	イー
うう	ウー
えい	エー
おう	オー

Examples

1. スーってだれですか。   Who is Sue?
2. カーキーって？   What is "Car Key"?
3. アーサーってだれですか。   Who is Arthur?
4. エコカーっていいですか。   Is an eco(-friendly) car any good?

BTL 3 Borrowed words

It is not always easy to predict what will happen when a word is borrowed into Japanese. There are likely to be changes in pronunciation (more on this in the following BTLs) as well as meaning. The English word *smart* (borrowed as スマート), for example, does not mean 'intelligent'; rather it means 'slim.' ジンクス comes from English *jinx*, but it is not necessarily bad; it may mean something lucky. Words are also often shortened beyond recognition to an English speaker: アメフト 'American football,' アマ 'amateur,' エコ 'ecology, ecological,' and リモコン 'remote control' are some examples.

Remember, too, that katakana is used not only for borrowed words but in any context where the writer wants the language to stand out: animal sounds, brand names, mistakes in learners' pronunciation, and even the Japanese names of people who are of Japanese descent but are not citizens.

BTL 4 Morae ending in consonants

Because Japanese morae (with the exception of the mora /n/) are always [consonant + vowel], borrowed words with morae that end in consonants acquire a vowel in Japanese. If the mora ends in /p/, /b/, /s/, /z/, /k/, or /g/ the added sound will be usually /u/.

Examples (people's names)

1. セスでもいいですか？   Is it okay if it's Seth
2. カークでもいい？   Is it okay if it's Kirk?
3. アイクでいいですか？   Is it okay if it's Ike?

Other examples

1. アイスってこれぐらいですか。   Is the ice (cream) this much?
2. スキーのコースはどちらですか。   Where is the ski course?
3. わりとおいしいソースですよ。   The sauce is quite good.

4.　ＢＡＲオークにございます。　　　　It is (available) in Bar Oak.

5.　エースはだれですか?　　　　　　Who is the ace?

BTL 5 /ar/, /er/, /ir/ and /ur/

The morae /ar/, /er/, /ir/ and /ur/ (as in *car, learn, sir, fur*) are likely to become long /a/ morae (アー, カー, サー, etc.). The mora /or/ (as in *normal, ford, corn*) is likely to become a long /o/ mora (オー, コー, ソー, etc.) in the middle of a word and /oa/ at the end of words such as *score, more*.

Examples

1.　「アーク」って?　　　　　　　What is Arc?

2.　だれのスコアですか?　　　　　Whose score is it?

3.　２００３のオスカーはだれ?　　Who won the Oscar in 2003?

BTL 6 /th/

The /th/ of *thin* becomes /s/ in Japanese.

Examples (names)

1.　セオです。はじめまして。　　　　　I'm Theo. Nice to meet you.

2.　キースさん、はじめまして。　　　　Nice to meet you, Keith-san.

3.　アーサーさんがいらっしゃいます。　Arthur-san is coming.

#16.　タ　　　　た

#17.　チ　　　　ち

#18.　ツ　　　　つ

#19.　テ　　　　て

タ
チ
ツ
テ

#20.	ト	と
#21.	ナ	な
#22.	ニ	に
#23.	ヌ	ぬ
#24.	ネ	ね
#25.	ノ	の

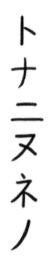

Examples

People's names

1. アナです。　　　　　　　　　　　　　　I'm Anna.
2. ノアです。よろしく。　　　　　　　　　　I'm Noah. Nice to meet you.
3. アニタです。どうぞよろしく。　　　　　　I'm Anita. Nice to meet you.
4. カーターです。どうも。　　　　　　　　　I'm Carter. Nice to meet you.
5. サニーさん、よろしく。　　　　　　　　　Nice to meet you, Sunny-san.
6. ケニーさん、どうも。　　　　　　　　　　Nice to meet you, Kenny-san.
7. トニーさん、どうぞよろしく。　　　　　　Nice to meet you, Tony-san.
8. コニーさん、どうぞよろしくおねがいします。　Nice to meet you, Connie-san.

Places

9. カナダにおります。　　　　　　　　　　I'm in Canada.
10. ケニアにいます。　　　　　　　　　　　I'm in Kenya.
11. テネシーにいらっしゃいます。　　　　　He is in Tennessee.
12. テキサスにいてください。　　　　　　　Please be in Texas.

Others

13. テニスしてください。　　　　　　　　　Please play tennis.
14. カヌーはできますか。　　　　　　　　　Can you canoe?

5-7R

お願いしてもいいですか。

226

15.	このスーツっていくらですか。	How much is this suit?
16.	このツアーはいくらですか。	How much is this tour?
17.	コーチをしてくださってありがとうございます。	Thank you for coaching me.
18.	タクシーでいらしてください。	Please come by taxi.

BTL 7 More on morae ending in consonants

Recall that borrowed words with morae that end in consonants acquire a vowel in Japanese. If the mora ends in /p/, /b/, /s/, /z/, /k/, or /g/ the added sound will be /u/. If the mora ends in /t/ or /d/, the added sound will be /o/.

Examples

Names

1.	コートニーはないです。	Courtney doesn't have any.
2.	ネートでもネイトでもいいですよ。	Either *Neeto* or *Neito* (Nate) is fine.
3.	ケートもケイトもいいですよ。	*Keeto* and *Keito* (Kate) are both good.

Others

4.	いいアートですね。	It's good art.
5.	オートですか。	Is it auto(matic)?
6.	カートがございますから······。	I have a cart, so . . .
7.	このコースがしやすいですね。	This course is easy to do.
8.	このシートですね。	This sheet, right?
9.	あのう、ソートって······。	Um, (what do you mean by) "sort"?
10.	あのノートはいくらですか。	How much is that note(book)?
11.	テストしていただけますか。	Could I have you conduct the test?
12.	そのトースト、おいしいですか。	Is that toast good?
13.	スカートはないです。	They don't have skirts.
14.	スタートしてください。	Please start.
15.	アシストしますよ。	I will assist.

5-7R

お願いしてもいいですか。

BTL 8 /w/

Since there is no /wi/, /wu/, /we/, or /wo/ in contemporary Japanese, borrowed words that contain these morae are represented by ウ plus a vowel.

Examples

1.	キウイをおいしくいただきました。	I enjoyed eating kiwis.
2.	ウエストは８６cmです。	(My) waist is 86 cm.
3.	ウイスキーはあまり‥‥‥。	(I don't drink) much whiskey.

BTL 9 Voiced consonants (濁音(だくおん)゛ or 点(てん)々(てん))

As with hiragana, two small slashes indicate voiced consonants.

/k/	カ キ ク ケ コ	/g/	ガ ギ グ ゲ ゴ
/s/	サ シ ス セ ソ	/z/	ザ ジ ズ ゼ ゾ
/t/	タ チ ツ テ ト	/d/	ダ ヂ ヅ デ ド

ヂ and ヅ, pronounced /ji/ and /zu/, are rarely used in Modern Japanese. Instead you will see ジ and ズ.

Compare:	カート	cart	カード	card	ガード	guard
	シート	seat, sheet	シード	seed		
	ケート	Kate	ゲート	gate		
	テニス	tennis	デニス	Dennis		

Examples

Names

1.	ガイさんといます。	I'll be with Guy-san.
2.	どこですか?ダグさんは?	Where is he—Doug-san?
3.	エドさんもいてくださってありがとうございます。	Thank you, Ed-san, for also being here.
4.	ジニーさんもいらっしゃいますか。	Is Ginny-san also coming?
5.	ダニーでもいいですよ。	Even Danny is okay.
6.	やっぱりアガサでしょう?	It's Agatha after all?

お願いしてもいいですか。

7. やっぱりゲイツですね。	It's Gates after all, right?
8. もちろんデニスです。	Of course, it's Dennis.
9. ジーナはこっちです。	Gina's here.
10. ゾーイはあっちです。	Zoe is over there.
11. シーザーさんはそっちです。	Caesar-san is near you.
12. エドガーでもだめですか。	Even Edgar is no good?
13. ゲイリーさんでもだめでしょう。	Even Gary-san is likely no good.
14. デイジーはだめです。	Daisy is no good.

Places

15. シカゴだったでしょう?	It was Chicago, right?
16. ドイツがいいです。	Germany is good.
17. カナダにはありませんよ。	It isn't in Canada.
18. ギニアには９つあります。	Guinea has nine.
19. ガーナだけです。	It's only Ghana.
20. ノースダコタにありますよ。	North Dakota has one.
21. サウスダコタにもありますよ。	South Dakota has one, too.

Others

22. ドアが３つあります。	There are three doors.
23. チーズを３つおねがいします。	Please give me three blocks of cheese.
24. ガイドがいりますか。	Do you need a guide?
25. タイガーじゃなくて「tiger」ですよ。	It's not *taigaa*, it's "tiger." (correcting the English pronunciation)
26. デザートがなくてもいいですか。	Is not having dessert okay?

BTL 10 促音（そくおん） (small ッ)

As with hiragana, the small ッ represents double consonants.

Compare:	カート	cart	カット	cut
	カーター	Carter	カッター	cutter
	セーター	sweater	セッター	setter (volleyball)

Examples

Names

1.	ザックがしました。	Zack did it.
2.	ウッドさんがしました。	Wood-san did it.
3.	クックさんはしました。	Cook-san (at least) did it.
4.	キットはしませんでした。	Kitt (at least) didn't do it.
5.	テッドもしました。	Ted also did it.
6.	ニックさんもしましたよ。	Nick-san also did it.
7.	ニッキーさんはしませんでした。	Nickie-san didn't do it at least.
8.	オットーさんまでしました。	As far as Otto-san did it.
9.	サックスをしました。	I played sax(ophone).
10.	アイザックからしました。	We started from Isaac.

Others

11.	ネットでしました。	I did it on the internet.
12.	すごいキック!!	A powerful kick!
13.	このデッキにはない。	This deck doesn't have one.
14.	あのデスクにもない。	The desk over there doesn't have one either.
15.	いつものセット	The usual set
16.	オッケーだよ。	It's okay.
17.	サッカーをしましょう。	Let's play soccer.
18.	かわいいソックス	cute socks
19.	おいしいクッキー	delicious cookies
20.	いくらのチケット?	A ticket (that is worth) how much?
21.	つまらないカセット	boring cassette
22.	ツイッターにありました。	It was on Twitter.
23.	ダイエットしてください。	Please go on a diet.
24.	コネチカットのどちらからですか。	Where in Connecticut are you from?

5-7R

お願いしてもいいですか。

230

Summary of Symbols in ACT 5

n	w	r	y	m	h	n	t	s	k	
						な ナ *na*	た タ *ta*	さ サ *sa*	か カ *ka*	あ ア *a*
						に ニ *ni*	ち チ *chi*	し シ *shi*	き キ *ki*	い イ *i*
						ぬ ヌ *nu*	つ ツ *tsu*	す ス *su*	く ク *ku*	う ウ *u*
						ね ネ *ne*	て テ *te*	せ セ *se*	け ケ *ke*	え エ *e*
						の ノ *no*	と ト *to*	そ ソ *so*	こ コ *ko*	お オ *o*

Now go to the Activity Book for 練習 Practice.

Then do 評価 Assessment activities, including 読んでみよう Contextualized reading, 書き取り Dictation, and 書いてみよう Contextualized writing.

Note

1 Depending on your operating system and whether you are using a computer or a smart phone, conversion to katakana may vary. Input follows the same process as hiragana. You may have the option of choosing katakana input; you may have to hold the shift key for katakana, or you may see both hiragana and katakana options as you input.

5-7R

お願いしてもいいですか。

いつもお世話になっております。

We always appreciate your helpfulness.

明日の百より今日の五十
A bird in the hand is worth two in the bush.

◆ 話(はな)す・聞(き)く Speaking and listening

Scene 6-1 留学生(りゅうがくせい)センターで勉強(べんきょう)しています。
I'm studying at the International Student Center.

Brian has joined a community aikido school near his homestay house, where his homestay brother also goes. After training, the members are gathered for a small welcome party. Kawakami-san, the leader of the aikido school, asks Brian to introduce himself.

 The script

川上(かわかみ)	ブライアン
もうみんな来(き)ていますね?	
はい、みなさん、新(あたら)しいメンバーです。	
ブライアン君(くん)、ひとこと自己紹介(じこしょうかい)をお願(ねが)いします。	はい、ブライアン・ワンです。アメリカのオレゴン州(おれごんしゅう)から来(き)ました。今(いま)福沢大学(ふくざわだいがく)の留学生(りゅうがくせい)センターで勉強(べんきょう)しています。白井一郎(しらいいちろう)君(くん)のところでホームステイしています。あと、合気道(あいきどう)はオレゴン(おれごん)でちょっとだけしていましたけど、まだ下手(へた)です。よろしくお願(ねが)いします。
ありがとうございます。	

Kawakami	Brian
Everyone is here now, right?	
All right, everyone, there's a new member.	

235

| Brian, please introduce yourself and say something. | Yes, I'm Brian Wang. I came from Oregon in America. I am studying now at the International Student Center at Fukuzawa University. I am doing a homestay at Ichiro Shirai's place. And also, I was doing a little aikido in Oregon, but I'm still really bad at it. Nice to meet you. |
| Thank you. | |

 ## 単語と表現 Vocabulary and expressions

Nouns

みなさん	everyone (used in addressing a group)
メンバー	member
ひとこと	something (to say)
自己紹介(します)	self-introduction
アメリカ	America
日本・日本	Japan
カナダ	Canada
メキシコ	Mexico
ブラジル	Brazil
中国	China
韓国	Korea
イギリス	England, U.K.
ドイツ	Germany
ケニア	Kenya
オレゴン州	Oregon
州	state, as in the US
省	provinces in China
広東省	Guangdong Province
留学生センター	International Student Center
留学生	study abroad student

りゅうがく 留学（します）	study abroad
がくぶ 学部	academic division, undergraduate
ぶんがくぶ 文学部	faculty of arts and humanities
ほおむすてい ホームステイ	homestay
あいきどう 合気道	aikido (martial art)
へた 下手	unskillful, bad at
じょうず 上手	skillful, good at

Classifiers

| ねんせい
〜年生 | classifier for grade, level in school |

Special expressions

NAME くん NAME 君	[informal title]
もう	already, yet, anymore
まだ	still, yet

拡張 Expansion

1. Find out what the country and state/province you are from are called in Japanese.
2. Select a martial art that you or one of your friends may be interested in. Using a picture, ask a Japanese acquaintance what it is called in Japanese.

Behind the Scenes

BTS 1 Verb 〜ています・〜ていました

Here you see Verb 〜て forms in combination with some forms of います. In speaking, the い of います is frequently dropped (〜てます・〜てました). There are two possible English equivalents for this combination:

a. Be X-ing

This interpretation indicates a past, current, or future ongoing action.

237

友だちはラーメンを食べています。	My friend is eating ramen.
この部屋、使っていませんね。	You're not using this room, right?
留学生センターで待っていますから ……。	I'll be waiting for you at the International Student Center, so . . .

The Verb います may occur in other forms, including the honorific form いらっしゃいます.

5時から10時まで勉強していました。	We were studying from 5:00 until 10:00.
神田さんのオフィスの前で待っていてください。	Please be waiting in front of Kanda-san's office.
隣の会議室を使っています。	We'll be using the conference room next door.
毎日は、ジョギングしていませんが ……。	I'm not running every day exactly, but . . .

b. Have X-ed or is/am/are X-ed

This interpretation generally indicates a resulting state or a repeated action, especially for Verbs of motion (行く, 来る, 帰る, 出る).

コピーができています。	The copies are done.
サーシャは帰っていて、ここにはいません。	Sasha, having gone home, is not here.
ヒルさん、来ていますか?	Is Hill-san here? or Has Hill-san come?
神田君、きのう会社に出ていましたよね?	Kanda-kun, you were at the office yesterday, weren't you?
毎日学校へ行っています。	I go to school every day.

Also note the difference between the two responses below:

A: どこの学生ですか?	Where are you from (as a student)?
B₁: 早稲田大学に行っています。	I go to Waseda University. (I'm a Waseda student.)
B₂: 早稲田大学に行きます。	I will go to Waseda University (but I'm not a student there yet).

Finally, there are a few verbs whose ～ています form is a simple present in English. 持っています meaning 'I have' is one of these.

BTS 2 もう + Sentence: already, yet, anymore

The word もう before a Sentence indicates a change in circumstances or that the Sentence has already taken place. The English equivalent might be 'already,' 'yet,' 'anymore,' and sometimes 'now' depending on whether the Sentence is affirmative or negative:

a. もう + affirmative

もうお昼食べましたか?	Did you already eat lunch?
もう帰りましたか?	Did he go home already?
もういいです。	It's good/enough already. (This is often used to indicate one doesn't need any more or is fed up.)
もうみんな来ていますね?	Everyone is here now, right?
あ、もう9月だね?	Oh, it's September, already, isn't it?

b. もう + negative

もうコーヒーは飲まなくなりました。	I've gotten to the point that I don't drink coffee anymore.
もう安くないね。	It's not cheap anymore, is it.
数学はもう勉強してないから……。	I no longer study math, so . . .

BTS 3 まだ + Sentence (unchanged situation)

The word まだ with a Sentence indicates a continuation in circumstances or that something is still or yet (not) the case. It typically occurs with the 〜ています form of a Verb, or an Adjective or [Noun です] that describes a situation.

a. まだ + affirmative

まだ古い携帯、使っていますか?	Are you still using the old cell phone?
鈴木さんはまだロンドンにいますね。	Suzuki-san is still in London, isn't she.
8月20日はまだお休みですか?	On August the 20th, will you still be on vacation?

b. まだ + negative

まだ日本に行っていないです。	I haven't gone to Japan yet.
勉強しましたが、まだ分かりません。	I studied, but I still don't understand.
みんな帰りましたけど、ブライアンはまだ食べていました。	Everyone went home, but Brian was still eating.

まだ does not occur with the simple affirmative past. Unlike もう, まだ combines with forms of です to indicate 'not yet':

Q: 中村さんからの電話は?	How about the phone (call) from Nakamura-san?
A: まだです。	Not yet. It hasn't happened yet.

Note that in responding to questions, an affirmative answer with もう will use the simple past, but a negative answer with まだ typically uses 〜ています・いました.

Q: 宿題、出しましたか?	Did you turn in your homework?
A₁: もう出しました。	I already turned it in.
A₂: まだ出していません。	I haven't turned it in yet.
Q: お昼食べましたか?	Did you eat lunch?
A₁: もう食べました。	We've already eaten.
A₂: まだ食べていません。	We haven't eaten yet.

BTS 4 自己紹介 Self-introduction

Self-introductions are very important and much appreciated in Japan, especially getting up in front of a group and telling your hosts who you are. Self-introductions follow a formula and should include: your name (even if it has already been mentioned), affiliation (country, school, and/or company), some information about yourself (such as hobbies or interests, how long you have been in Japan, etc.), and a ritual expression such as どうぞよろしく（お願いします）(with a bow) to close.

Now go to the Activity Book for 練習 Practice and 腕試し Tryout.

Scene 6-2 鈴木彩乃（すずきあやの）といいます。 My name is Ayano Suzuki.

After Brian introduces himself to the aikido group, Kawakami-san asks the other members to do a short self-introduction.

 The script

川上（かわかみ）	鈴木彩乃（すずきあやの）
じゃあ、みんなも一人（ひとり）ずつ自己紹介（じこしょうかい）してください。右（みぎ）からでいいですか?	はい。ええ、鈴木彩乃（すずきあやの）といいます。2週間前（しゅうかんまえ）に初段（しょだん）になりました。合気道（あいきどう）は今年（ことし）でもう5年目（ねんめ）になります。近（ちか）くの高校（こうこう）で生物（せいぶつ）の教師（きょうし）をしています。どうぞよろしく。

Kawakami	Ayano Suzuki
Well then, everyone introduce yourself one by one. Is it all right to start from the right?	Yes. Uhhh, my name is Suzuki Ayano. Two weeks ago I became first rank. As of this year, it's five years (that I've done) aikido. I usually work as a biology teacher at a high school nearby. Nice to meet you.

単語と表現 Vocabulary and expressions

Nouns

右 みぎ	right
左 ひだり	left
初段 しょだん	first or lowest rank black belt in martial arts, calligraphy, *shōgi*, *igo*, etc.
近く ちか	nearby, vicinity, neighborhood
向こう む	opposite side, other side, over there
隣 となり	next door, beside
上 うえ	top, over
下 した	bottom, under
中 なか	inside
外 そと	outside
店 みせ	store, shop
生物 せいぶつ	biology
教師 きょうし	instructor, teacher
マネージャー まねえじゃあ	manager
リーダー りいだあ	leader
医者 いしゃ	(medical) doctor
開発(する) かいはつ	development
企画(する) きかく	plan, project, design
デザイン(する) でざいん	design
マーケティング まあけていんぐ	marketing
セールス せえるす	sales

Verbs

申します↓(申さない；申して) もう　　　もう　　　もう	say (humble)
おっしゃいます↑(おっしゃらない；おっしゃって)	say (honorific)

Phrase particles

~と (言います・申します↓・おっしゃいます↑)　　Particle

Classifiers

~人・~人	classifier for counting people	六人	6 people
一人	1 person	七人・七人	7 people
二人	2 people	八人	8 people
三人	3 people	九人・九人	9 people
四人	4 people	十人	10 people
五人	5 people	何人	how many people

~分・分間	classifier for counting minutes
~日・~日間・日	classifier for counting days
~年間	classifier for counting years

Special expressions

一人ずつ	one (person) at a time
右からでいい	from the right is good
AMOUNT OF TIME~間	number of hours, days, weeks, years

拡張 Expansion

If you work, find out how your occupation would be described, using the ~ています pattern.

Behind the Scenes

BTS 5 Phrase particle + です

In Act 5 you saw ~て forms used for permission, including [Noun で] (これでいいですか? Is this one all right?). Here you see [Noun + Particle で] in the same pattern.

右からでいいですか? Is it all right (to start) from the right?

30ページまででいいです。 (If you read/complete) it will be fine up to page thirty.

In this pattern, で is a form of です. So in fact, the で in 右からで is the て form of 右からです。 'It's from the right.' Other [Noun + Particle です] combinations do the same thing:

30ページまでです。 (It goes) up to page thirty.

Particles が and を occur in this pattern but with some limitations. They only occur in response to statements where information is missing:

Q: 来ましたよ。 She's here!
A: 誰がですか? Who?
Q: きのう買いました。 I bought it yesterday.
A: 何をですか? What?

Phrase Particles に and までに rarely occur in this pattern.

BTS 6 Name + といいます・おっしゃいます・申します

You saw the Verb 言います in Act 3 日本語で何といいますか? 'What's it called in Japanese?' The Verb 言います and its honorific and humble equivalents—おっしゃいます↑ and 申します↓—mean 'say,' 'tell,' or 'is called.' When we identify things and people, this pattern is used. You have seen 言う in the Introduction in the 〜て form 言ってください。 'Please say it.'

鈴木といいます。 My name is Suzuki.
ロバート・ホールっていいましたか? Was his name Robert Hall?
日本語で自己紹介といいます。 In Japanese it's called a *jikoshookai* (self introduction).
これ、何ていいますか? What is this called?

Note that between the name and いいます you have a Phrase Particle: と, or less formally（っ）て (with って occurring after vowels, and て occurring after ん).

Because introductions tend to be formal, the humble form is often used for telling your own name, and the honorific for naming other people, especially superiors. See more on this humble and honorific distinction in Scene 6-4.

244

モリスと申します。 My name is Morris. (lit. I am called Morris.)

鈴木先生とおっしゃいます。 Her name is Prof. Suzuki. (lit. She is called Prof. Suzuki.)

BTS 7 Change of state: noun + になります・なりました

In Act 5, you saw Adjectives in their く form in combination with なります 'become, get to be,' The combination [Noun + になります] is used to indicate an end state or goal.

大変になりました。 It became terrible (i.e. when the store relocated).

友達になりました。 We got to be friends.

いい教師になりました。 She became a good teacher.

5時になりました。 It is (lit. has become) 5:00. (announcement before the news)

BTS 8 Locations

Location Nouns such as 右・左、上・下、中・外、隣 and 向こう are all relative to where the speaker is. If we are facing each other, my right is your left. If I am on the tenth floor and you are on the first floor, I must go down to the conference room on the fifth floor but tell you to come up. Keep perspective in mind as you give directions, and always be sure that you know where both parties are located.

神田さんは、サーシャさんの右です。 Kanda-san is on the right of Sasha-san.

チケットは電車の中で買いました。 We bought our tickets inside the train.

隣のスーパーに小さい本屋がありますよ。 There's a small bookstore in the supermarket next door.

BTS 9 Time classifier 〜間

A time classifier plus 〜間 always indicates the amount of time. You have already seen 〜時間 (1 時間 'one hour,' 2 時間 'two hours,' etc) and 〜週間(1 週間 'one week,' 2 週間 'two weeks'). Other classifiers that combine with 間 are:

〜分: 1 分間 'one minute,' 2 分間 'two minutes,' etc.

〜年: 1 年間 'one year,' 2 年間 'two years,' etc.

the calendar days (except 1日, which already indicates an amount of time in contrast to 1日):

2日間 'two days,' 3日間 'three days,' etc.

Note that for 分, 年, and 日 the classifier alone (without 間) might be either naming or counting. 間 simply clarifies that it is an amount of time. Thus, 5分 names a time in (5:05). But 5分 (間) あります 'we have five minutes' tells an amount of time. Likewise, 年 names a year in 明治2年 'Meiji 2,' while 10年(間) tells how many years. And 日 names a date in 4日 'the 4th,' while 14日間）いました。 'I was there for fourteen days.' tells an amount of time. The 間 is necessary in the case of 〜時間 and optional in the case of 〜週間 (though 〜週間 is definitely preferred).

Now go to the Activity Book for 練習 Practice and 腕試し Tryout.

Scene 6-3 みんなで写真撮りませんか？
Why don't we take a picture together?

Brian suggests taking a group photo of the aikido group.

The script

Pay attention to where everyone is standing when you rehearse this Scene.

ブライアン	鈴木
あの、みんなで写真撮りませんか？	いいですね。そうしましょう。
	じゃあ、みんなこっちの方に来て。 背が高い人は後ろに立って。 そこの緑と白の人、もっと右、じゃなくて左に寄ってください。 オッケー、行きますよ！1、2、3、はい、チーズ！
（みんなで）チーズ！	はい、もう一枚……。 はい、どうもお疲れ様でした。
ありがとうございました。	

Brian	Suzuki
Umm, shall we take a picture together?	Good! Let's do that.
	Well then, everyone come here. Taller people, stand in back. The person/people in green and white there, lean more to the right. I mean the left.
	Okay, here we go. one, two, three, cheese!!
[Everyone] Cheese!	Okay, one more. . . . Okay, good job.
Thank you.	

いつもお世話になっております。

単語と表現 Vocabulary and expressions

Nouns

写真 (しゃしん)	photo
方 (ほう)	way, direction, alternative (of two)
背 (せ)	back, spine
後ろ (うし)	back, behind
前 (まえ)	front
真ん中 (ま なか)	middle
出口 (で ぐち)	exit
入り口・入口 (い ぐち いりぐち)	entrance
窓 (まど)	window
人 (ひと)	person
方 (かた)	person (honorific)
女の人 (おんな ひと)	woman
男の人 (おとこ ひと)	man
チーズ (ち い ず)	cheese

Color nouns

緑 (みどり)	green
紫 (むらさき)	purple
茶色 (ちゃいろ)	brown
黄色 (き いろ)	yellow
グレー (ぐ れ え)	gray
ピンク (ぴ ん く)	pink
赤 (あか)	red
白 (しろ)	white
青 (あお)	blue, green
黒 (くろ)	black
色 (いろ)	color
何色 (なにいろ)	what color

いつもお世話になっております。

Verbs

撮(と)ります（撮(と)らない;撮(と)って）	take (a photo)
見(み)えます（見(み)えない;見(み)えて）	appear, be visible
立(た)ちます（立(た)たない;立(た)って）	stand
座(すわ)ります（座(すわ)らない;座(すわ)って）	sit
寄(よ)ります（寄(よ)らない;寄(よ)って）	get close to, drop by, lean on

Adjectives

(背(せ)が)高(たか)い	tall (in stature)
(背(せ)が)低(ひく)い	short (in stature)

Special expressions

背(せ)が高(たか)い人(ひと)	tall person/people
もっと	more
もう一枚(いちまい)	one more sheet
もうちょっと	a little more
右(みぎ)、じゃなくて左(ひだり)	right, I mean left
行(い)きますよ。	Here we go!
いち、に、さん!	One, two three!
チーズ!	Cheese!

Behind the Scenes

BTS 10 Verb 〜て for informal commands

You have seen Verb 〜てください used for requests. For a direct command in very informal situations, ください can be dropped. The command can be made more insistent with the addition of Sentence Particle よ.

待(ま)って!	Hold on!
見(み)てよ。	Look!

もう少し勉強して。   Study a little more.

あした来てね。   Come tomorrow, okay?

BTS 11 Colors: adjective and noun forms

You have now seen that some colors can have both an Adjective (赤い, 青い, 白い, 黒い) and a Noun (赤, 青, 白, 黒) form. Others, such as 緑, have only a Noun form. There is a slight difference in the Adjective and Noun form of colors such as 赤(い). The noun form enters into compounds such as 赤ワイン. Also, when talking about color as a concept, it is always the Noun form that is used: 赤がすきです。'I like red.'

赤と白のストラップ   a red and white (decorative) strap

外が雪 で白くなりましたね。   It's snowed outside and turned white.

この青、すごくきれいじゃないですか?   Isn't this a beautiful blue?

BTS 12 More: もう and もっと

There are two patterns for indicating 'more' or additional quantity in Japanese.

a. もう + amount

The word もう combines with a quantity or amount to indicate how much more.

もう一回   one more time

もう少し食べませんか。   Won't you have a little more?

もう二個ください。   Two more, please.

Notice that in English, 'more' follows the number ('one more time'), but in Japanese it precedes (もう一度).

b もっと + Sentence

The word もっと combines with a Sentence (Verb, Adjective, Noun です) to indicate an even greater degree than what has been mentioned.

もっと食べました。   They ate (even) more.

もっと高いです。   It's (even) more expensive.

もっときれいです。   It's (even) prettier (more pretty).

Compare the following:

もう少し飲みませんか。   Won't you drink a little more?

もっと飲みませんか。   Won't you drink more?

The first is a slightly more polite way of inviting someone to have more to drink.

BTS 13 Describing people: 背が高い・背が低い人 a short/tall person

In Act 2 you learned that Adjectives can directly modify Nouns: 古い店 'an old shop' or 'a shop that's old.' In fact, an Adjective Sentence in the informal can directly modify a Noun.

あまり新しくない店   a shop that's not so new

エンジンがいい車   a car with a good engine

ランチがおいしいレストラン   a restaurant where the lunch is good

Now go to the Activity Book for 練習 Practice and 腕試し Tryout.

いつもお世話になっております。

Scene 6-4 名刺交換 Exchanging business cards

大垣商会

企画部長

八木 礼子
REIKO YAGI
Planning Department Manager

〒123-4567 東京都東京区東京 1-23-4
Ogaki Firm Inc. 1-23-4 Tokyo, Tokyo-ku, Tokyo 123-4567, Japan
Phone (01) 2345-6789, Fax (01) 2345-6789

Sasha is introduced to someone at a reception.

The script

サーシャ	白井
(handing over her *meishi* and accepting his) 大垣商会のサーシャ・モリスと申します。いつもお世話になっております。	(handing over his *meishi* and looking at hers) はじめまして。吉田運送の白井と申します。こちらこそどうぞよろしくお願い致します。
ありがとうございます。	あ、申し訳ございません。こちらの番号が新しくなりまして……。
あ、そうですか。	はい。８９の７７２０です。
７７２０ですね。どうもありがとうございます。	よろしくお願い致します。
こちらこそ、どうぞよろしくお願い致します。	

Sasha	Shirai
My name is Sasha Morris from Ogaki Trading Company. We always appreciate your helpfulness.	How do you do, Ms. Morris. My name is Shirai from Yoshida Transport. It's we who appreciate you.

252

Thank you.	Oh, I'm terribly sorry but this number has changed.
I see.	Yes. It's 89-7720.
So, it's 7720, right? Thank you.	Nice to meet you.
It's I who am pleased to meet you.	

単語と表現 Vocabulary and expressions

Nouns

名刺	business card
交換	exchange
(お)世話(します)	help, aid, assistance
吉田運送	Yoshida Transport
番号	number
(お)電話番号	telephone number (your telephone number)
(お)名前	name (your name)
メール	email
アドレス	(email) address
連絡先	contact information

Verbs

おります↓	be (humble form of います 'be') The 〜ない and 〜て forms are rarely used today.
いらっしゃいます↑(いらっしゃらない；いらっしゃって)	be (honorific form of います 'be')

Special expressions

はじめまして。	How do you do.
いつもお世話になっております↓。	I/we are always in your debt.
申し訳ございません↓。	I am terribly sorry. (lit. 'I have no excuse.')
０５５２、８９の７７２０	(0552) 89-7720

Do a search on the internet for visual or motion picture representations of Japanese people exchanging business cards. (Avoid comedic or satirical situations.) Discuss the situation with your Japanese teacher or colleague. Find out in what context(s) the behaviors you see are appropriate.

Behind the Scenes

BTS 14 名刺交換 Exchanging business cards

Business cards 名刺 are commonly seen in Japan. Even students sometimes use 名刺. There is a great deal of information on these cards that helps people to determine what their relationship to the other person is—company or affiliation, unit, rank—and therefore how they should address one another. Japanese names are notoriously varied in the kanji that are used to represent them, and this information is also available from the business card.

When you hand over your business card in Japan, the card should be turned so that the other person can easily read it. Using two hands—both to give your card to the other person and to take the other person's card—is conventional in a formal setting. When you accept someone's card, it is polite to look at the information contained on it, and either put it away or, if you are at a meeting, place it on the table in front of you (so that you can remember the names of those in attendance).

Note that numbers which are ordinarily one mora (2 and 5) are lengthened when they occur in a telephone number—or any other list (credit card numbers, room numbers, etc.).

教室は３２５です。	The room is 325.
ええっと、５７０ですか、５０７ですか?	Umm, is it 570? Or 507?

BTS 15 More on politeness

This Scene is a very formal meeting between two people who do not know each other and who have a good deal at stake in the relationship. Both speakers introduce themselves using the humble 申します↓. You see two other humble Verbs: おります↓ (humble form of います) and いたします↓ (humble form of します). Sasha uses the humble Verb お願いします, and Shirai-san responds using the even more humble お願いいたします. Below you see the polite forms for these Verbs.

6-4

いつもお世話になっております。

Plain	Polite-honorific↑	Polite-humble↓
言います	おっしゃいます↑	申します↓
います	いらっしゃいます↑	おります↓
します	なさいます↑ (see Act 7)	いたします↓

BTS 16 Formal 〜まして forms: 新しくなりまして

In this Scene you see the 〜て form of a Verb in the formal form: 新しくなりまして. This use of formal 〜まして forms is typical of ritual speech, such as introductions and public speaking.

はじめまして。	How do you do. (from 始めます 'begin')
遅くなりまして、申し訳ございません。	I am terribly sorry for being late.

Now go to the Activity Book for 練習 Practice and 腕試し Tryout.

6-4

いつもお世話になっております。

Scene 6-5 お話ししたいんですが ……。

Sasha wants to discuss her future plans with Yagi-bucho, so she makes an appointment to see her.

The script

サーシャ	八木部 長
部長、今週お忙しいですか?	何ですか?
いつかちょっとお話ししたいんですが ……。	何か難しい話?
いえ、ちょっと来年のことについて ……。	わかりました。じゃあ、木曜はどうですか?午後はずっと空いてますから。
そうですか?では2時ごろいかがでしょうか。	いいですよ。じゃあ、あさっての2時に。
よろしくお願いします。	

Sasha	Yagi-bucho
Chief, are you busy this week?	What is it?
I'd just like to have a word, but . . .	Is it something that's hard to talk about?
No, but there's something I'd like to talk about regarding next year.	I understand. Well then, how about Thursday? The whole afternoon is open, so . . .
Is it? Well, how would about 2:00 be?	That's just fine. So then, the day after tomorrow at 2:00.
Thank you. (lit. 'Please treat me favorably.')	

単語と表現 Vocabulary and expressions

Nouns

課長 かちょう	section chief
社長 しゃちょう	company president
所長 しょちょう	head of a laboratory, research center
学長 がくちょう	school president
(お)話 はなし	talk
(ご)相談(する) そうだん	consultation
(ご)報告(する) ほうこく	report
アポ あぽ	appointment
留守 るす	away from home or work

Verbs

お話しします↓ はな	talk (humble)
空きます(空かない；空いて) あ　　　あ　　　あ	become free, empty
休みます(休まない；休んで) やす　　やす　　やす	take a break, go on vacation/holiday
いたします↓(いたさない；いたして)	do (humble)

Adjectives

Verb～たい	want to VERB

Special expressions

いつか	sometime
何か なに	something
Xについて	with regard to X
いかが	how (polite)
ずっと	continuously, by far, the whole time

いつもお世話になっております。

Behind the Scenes

BTS 17 Polite adjectives

You have seen polite prefix お〜 with Nouns (お電話、お茶、おすし), but here you see Sasha asking her division chief if she is busy using an Adjective with the same polite prefix: お忙しい. Not all Adjectives will add this polite お〜, but some others that you may hear (especially from service personnel) are お早い, お高い, and お安い. Polite Adjectives are never used when talking about yourself.

BTS 18 Question word + か：何か、どれか、どこか、 どちらか、誰か

A question word plus Sentence Particle か makes an indefinite expression usually equivalent to English 'some-X' or 'any-X':

何か	something/anything
だれか・どなたか	someone/anyone
どこか・どちらか・どっちか	somewhere/anywhere
どうか	somehow/anyhow
どれか	something/any one (of a group)
いつか	sometime (an uncertain time in the future)
いくつか	some number of

These expressions may occur with (or without) Phrase Particles just as other Nouns do.

あ、だれか（が）来た！	Oh, someone's here!
何か、食べませんか？	Do you want to eat something?
本田さんはどこかに行きました。	Honda-san went somewhere.

This combination can also precede a Noun phrase to make it indefinite.

何か難しい話	something difficult to talk about
どこかおいしいラーメン屋	some delicious ramen shop
いつか休みの日	some day that's a holiday

いつもお世話になっております。

BTS 19 Adjective んです

Any of the three Core Sentence types (Verb, Adjective, and Noun です) can occur in combination with んです. In this Act we cover Adjectives plus んです.

高^{たか}いんです。	The fact is, it's expensive.
高^{たか}くないんです。	The fact is, it's not expensive.
高^{たか}かったんです。	The fact is, it was expensive.
高^{たか}くなかったんです。	The fact is, it wasn't expensive.

Sentence んです is a [Noun です] sentence, which means that the informal form will use だ instead of です (んだ). This will be covered in more detail in the next Act.

Sentence んですhas a number of uses, all of which can be subsumed under the idea of "fact, matter, thing (intangible)." Let's divide the use of this form into questions on the one hand and statements on the other.

• んです in questions

When んです is used in a yes-no question, you must have evidence to believe that the main sentence is true. This is not unlike the use of "What, _____?" in English. Seeing that your friend is struggling with his Japanese homework, you might say, "What, is it tough?" The same question in Japanese would be 難^{むずか}しいんですか。Other English constructions that accomplish the same thing include affirmative tag questions ("It's tough, is it?" "It's tough, huh?").

• んです in statements

In statements, too, んです refers to the situation within which the main sentence occurs. It is often used to express reasons or provide rationales—direct or underlying. In this sense, it is very different from [Sentence + から] which is a direct reason. んですasks the listener to take in the entire situation and draw a conclusion. Thus if your teacher asks why you haven't bought the textbook yet, you might reply, 高^{たか}いんです。'It's that it's expensive.' The price of the textbook is a direct reason for your not buying it, but use of んです here is a softer alternative than [Sentence + から]. On the other hand, you might give a less direct, more oblique rationale:アルバイトがないんです。'I don't have a part-time job.' No job means no money means I can't afford it. You will find that Japanese people often use んです in ways that require you to make these logical connections. Again, it is a virtue in Japan to be vague, but it is also a virtue to listen carefully for the underlying message!

One related—and frequent—use of んですis to set the stage with background information. You see an example in this Scene when Sasha tells her supervisor that she would

いつもお世話になっております。

259

like a little of her time: ちょっとだけお話ししたいんですが …… 'I'd like to have a word, but . . .' This sentence frames or forms background for what is to follow—she wants to ask about next year. English speakers sometimes do this with phrases such as "you know," "well, you see," "here's the thing," etc.

BTS 20 Verb 〜たい

A Verb in the 〜たい form means 'want to' or 'would like to.' It is formed by adding 〜たい to the Verb stem .

〜ます form	〜たい form	
食べます	食べたい	to eat
飲みます	飲みたい	to drink
使います	使いたい	to use

This 〜たい form is an Adjective, so all of its forms parallel that of Adjectives.

	Affirmative	Negative
Non-past	食べたいです	食べたくないです
	want(s) to eat	食べたくありません
		do(es)n't want to eat
Past	食べたかったです	食べたくなかったです
	wanted to eat	食べたくありませんでした
		didn't want to eat

Because a 〜たい form is an explicit expression of what the speaker wants, it is very often backgrounded by embedding it into an んです sentence:

ちょっとお聞きしたいんですが ……。 'I'd like to ask you a question, but . . .' (offered as a reason for stopping a stranger to ask for directions).

Either Phrase Particle を or が might mark the direct object of a 〜たい form:

新しい車(を・が)買いたいんですけど ……。 'We'd like to buy a new car, but . . .' (offered as a reason for applying at the bank for a loan).

Remember that 〜たい forms rarely refer to what someone else wants, and are not generally used as invitations the way that "do you want to" forms are in English. For invitations, it is safer to use a negative question.

260

Note also that some Verbs do not normally occur in the 〜たい form. These include あります, できます, and 分かります. What these Verbs have in common is that they aren't volitional or a matter of will. You cannot decide that something exists or that you will be able to do or understand something.

BTS 21 Humble verbs

Most Verbs have a humble equivalent that shows deference (and a certain sense of benefit) to the listener or someone else in the context. They can be formed by adding the prefix お〜 to the stem (drop 〜ます from the formal form) and adding some form of します.

お話しします↓	I/we will talk/speak (to someone for you)
お手伝いします↓	I/we will help (you)
お作りします↓	I/we will make it (for you)

Note that you can substitute いたします↓ for します in any humble form and make it doubly polite. Thus お手伝いします↓ is humble but お手伝いいたします↓ is even more humble.

Now go to the Activity Book for 練習 Practice and 腕試し Tryout.

6-5

いつもお世話になっております。

Scene 6-6 よくご存知ですね！ You know a lot, don't you!

Kanda-san is joining Sasha for lunch at a new restaurant near their office.

The script

神田	サーシャ
どうもお待たせしました。	いえいえ。
何か、もう頼みました？	いえ、まだ何も。カレーか今日のランチかで迷ってます。
それはカレーでしょう！	え？ランチよりカレーの方がおすすめですか？
ええ。ランチもいいんですけどね、カレーほどすごくないですよ。他の店のものとあまり違わないですね。	へえ。さすがグルメの神田さん、よくご存知ですね！
いえいえ。	じゃあ、カレーにします。やっぱり神田さんに聞いて、よかった！

Kanda	Sasha
Sorry to make you wait.	No, no.
Did you already order something?	No, nothing yet. I'm torn over whether it should be curry or the lunch of the day.
That should be curry!	Oh? You recommend curry over the lunch of the day?
Right. The lunch of the day is okay, but not as awesome as curry, you know. It isn't all that different from stuff at other places, you know.	Wow! True to his reputation, Kanda-san the gourmet knows a lot!
No, no.	Well then, I'll have the curry. Glad that I asked you, Kanda-san!

いつもお世話になっております。

6-6

単語と表現 Vocabulary and expressions

Nouns

ランチ	lunch, lunch of the day
定食	set meal
(お)勧め	recommendation, suggestion
他・外	other, else, besides
別	different, separate, distinct
もの	thing (tangible)
グルメ	gourmet, connoisseur

Verbs

頼みます (頼まない; 頼んで)	order (at a restaurant, online, etc.), request
迷います(迷わない; 迷って)	become confused, lost
困ります(困らない; 困って)	be troubled; be bothered; be embarrassed
存じます↓(存じない; 存じて)	know, find out (humble)
知ります(知らない; 知って)	know, find out
知っています	know
Xに勧めます・薦めます (勧めない・薦めない; 勧めて・薦めて)	recommend to X, advise X, encourage X

Particles

より	compared to [comparison particle]
ほど	as much as [comparison particle]

Special expressions

お待たせしました。	Sorry to make you wait.
何も	nothing
カレーか今日のランチか	curry or the lunch of the day
ランチよりカレーの方がお勧め	curry rather than the lunch of the day is the recommendation

カレーほどすごくない	not as awesome as curry
Xと違わないです	not different from X
さすが (Noun)	true to (your reputation, what I expected, etc.)
ご存知です↑	know (honorific)
Xにします	decide on X
Xに聞きます	ask X
Xに・と相談します	consult with X
Xに報告します	make a report to X

拡張 Expansion

What kinds of items do you usually carry with you when you go to work or school? Find out what to call these items in Japanese, and practice saying the words.

Behind the Scenes

BTS 22 何も Question word + も

A question word combines with Phrase Particle も to indicate all of a category (with affirmative Sentences) or none of a category (with negative Verbs). Not all combinations are possible, as the following table shows.

	with AFFIRMATIVE	with NEGATIVE
何も	[rare]	nothing, not anything
だれも	[rare]	nobody, no one, not anybody
どこも	everywhere	nowhere, not anywhere
いつも	always	never
どれも	every one	not (a single) one
どちらも	both	neither, not either
どの X も	every X	no X
どんな X も	every kind of X	no kind of X
どの連絡先もまずいです。	All of the forwarding addresses are bad?	
この携帯、どちらもだめです。	Both of these cell phones are broken.	
何も報告しませんでした。	They didn't report anything.	

The same Phrase Particles that can be followed by も in other contexts (にも、でも、から も、etc.) can take も in this pattern. Here are some examples:

どこまでも頑張ります。	I'll do my best all the way, no matter how far.
いつまでも待ちます。	I'll wait forever.
だれからも何も聞いていませんが ……	I haven't heard anything from anyone, but . . .

When the question word refers to quantity, the meaning is 'no large number/amount' (with negative sentences) or 'a large number/amount' (with affirmative sentences).

	with AFFIRMATIVE	with NEGATIVE
いくらも	a large amount	no large amount
いくつも	a large number	no large number
何-CLASSIFIER も (including 何個も、何本も、何枚 も、何人も etc.)	a large number	no large number

Here are some examples:

日本人が何人も来ました。	Any number of Japanese people came.
こんな紙、宿題に何枚も使いましたけど。	I used any number of sheets of this kind of paper for my homework, but . . .
消しゴムはいくつもないから ……。	There aren't a lot of erasers, so . . .

BTS 23 Noun$_X$ か noun$_Y$ (か) either X or Y

Particle か follows Nouns in a list of two or more alternatives; か is optional on the final item in the list. Thus 毎日サンドイッチかピザかハンバーガー(か)を食べました。 'Every day I ate a sandwich, pizza or a hamburger.'

神田さんか部長に報告してください。	Please report either to Kanda-san or the division chief.
中国か韓国からの留学生ですね。	They are study abroad students from either China or Korea.

BTS 24 Comparison of two items

In comparing items, there is no *-er* (*taller*) or *-est* (*tallest*) in Japanese. Rather, when you mention the two items being compared, both are followed by と: XとYと and what follows tells how they are to be compared. If the comparison is a question, it typically begins with どちら(の方). You saw 方 in Scene 3 of this Act meaning 'direction, way.' In this pattern, 方 is used to indicate one alternative of two in making the comparison, and is optional.

課長と部長とどちらの方がよくわかると思う?	Who do you think would understand better, the section chief or the division chief?
103号室と107号室とどちらが使いやすいでしょうか。	Which would be easier to use, room 103 or room 107?

Is indicating a preference of one thing over another, the word より can be translated 'rather than' or 'compared to.' When it is used for comparisons, より marks the point from which the comparison is made: そこより 'compared to that place,' 私より 'compared to me.' (Note that より comes up in the *kotowaza* for this Act: 明日の百より今日の五十 literally 'Better fifty today than a hundred tomorrow.') Like other particles, よりcan take は or も.

アイスクリームより甘いです。	It's sweeter than ice cream. (Compared to ice cream, it's sweet.)
英語よりも難しかったです。	It was harder than English, too (in addition to being harder than something else). (Compared to English, too, it was hard.)
寒いけど、去年よりはいいんじゃないですか?	It's cold, but compared to last year, at least, isn't it better?
今学期は数学より物理のテストのほうがやさしいね。	This term, the tests for physics are easier than the tests for math, aren't they. (This term, compared to math, the tests for physics are hard.)

In negative comparisons, an item can be described as 'not as much as': X ほど.

私、神田さんほど上手じゃないです。	I'm not as good (at X) as Kanda-san.
お肉は嫌いじゃないですが、魚ほど好きじゃないです。	I don't hate meat, but I don't like it as much as fish.

いつもお世話になっております。

BTS 25 Noun + と + Sentence

When two items are compared or contrasted using 別, 違います, or 同じ, the point of comparison takes Phrase Particle と.

これは先生のと違います。   This is different from the teacher's.

私の車は山口さんのと同じです。   My car is the same as Yamamoto-san's.

Recall that Phrase Particles such as と (including から、まで、で) combine with も for additional elements as well as は in its comparative meaning.

あ、山本さんのとは違います。   Oh, it's different from Yamada-san's.

私のとも違いますよ。   It's also different from mine.

私のアパートは山口さんのとは別です。   My apartment is different from Yamaguchi-san's.

A Noun plus と can precede a basic sentence in a general sense of 'with' or 'to.'

課長と話して、帰りました。   I talked to my section chief and went home.

先輩と相談しましたが ……。   I conferred with my senior, but . . .

八木部長とずっと待っていました。   I was waiting the whole time with Division Chief Yagi.

Some Verbs, such as 相談します and 会います, take Phrase Particle に or と with a slight difference in meaning. [Noun + に相談します] sounds as if the communication is one-way—I'm going to get advice from X. [Noun + と相談します] sounds a bit more collaborative, because of the 'with' meaning of Phrase Particle と.

BTS 26 さすが

さすが is used in combination with a Noun (さすがグルメの神田さん) when you are favorably impressed with the knowledge, accomplishment, or behavior of another. There is a sense of 'I expected no less' when Sasha compliments Kanda on his knowledge of what to order in this Scene. You will also hear さすが(です) 'Excellent! Just like you!' on its own as a compliment.

The Verb 知^しります in the simple affirmative, present or past, means 'find out':

それ、いつ知^しりましたか。 When did you find that out?

But in its 〜ています form, the English equivalent is 'know':

この漢字^{かんじ}、知^しっていますか。 Do you know this kanji?

The negative response to questions about knowing is not a 〜ています form, but a simple negative:

いいえ、知^しりません。 No, I don't know it.

Note that 知^しっています is used for factual knowledge or learning, while わかります is used for understanding or recognition. There is some overlap in these two, since either can be used in talking about, for example, someone's name.

The polite forms of 知^しります are, 存^{ぞん}じます↓ and ご存知^{ぞんじ}です↑. The honorific form of the question above is ご存知^{ぞんじ}ですか.

この漢字^{かんじ}、ご存知^{ぞんじ}ですか。 Do you know this kanji?

Note that the honorific is a Noun rather than a Verb. Its negative is ご存知^{ぞんじ}じゃないです or ご存知^{ぞんじ}ないです.

The humble affirmative and negative responses to a question are:

はい、存^{ぞん}じています。 Yes, I know it.
いいえ、存^{ぞん}じません。 No, I don't know it.

Note that you have already seen a humble polite form of います in おります. So the foregoing affirmative response can be made even more polite with this substitution:

はい、存^{ぞん}じて↓おります↓。 Yes, I do know it.

This is further evidence that politeness is not a matter of 'on' and 'off' but something that can be amplified and reduced.

BTS 28 Particle に for decisions: カレーにします。
I'll have curry.

Note that [Noun + にします] is a new way of saying 'decide.'

ここのラーメン、おいしそうだから、	The ramen here looks good, so let's choose ramen.
ラーメンにしましょう。	Let's have ramen.
8時からにしましょう。	Let's make it from 8:00.
105号室にしました。	We decided on room 105.

Now go to the Activity Book for 練習 Practice and 腕試し Tryout.

Then do 評価 Assessment activities.

6-6

いつもお世話になっております。

◆ 読み書き Reading and writing

This lesson introduces the remaining 21 katakana symbols, along with additional information.

Scene 6-7R メニュー Menu

Brian and his colleague are deciding what to order over texts.

 ## テキスト Text

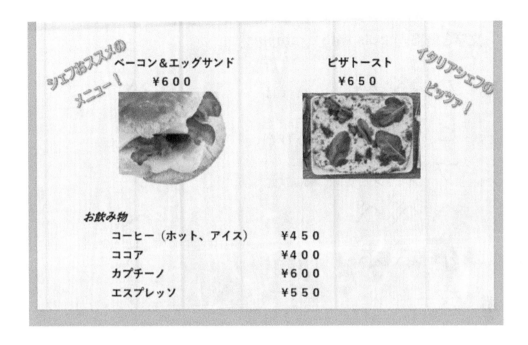

シェフおススメの
メニュー！

ベーコン＆エッグサンド
¥600

ピザトースト
¥650

イタリアシェフの
ピッツァ！

お飲み物

コーヒー（ホット、アイス）	¥450
ココア	¥400
カプチーノ	¥600
エスプレッソ	¥550

Have you already ordered?	
	No, not yet. Everything looks so good . . . Here is the menu.

Hamburger	¥750	Cheeseburger	¥750
Juicy hamburger!		Very juicy! Very tasty cheese!	
Ham and egg sandwich	¥600	Pizza toast	¥650
Chef's recommended menu!		Pizza by an Italian chef	

Set Menu

Drinks
Coffee (hot, iced)	¥450
Hot chocolate	¥400
Cappuccino	¥600
Espresso	¥550

6-7R

いつもお世話になっております。

文字と例 Symbols with examples

#26.	ハ	バ	パ	はばぱ	
#27.	ヒ	ビ	ピ	ひびぴ	
#28.	フ	ブ	プ	ふぶぷ	
#29.	ヘ	ベ	ペ	へべぺ	
#30.	ホ	ボ	ポ	ほぼぽ	
#31.	マ			ま	
#32.	ミ			み	
#33.	ム			む	
#34.	メ			め	
#35.	モ			も	

ハ
ヒ
フ
ヘ
ホ
マ
ミ
ム
メ
モ

Examples

Names

1.	ハナはまだいますよ。	Hannah is still here.
2.	トムはまだいませんよ。	Tom is still not here.
3.	サムはもういますよ。	Sam is already here.
4.	ジムはもういませんよ。	Jim is no longer here.
5.	トニーさんとおっしゃいます。	He is Tony-san.
6.	ペギーさんはまだしています。	Peggy-san is still doing that.
7.	トーマスはまだです。	Thomas hasn't done this.

8.	ピートといいます。	I'm Pete.
9.	パットとおっしゃいます。	She is Pat.
10.	ナオミっていいます。	I'm Naomi.
11.	スミスさんっていいます。	He is Smith-san.
12.	ピーターさんっておっしゃいます。	He is Peter-san.

Places

13.	ネバダにはまだありますよ。	Nevada still has it.
14.	アイダホにもまだありますよ。	Idaho also still has it.
15.	オハイオにはもういません。	I'm no longer in Ohio.
16.	ミネソタにももういません。	I'm also no longer in Minnesota.
17.	エジプトにまだいました。	He was still in Egypt.
18.	メキシコにもういました。	He was already in Mexico.
19.	ミシシッピーでもうしました。	I already did this in Mississippi.

Food and drinks

20.	ピザはまだありますよ。	We still have pizza.
21.	パイはもうないです。	We no longer have pies.
22.	バターはまだです。	I still haven't used the butter.
		I still don't have butter.
23.	いつものコーヒー	the usual coffee
24.	ビスケットが1つ	one biscuit
25.	カプチーノってまだありますか。	Do you still have cappuccino?
26.	ピーチパイってまだおいしいですか。	Is the peach pie still tasty?
27.	チーズバーガーってもうありませんか。	Is the cheeseburger no longer available?
28.	ホットコーヒーってまだですか。	Has the hot coffee still not arrived?
29.	アイスコーヒーお1つですね。	One iced coffee, right?
30.	ハム＆エッグはもうないよ。	The ham and egg sandwich is no longer available.

6-7R
いつもお世話になっております。

BTL 1 /v/

There is no /v/ in Japanese so it is usually realized as /b/ (バ、ビ、ブ、ベ、ボ) in katakana. バット might be 'bat' or 'vat' (You will encounter an innovative way of representing /v/ in Act 7).

Examples

Names

1.	ベスはおりません。	Bess/Beth is not here.
2.	ビクターはまだおりますが ……。	Victor is still here.
3.	バートさんはいらっしゃいますか。	Is Bart/Burt-san here?
4.	ボビーさんってまだいらっしゃいますか。	Is Bobbie/Bobby-san still here?
5.	バーニーさんはもういらっしゃいますか。	Is Barney/Bernie-san already here?
6.	ベネットのとなりにございます。	It's next to Bennett.
7.	ビッキーのとなりにあります。	It's next to Vickie.
8.	バーナードさんのとなりにまだありますか。	Is it still next to Bernard-san?

Places

9.	バージニアにはまだございます。	It's still in Virginia at least.
10.	ウエストバージニアのとなりにもあります	It's also next to West Virginia.

#36.	ヤ	や	ヤ
#37.	ユ	ゆ	ユ
#38.	ヨ	よ	ヨ
#39.	ラ	ら	ラ
#40.	リ	り	リ

#41.	ル	る	ル
#42.	レ	れ	レ
#43.	ロ	ろ	ロ
#44.	ワ	わ	ワ
#45.	ヲ	を	ヲ
#46.	ン	ん	ン

BTL 2 /l/ and /r/

Since Japanese does not distinguish between /l/ and /r/, both of these are usually realized as /r/ morae in Japanese. Compare these sentences.

1.	きれいなライトです。vs. ライトにいます。	It's a pretty light. vs. He is in the right field.
2.	すごいカーレース vs. きれいなレース	an amazing car race vs. pretty lace
3.	ライターがあります。vs. ライターをしています。	There is a lighter vs. I'm working as a writer.
4.	レーザーポインターです。vs. レーザーカット、おねがいします。	It's a laser pointer vs. Please give me a razor (cut).
5.	アメリカのリーダー、いますか。vs. ブックリーダーってありますか。	Is the American leader here? vs. Do you have an e-book reader?

Examples

Names

1.	ロイがします。	Roy will do it.
2.	リリーがしています。	Lily is doing that.
3.	ローラはしていません。	Laura is not doing this.
4.	ロペスさんももうしていません。	Lopez-san is also not doing it any more.

5.	リンジーさんはまだしていません。	Lindsay-san hasn't done that yet.
6.	ビバリーさんはまだいりません。	Beverly-san still doesn't need it.
7.	タイラーさんはまだしていないです。	Tyler-san still hasn't done this.
8.	ルイーズはもうしていないよ。	Louise is no longer doing it.
9.	レベッカさんから１つずつしています。	They are doing it one by one starting from Rebecca.

Places

10.	イランにいたいです。	I want to be in Iran.
11.	シリアにいたかったなあ。	I wanted to be in Syria.
12.	ロシアにまだいたかった。	I wanted to continue to be in Russia.
13.	インドでしたいなあ。	I want to do that India.
14.	アメリカでもしたかったよ。	I wanted to do it also in the U.S.
15.	イタリアではしたくないです。	I don't want to do it in Italy.
16.	スペインからしたいけど ……。	I want to do that from Spain but . . .
17.	フランスでしたいですけど ……。	I want to do this in France but . . .
18.	イギリスでしたいんですけど ……。	It's that I want to do it in England but . . .
19.	ブラジルではしたくないんですけど ……。	It's that I don't want to do this Brazil but . . .
20.	ヨーロッパにいらっしゃらないんですか。	So you won't be in Europe?
21.	オーストラリアにいたいんですか。	Is it that you want to be in Australia?
22.	シンガポールにずっといたいんだ。	It's that I want to be in Singapore forever.

U.S. States

23.	ユタでもいいですか。	Is it okay even in Utah?
24.	ハワイでもいいんですか。	Is it that it's okay even in Hawai'i?
25.	カンザスにいてもいいですか。	Is it okay if I stay in Kansas?
26.	ミシガンにいてもいいんですか。	Is it that it's okay if I stay in Michigan?
27.	オレゴンにはないです。	It's not in Oregon.
28.	コロラドにはないんです。	It's that it's not in Colorado.
29.	フロリダからだから ……。	It's from Florida, so . . .
30.	ワシントンからありますから ……。	It starts in Washington, so . . .

| 31. | ケンタッキーまでございますから……。 | It's as far as Kentucky, so . . . |
| 32. | ペンシルバニアまでだから……。 | It's as far as Pennsylvania, so. |

Cities

33.	パリにだれかいないんですか。	So isn't there someone in Paris?
34.	ホノルルになにかないんですか。	So isn't there something in Honolulu?
35.	ベルリンのどこかにないんですか。	So is it not somewhere in Berlin?
36.	セントルイスにいつかいらっしゃらないんですか。	So you won't be visiting St. Louis sometimes?
37.	どれもポートランドにはないんですか。	So none of these are found in Portland?
38.	ロサンゼルスにはなにもないんですか。	So there is nothing in Los Angeles?
39.	サンフランシスコにはだれもいないんですか。	So there is no one in San Francisco?

BTL 3 /th/

The /th/ of *leather* becomes /z/ and is usually represented by ザ, ジ, or ズ.

Examples

1.	わりといいリズム♬♪(^^♪	Pretty good rhythm!
2.	すごい！「レーザービーム」だ！	Wow! It's a laser beam!
3.	アナザーラブストーリー🖤	another love story
4.	「ザ・ゲスト」ってわりとよかったよ。	"The Guest" was quite good.
5.	もう「ジ・エンド」だね。	It's already "the end."

BTL 4 /wh/

English /wh/ (as in *what*) is sometimes represented by ホ.

Examples

1.	グレーのホイールがいい。	I want the grey wheel.
2.	ホワイトがいいんだけど。	It's that I want the color white.
3.	ホイットニーさんとしたいんだけど……。	It's that I want to do this with Whitney-san, but . . .

BTL 5 *Yoo-on* 拗音 <ruby>拗音<rt>ようおん</rt></ruby> (small ヤ、ユ、ョ)

As with hiragana, the small ヤ、ユ、ョ represent [consonant + y + vowel]:

キャ　キュ　キョ　ギャ　ギュ　ギョ

Examples

1.	おもしろいギャグ知らない？	Do you know a funny joke?
2.	キューバについて知ってますか。	Do you know about Cuba?
3.	キャサリンはなにも知りませんよ。	Catherine doesn't know anything (about it).
4.	ドキュメンタリーについておととい知りました。	I found out about the documentary two days ago.

シャ　シュ　ショ　ジャ　ジュ　ジョ

Examples

1.	ジョンを知ってますか。	Do you know John?
2.	ジャックについてなにか知ってますか。	Do you know anything about Jack?
3.	ジョージアについてなにも知りません。	I don't know anything about Georgia.
4.	シャンハイのことはきのう知りました。	I found out about Shanghai yesterday.

いつもお世話になっております。

5. あさってのスケジュール知りたいんですが ……。　It's that I want to find out about the schedule for the day after tomorrow . . .

6. シャワーのことはだれも知らないよ。　No one knows about the shower.

チャ　チュ　チョ

Examples

1. さすがチャールズさん　True to your reputation, Charles-san.
2. チューターはもういないんです。　I no longer have a tutor.
3. チョコレートはまだないんです。　It's that I still don't have any chocolates.
4. マサチューセッツにもいたいんですが ……。　I want to stay in Massachusetts, too, you see.

ニャ　ニュ　ニョ

Examples

1. ソーニャのほうがいいです。　I prefer Sonya.
2. ニョッキのほうがいいんだけど。　It's that I prefer gnocchi.
3. ニューヨークのほうがよかったなあ。　New York was better.
4. このニュース、きのうのとおなじです。　This news is the same as the one from yesterday.
5. ニュージャージーとちがいます。　It is different from New Jersey.

ヒャ　ヒュ　ヒョ　ビャ　ビュ　ビョ　ピャ　ピュ　ピョ

Examples

1. ヒューさんがしてもいい?　Is it alright if Hugh-san does it?
2. ヒューロンにしてもよろしいですか?　Is it alright if we decide on Huron?
3. このコンピュータにしていい?　Is it alright if we decide on this computer?
4. インタビューをしてもよろしいですか。　Is it alright if I interview you?
5. ランチはビュッフェにしない?　Shall we go to a buffet for lunch?

ミャ　ミュ　ミョ

いつもお世話になっております。

Examples

1. ミャンマーにしましょう。   Let's decide on Myanmar.
2. ミュージック、スタート!   Start the music!
3. このミュージカルにしない?   Shall we decide on this musical?

リャ　リュ　リョ

Examples

1. スクリューがないんです。   It's that there aren't any screws.
2. ドイツのリューベックでしましょう。   Let's do that in Lübeck in Germany.
3. ITソリューションって?   What is "IT solution"?

Additional examples (by semantic category)

Food and drink

1. ミルクだけです。   It is just milk.
2. ビールはこれだけですか。   Is this the only beer?
3. ワインはあれだけでしょう?   That's the only wine, right?
4. ジャムをもう1つください。   One more (jar of) jam, please.
5. パスタをもっとください。   More pasta, please.
6. サラダ、もっとおねがいします。   Please give me more salad.
7. メニュー、もう1つおねがいします。   Please give me one more menu.
8. このランチスペシャルのステーキ、いかがですか。   How about this special steak meal?
9. Premium Steak! ステーキバイキング   Premium steak! All-you-can-eat steak
10. Enjoy! コカコーラ   Enjoy! Coca-cola
11. ランチがおいしいレストラン   a restaurant that has tasty lunch
12. どのチョコレートもおいしそうでこまってます。   All the chocolates look good, so I'm stuck.
13. どのハンバーガーもおいしいですよ。   Every hamburger is tasty.
14. サンドイッチはどれもいいですよ。   All the sandwiches are good.

15.	おススメのアップルパイにします。	I will have the apple pie that was recommended.
16.	チーズケーキはもうオーダーしました？	Have you already ordered the cheesecake?
17.	オレンジジュースはまだです。	My orange juice hasn't arrived yet.
18.	このバニラアイスクリーム、どうしましょう。	What shall I do with this vanilla ice cream?
19.	ストロベリーヨーグルトがおススメですよ。	I suggest you get the strawberry yogurt.

Clothing and accessories

20.	グレーのコート	a grey coat
21.	みどりのドレス	a green dress
22.	みどりさんのベルト	Midori-san's belt
23.	センパイのジーンズ	a senior colleague's jeans
24.	むらさきのＴシャツがいります。	I need a purple T-shirt.
25.	Ｙシャツ（ワイシャツ）はワンさんがいります。	It is Wang-san that needs a dress shirt.
26.	セーターがしろいモリスさん	Morris-san whose sweater is white
27.	あかのスカーフのモリスさん	Morris-san with a red scarf (for women)
28.	くろのブラウスのスミスさん	Smith-san with a black blouse
29.	ジャケットがくろいスミスさん	Smith-san whose jacket is black
30.	このポロシャツは¥1,980でした。	This polo shirt was ¥1,980.
31.	あのきいろのワンピースは¥7,980ですか。	Is that yellow one-piece (dress) ¥7,980?
32.	ハイヒールはあかいのにしましょう。	As for high heels, let's wear the red ones.
33.	このタキシードにしたいんですが ……。	It's that I want to decide on this tuxedo, but . . .
34.	ピンクのネックレスが１つありますけど ……。	I have one pink necklace, but . . .
35.	グレーのハンドバッグにしてください。	Please decide on the grey handbag.
36.	アクセサリーはどれもきれいだよ。	The accessories are all pretty.
37.	ジャンさんのショルダーバッグがないんですけど ……。	It's that Zhang-san's shoulder bag is missing . . .

いつもお世話になっております。

Sports （スポーツ）

38.	ヨガをしました。	I did yoga.
39.	スキーにしました。	I decided on skiing.
40.	スノボ (short for スノーボード) がいいですよ。	Snowboarding is good.
41.	「ピンポン」って知ってますか?	Do you know "ping pong"?
42.	アメフト (short for アメリカンフットボール)のルールを知らない。	I don't know the rules for American football.
43.	プロレス (short for プロレスリング)のルールについてはきのう知りました。	I found out about the rules for professional wrestling yesterday.
44.	ボーリングはあまりしませんね。	I don't go bowling much.
45.	ハイキングをしましょう。	Let's go hiking.
46.	ジョギングにしましょうか。	Shall we decide on jogging?
47.	サイクリングをしています。	I do cycling.
48.	バドミントンがしやすいネット	a net that is easy to play badminton with
49.	バレーボールがしにくいネット	a net that is difficult to play volleyball with
50.	バスケットボールはまだへたです。	I'm still not good at basketball.

Computer and office

51.	カメラがいいスマホ	a smartphone with a good camera
52.	ビデオをとりましょう。	Let's film (lit. video) it.
53.	テレビがあたらしくなりました。	The television became like new.
54.	あたらしいパソコンはまだいらないんです。	So I still don't need a new personal computer.
55.	あのビデオカメラはもういらないんですか。	So you no longer need that (video) camcorder?
56.	みんながいそがしいスケジュール	a schedule that everyone is busy with
57.	ここからダウンロードしてください。	Please download it from here.
58.	ユーチューブでですか。	(You mean) on YouTube?
59.	インターネットでしなかったんですか。	Is it that you didn't do this on the Internet?

Katakana words not borrowed from American English

60.	¥１００のパン	¥100 bread
61.	¥３９０のホッチキス	¥390 stapler
62.	アルバイトがまよってます。	The part-time worker is lost.
63.	このマフラーのいろはどうですか。	How about the color of this (knitted) scarf?

U.S. presidents

64.	バラク・オバマについてなにか知ってますか。	Do you know anything about Barack Obama?
65.	ジョージ・ブッシュのこと、知らない？	Don't you know George Bush?
66.	ドナルド・トランプも知らないの？	Even Donald Trump doesn't know?
67.	だれかロナルド・レーガンについて知ってますか。	Does anyone know Ronald Reagan?
68.	ジョージ・ワシントンについてきのう知りました。	I found out about George Washington yesterday.
69.	アブラハム・リンカーンのことはあまり知りません。	I don't know much about Abraham Lincoln.

Buildings

70.	あのビルのむこうです。	It's over on the other side of that building.
71.	ホテルのうしろにいらっしゃいますよ。	He is behind the hotel.
72.	ロビーのなかにおります。	I'll be inside the lobby.
73.	トイレはどこですか。	Where is the restroom?
74.	いつものスーパーでショッピングしてきます。	I'll be shopping at the usual supermarket.
75.	アパートの２Ｆがあたらしくなりました。	The second floor of the apartment became like new.
76.	エスカレーターでまいりました。	I came by the escalator.
77.	ガソリンスタンドまではあとどのぐらいですか。	How long until the gas station?

いつもお世話になっております。

Transportation

78.	バスでまいりましょう。	Let's use the bus.
79.	タクシーでいらしてください。	Please come by taxi.
80.	レンタカーっていくらぐらいですか。	About how much is the rental car?
81.	モノレールでもいいですよ。	It's also okay (to come) by monorail.
82.	ヘリコプター、のりましょうか。	Shall we ride the helicopter?

Musical instruments

83.	へたなギター	unskilled guitar (performance)
84.	ピアノのパフォーマンス	piano performance
85.	¥300,000 のサックス	a 300,000-yen sax
86.	フルートはちょっと ……。	(I don't play) flute . . .
87.	バイオリンのインストラクター	a violin instructor
88.	トランペットってむずかしいですか。	Is (playing) the trumpet difficult?
89.	パイプオルガンはできますか。	Do you play the pipe organ?

BTL 6 ヲ

The distinction in pronunciation between オ and ヲ disappeared in the history of the Japanese language, and katakana ヲ is rarely used now. Sometimes it is used purposefully in place of オ to make it stand out in such words as ヲタク (also オタク) 'someone with an obsessive interest in manga and anime.' Certain proper nouns continue to use ヲ, including 深草ヲカヤ町 Fukakusa Okayacho, an area of Kyoto. Japanese spoken by foreigners and robots is sometimes written entirely in *katakana* and ヲ can be found in those utterances: コンピューターヲカイマシタ 'I bought a computer.'

Summary of hiragana and katakana

n	w	r	y	m	h	n	t	s	k	
ん	わ	ら	や	ま	は	な	た	さ	か	あ
ン	ワ	ラ	ヤ	マ	ハ	ナ	タ	サ	カ	ア
n	*wa*	*ra*	*ya*	*ma*	*ha*	*na*	*ta*	*sa*	*ka*	*a*

284

		り リ *ri*		み ミ *mi*	ひ ヒ *hi*	に ニ *ni*	ち チ *chi*	し シ *shi*	き キ *ki*	い イ *i*
		る ル *ru*	ゆ ユ *yu*	む ム *mu*	ふ フ *fu*	ぬ ヌ *nu*	つ ツ *tsu*	す ス *su*	く ク *ku*	う ウ *u*
		れ レ *re*		め メ *me*	へ ヘ *he*	ね ネ *ne*	て テ *te*	せ セ *se*	け ケ *ke*	え エ *e*
を ヲ *o*	ろ ロ *ro*	よ ヨ *yo*	も モ *mo*	ほ ホ *ho*	の ノ *no*	と ト *to*	そ ソ *so*	こ コ *ko*	お オ *o*	

Now go to the Activity Book for 練習 Practice.

Then do 評価 Assessment activities, including 読んでみよう Contextualized Reading, 書き取り Dictation, and 書いてみよう Contextualized Writing.

いつもお世話になっております。

Appendix A: Japanese-English glossary in *gojuuon* order

List of abbreviations

N = Noun
V = Verb
Adj = Adjective
Sp. Exp. = Special Expressions

	あ、	あ、	Sp. Exp.	Oh	1	10
	ああ	ああ	Sp. Exp.	ahh, oh	2	7
	あいきどう	合気道	N	aikido (martial art)	6	1
	あいだ	Amount of time～間	Sp. Exp.	number of hours, days, weeks, years	6	2
+	あいまい	曖昧(な)	N	ambiguity (BTS 12)	4	2
+	あう	会う(-U; 会った)	V	see, meet	3	4
+	あお	青	N	blue, green	6	3
+	あおい	青い	Adj	blue	3	5
+	アオイしゅっぱん	アオイ出版	N	Aoi Publishing	3	1
+	あか	赤	N	red	6	3
	あかい	赤い	Adj	red	3	5
	あかいの	赤いの	Sp. Exp.	the red one	3	5
	あく	空く・あく (-U; 空いた)	V	become free, empty	6	5
+	あさ	朝	N	morning	3	4
+	あさごはん	朝ごはん	N	breakfast	2	3
	あさって	あさって	N	day after tomorrow	3	4

+	あした	あした・明日	N	tomorrow	2	2
	あす	あす	N	tomorrow (slightly more formal than あした)	5	1
	あすのひゃくより きょうのごじゅう	明日の百より今日の 五十	Kotowaza	A bird in the hand is worth two in the bush.	6	0
+	あそこ	あそこ	N	over there, there (away from both of us), that place (that we both know about)	2	7
+	あたらしい	新しい	Adj	new	4	1
+	あちら	あちら	N	there (away from both of us), that thing (away from both of us), in that direction (away from both of us), that alternative (of two away from both of us), that place (that we both know about), that person over there (polite)	2	4
+	あっち	あっち	N	there (away from both of us), in that direction (away from both of us), that alternative (of two away from both of us), that place (that we both know about)	2	7
	あと	あと	Sp. Exp.	lastly, remaining, and then	4	2
	あと	あと・後	N	time after	5	6
	あとで	あとで	Sp. Exp.	later	2	2
	あとで	Xのあとで	Sp. Exp.	later, N のあとで = 'after N'	5	6
+	アドバイス	アドバイス	N	advice	5	6
+	アドレス	アドレス	N	(email) address	6	4
+	あなた	あなた	N	you	1	7
+	あの	あの+ N	Sp. Exp.	that N over there	3	5
	あのう	あのう	Sp. Exp.	umm (hesitation noise)	2	2
+	アパート	アパート	N	apartment	2	5
+	アプリ	アプリ	N	app, application	3	3
+	アポ	アポ	N	appointment	6	5
+	あまり・あんまり	あまり・あんまり+ negative	Sp. Exp.	not very much	4	2

	あめ	雨	N	rain	3	6
	アメリカ	アメリカ	N	America	6	1
+	アメリカじん	アメリカ人	N	American (person)	3	1
+	ありがとう。	ありがとう。	Sp. Exp.	Thank you. (non-past or past, informal)	1	2
	ありがとうございました。	ありがとうございました。	Day1 Phrase	Thank you. (past, formal)	0	0
	ありがとうございます。	ありがとうございます。	Sp. Exp.	Thank you. (non-past, formal)	1	2
	ある	ある(-U; あった; ない)	V	exist (inanimate)	2	8
	あるいて	歩いて	Sp. Exp.	on foot	5	4
	あるく	歩く(-U; 歩いた)	V	walk	5	4
+	あれ	あれ	N	that (thing over there)	2	1
+	いい	いい	Adj	good	2	1
+	いいえ	いいえ	Sp. Exp.	no	2	1
	いう	いう・言う (-U; 言った)	V	is called, say	3	1
+	いえ	いえ	Sp. Exp.	no	2	1
+	いえ	いえ・家	N	house, home	2	5
	いえいえ	いえいえ	Sp. Exp.	no, no	2	1
	いかが	いかが	Sp. Exp.	how (polite)	6	5
	いきますよ。	行きますよ。	Sp. Exp.	Here we go!	6	3
+	イギリス	イギリス	N	England, U.K.	6	1
+	いく	行く(-U; 行った)	V	go	2	2
	いくつ	(お)いくつ	Classifier	how many things/items	5	3
	いくら	いくら	N	how much	3	5
+	いしゃ	医者	N	(medical) doctor	6	2
	いそがしい	(お)忙しい	Adj	busy	2	4
	いそがばまわれ	急がば回れ	Kotowaza	More haste, less speed. (lit. 'If you are in a hurry, go the long way.')	3	0
+	いそぐ	急ぐ(-U; 急いだ)	V	hurry	5	1
+	いたす	いたす (-U; いたした)	V	do (humble)	6	5
	いただきます。	いただきます。	Sp. Exp.	I humbly receive. (eating ritual)	1	6

	いただく	いただく↓(-U; いただいた)	V	eat; receive (humble)	2	3
	いただける	いただける (-RU; いただけた)	V	can/may have someone do X	5	3
	いち	一・1	Numbers	1	3	2
	いち、に、さん!	いち、に、さん!	Sp. Exp.	One, two three!		
	いちおう	一応	N	for the time being, tentatively, more or less	5	3
	いちごいちえ	一期一会	Kotowaza	'Once in a lifetime' or 'carpe diem' (seize the day).	1	0
+	いちばん	一番	Sp. Exp.	most, best	4	5
	いちろう	一郎	N	[given name]	1	7
	いちろうくん	一郎君	Sp. Exp.	Ichiro	1	7
	いつ	いつ	N	when?	4	3
	いつか	いつか	Sp. Exp.	sometime	6	5
	いっしょ	一緒	N	together	3	4
	いっていらっしゃい。	行って(い)らっしゃい。	Sp. Exp.	See you later. (lit. 'Go and come back.')	1	8
	いってきます。	行ってきます。	Sp. Exp.	See you later. (lit. 'I'll go and come back.')	1	8
	いってください。	言ってください。	Inst. Exp	Please say it.	0	0
	いってください。	PERSON に言ってください。	Inst. Exp	Please say it to PERSON.	2	0
	いつも	いつも	N	always, usual(ly)	4	4
	いつもおせわになっております↓。	いつもお世話になっております↓。	Sp. Exp.	I/we are always in your debt.	6	4
	いつものN	いつものN	Sp. Exp.	the usual N (e.g., *basho* 場所 place, jikan 時間 time, *tokoro* ところ place,	4	4
+	いとう	伊藤	N	[family name]	3	9R
+	いのうえ	井上	N	[family name]	3	9R
+	イベント	イベント	N	event	4	4
	いま	今	N	now	2	2
	いや	いや	Sp. Exp.	no (informal); uhh (hesitation noise)	2	4
+	いらっしゃる	いらっしゃる↑ (-ARU; いらっしゃった)	V	be (honorific form of います 'be')	6	4

	いらっしゃる↑	いらっしゃる↑／いらっしゃって↑ or いらして↑ (-ARU; いらっしゃった or いらした)	V	go, come (honorific)	5	5
+	いりぐち	入り口／入口	N	entrance	6	3
+	いる	いる (-RU; いた)	V	be, exist (animate)	2	2
+	いる	いる (-U; いった)	V	need	4	6
+	いろ	色	N	color	6	3
	う～ん	う～ん	Sp. Exp.	well (hesitation)	2	7
+	ウーロンちゃ	ウーロン茶	N	oolong tea	2	3
+	うえ	上	N	top, over	6	2
	うかがう	伺う↓ (-U; 伺った)	V	visit (humble)	5	5
	うしろ	後ろ	N	back, behind	6	3
+	うち	うち	N	house, home; Scene 5-5 our company	2	5
	うち	うちのX	Sp. Exp.	our company's X	5	5
+	うどん	うどん	N	udon (wheat noodles)	2	3
+	うみのひ	海の日	N	Marine Day (BTS 18)	4	4
	え？	え？	Sp. Exp.	what?	2	3
+	えいご	英語	N	English (language)	3	1
+	ええ	ええ	Sp. Exp.	yes (suggesting agreement or indicating understanding; less formal than *hai*)	1	1
	ええと	ええと	Sp. Exp.	uhh (hesitation noise)	2	2
+	えき	駅	N	train station	2	5
	えり	恵理	N	Eri [female given name] (Eri is Sasha's housemate)	1	13
	えん	～円	Classifier	yen (Japanese currency)	3	5
+	えんぴつ	鉛筆	N	pencil	3	3
	おいしい	おいしい	Adj	delicious	2	3
	おいしそう	おいしそう	N	look(s) delicious	2	3
+	おおがきしょうかい	大垣商会	N	Ogaki Trading Company, Ltd.	3	1
+	おおきい	大きい	Adj	big	2	7
	おかえりなさい。	おかえりなさい・お帰りなさい。	Sp. Exp.	Welcome back	1	13
+	おく	億	Numbers	hundred millions (BTS 4)	4	1

+	おさきに	お先に	Sp. Exp.	I'll be x-ing (ahead of you)	1	12
	おさきにしつれい します。	お先に失礼します。	Sp. Exp.	I'll be leaving (ahead of you).	1	12
+	おしえる	教える(-RU; 教えた)	V	tell, teach	5	5
	おじかん	お時間	N	your time	5	6
+	おそい	遅い	Adj	late	3	4
+	おたく	お宅	N	home (polite)	2	5
+	おちゃ	お茶	N	tea	2	3
	オッケー	オッケー	Sp. Exp.	okay	3	4
+	おっしゃる	おっしゃる↑(-ΛRU; おっしゃった)	V	say (honorific)	6	2
	おつかれさま。	お疲れ様。	Sp. Exp.	Good work, hello. (informal)	1	11
	おつかれさまで した。	お疲れ様でした。	Sp. Exp.	Good work.	1	12
	おつかれさまです。	お疲れ様です。	Sp. Exp.	Good work, hello.	1	11
+	おとこのひと	男の人	N	man	6	3
+	おととい	おととい	N	the day before yesterday	4	3
+	おなじ	同じ	N	same	3	6
	おねがいします。	お願いします。	Sp. Exp.	please help me with this	1	3
	おねがいできます か?	お願いできますか?	Sp. Exp.	Can I ask a favor of you?	5	3
	おねがいできる	お願いできる (-RU)	V	can request	5	3
	おはなししする↓	お話しする↓	V	Talk (humble)	6	5
	おはよう。	おはよう。	Day1 Phrase	Good morning. (informal)	1	6
	おはようござ います。	おはようございます。	Day1 Phrase	Good morning. (formal)	0	0
	オフィス	オフィス	N	office	4	5
	おまたせしました。	お待たせしました。	Sp. Exp.	Sorry to make you wait.	6	6
	おもいやり	思いやり	N	consideration	3	4
	おもしろい	おもしろい	Adj	interesting	2	3
+	おもしろそう	おもしろそう	N	look(s) interesting	2	3
	おやすみなさい。	おやすみなさい。	Sp. Exp.	Good night.	1	14
	おる	おる↓(-U; おった)	V	be (humble form of いま す 'be') The 〜て form is rarely used today.	6	4

+	おれ	俺	N	I (masculine, informal) (BTS 15)	1	7
	オレゴンしゅう	オレゴン州	N	Oregon	6	1
	おわります。	終わります。	Inst. Exp	That's all for today. (used at the end of a class).	0	0
+	おわる	終わる (-U; 終わった)	V	end	2	2
+	おんなのひと	女の人	N	woman	6	3
	おんよみ	音読み	N	Chinese-based readings of kanji	1	BTL 2
	か	〜か?	S. Particle	[question particle]	2	1
+	が	〜が	S. Particle	but, and	2	4
	が	〜が	Particle	[subject particle]	4	3
+	かい	〜会	N	organization, club, association, group	3	1
	かい	〜階	Classifier	classifier for naming and counting floors	4	5
+	かいぎ	会議	N	(hold a) meeting	3	2
	かいぎしつ	会議室	N	meeting room	4	4
+	がいこくじん	外国人	N	foreigner	3	1
	かいしゃ	会社	N	office, company	2	5
+	がいじん	外人	N	foreigner (can be derogatory)	3	1
	かいてください。	書いてください。	Inst. Exp	Please write it.	0	0
+	かいはつ	開発(する)	N	development	6	2
+	かいもの	買い物	N	shopping	5	4
	がいらいご	外来語	N	loan words (BTS 14)	3	3
	かいわ	会話	N	conversation	5	6
+	かう	買う(-U; 買った)	V	buy	4	1
+	かえる	帰る(-U; 帰った)	V	return (home)	3	2
	かかる	かかる (-U; かかった)	V	take (time/money)	4	6
+	かかん・にちかん・にち	〜日間	Classifier	classifier for counting days	6	2
+	かき	書き	N	writing	5	6

+	かきとり	書き取り	N	dictation	5	6
+	かく	書く(-U; 書いた)	V	write	2	2
	がくせい	学生	N	student	3	1
+	がくちょう	学長	N	school president	6	5
+	がくぶ	学部	N	academic division, college	6	1
+	かげつ	〜ヶ月・〜カ月	Classifier	classifier for counting months	4	6
	かさ	傘	N	umbrella	3	6
+	かた	方(かた)	N	person (honorific)	6	3
	カタカナ	片仮名・カタカナ	N	katakana syllabary	1	BTL 1
+	かちょう	課長	N	section chief	6	5
	がつ	〜月(がつ)	Classifier	classifier for naming the months of the year	4	4
+	がっき	〜学期	Classifier	school /term	4	6
+	がっこう	学校	N	school	2	5
+	かとう	加藤	N	[family name]	3	9R
	かな	かな	N	syllabary	1	BTL 1
	かなあ	〜かなあ	S. Particle	[sentence particle indicating a shared question]	2	6
+	カナダ	カナダ	N	Canada	6	1
+	かばん	かばん	N	bag, briefcase	3	6
+	カフェ	カフェ	N	café	4	4
	かまう	構う (-U; 構った)	V	mind, care, be concerned about (most commonly occurs in the negative)	5	1
+	かみ	紙	N	paper	3	6
+	かよう(び)	火曜(日)	N	Tuesday	4	6
	から	〜から	Particle	from (starting point)	4	4
	から	REASON 〜から	S. Particle	because of REASON X	5	5
+	かりる	借りる (-RU; 借りた)	V	borrow	5	3
	ほとんど	ほとんど	N	almost; barely (plus negative)	4	6
+	カレーライス	カレーライス	N	curry rice	2	3
	かわいい	かわいい	Adj	cute	3	5

+	かんがえる	考える (-RU; 考えた)	V	think about, consider	4	3
+	かんこく	韓国	N	Korea	6	1
+	かんこくご	韓国語	N	Korean (language)	3	1
+	かんこくじん	韓国人	N	Korean (person)	3	1
	かんじ	漢字	N	kanji	1	BTL 1
+	がんじつ	元日	N	New Year's Day (BTS 18)	4	4
+	かんだ	神田	Name	Mr/s. Kanda	1	1
	かんださん ですか?	神田さんですか?	Sp. Exp.	Are you Mr./Ms. Kanda?	1	10
+	かんとんしょう	広東省	N	Guangdong Province	6	1
+	がんねん	元年	N	first year (of a new era) (BTS 18)	4	4
	がんばりましょう。	頑張りましょう。	Inst. Exp	Do your best.	2	0
	がんばる	頑張る (-U; 頑張った)	V	will do my best	2	1
	きいてください。	聞いてください。	Inst. Exp	Please listen.	0	0
	きいてください。	PERSON に聞いてください。	Inst. Exp	Please ask PERSON.	2	0
+	きいろ	黄色	N	yellow	6	3
+	きかく	企画(する)	N	plan, project, design	6	2
+	ききとり	聞き取り	N	listening	5	6
	きく	聞く (-U; 聞いた)	V	hear; listen	4	4
+	きく、Xに	Xに聞く	Sp. Exp.	ask X	6	6
	きくはいっときの はじ、きかぬはい っしょうのはじ	聞くは一時の恥、聞 かぬは一生の恥	Kotowaza	To ask may lead to shame for a moment, but not to ask leads to shame for a lifetime.	5	0
+	きのう	きのう	N	yesterday	4	3
+	きむら	木村	N	[family name]	3	9R
	きめる	決める (-RU; 決めた)	V	decide (something)	5	1
	きゅう・く	九・9	Numbers	9	3	2
+	きょう	きょう・今日	N	today	2	2
+	きょうかしょ	教科書	N	textbook	2	2
	きょうし	教師	N	instructor, teacher	6	2
+	きょうしつ	教室	N	classroom	4	4

	きょうまでだったでしょう?	今日までだったでしょう?	Sp. Exp.	It was until today, wasn't it?	5	2
+	きょねん	去年	N	last year	4	3
+	きれい	きれい (な)	N	pretty, clean	2	3
	ぎんこう	銀行	N	bank	5	4
+	きんよう(び)	金曜(日)	N	Friday	4	6
+	きんろうかんしゃのひ	勤労感謝の日	N	Labor/Thanksgiving Day (BTS 18)	4	4
+	くすり	(お)薬	N	medicine	2	3
	くださってありがとう(ございます)。	Xくださって↑ありがとう(ございます)。	Sp. Exp.	Thank you for doing X	5	5
	クッキー	クッキー	N	cookie	2	3
	くてん	句点	N	phrase point, comma	2	BTL 2
	くとうてん	句読点	N	Punctuation	2	BTL 2
	ぐらい・くらい	X ぐらい・くらい	Sp. Exp.	about X	4	1
+	クラスメート	クラスメート	N	classmate	3	6
	クラブ	クラブ	N	club	3	1
+	くる	来る (IRR; 来た)	V	come	2	1
	くるま	車	N	car	5	4
	グルメ	グルメ	N	gourmet, connoisseur	6	6
+	グレー	グレー	N	gray	6	3
+	くろ	黒	N	black	6	3
+	くろい	黒い	Adj	black	3	5
	くん	NAME ～君	Sp. Exp.	[informal title]	6	1
	くんよみ	訓読み	N	Japanese-based readings of kanji	1	BTL 2
	けさ	今朝	N	this morning	4	4
+	けいご	敬語	N	politeness, polite language (BTS 10)	5	5
+	けいざい(がく)	経済(学)	N	economics	4	2
+	けいたい	携帯/ケータイ	N	cell phone, mobile phone	2	2
	けいたいをみないでください。	携帯を見ないでください。	Inst. Exp	Please don't look at your phone.	0	0
+	けいろうのひ	敬老の日	N	Respect for the Aged Day (BTS 18)	4	4

+	ケーキ	ケーキ	N	cake	2	3
+	けしゴム	消しゴム	N	(pencil) eraser	3	6
	けっこう	けっこう	Sp. Exp.	a fair amount	4	2
+	げつよう(び)	月曜(日)	N	Monday	4	6
	けど	～けど	S. Particle	but	2	4
+	ケニア	ケニア	N	Kenya	6	1
+	けれど(も)	～け(れ)ど(も)	S. Particle	but	2	4
	げんこうようし	原稿用紙	N	Japanese writing paper	1	BTL 5
+	げんごがく	言語学	N	linguistics	4	2
+	けんこくきねんび	建国記念日	N	Foundation Day (BTS 18)	4	4
+	けんじょうご	謙譲語	N	humble language (BTS 10)	5	5
	げんち	現地	N	the place, destination	3	4
+	けんぽうきねんび	憲法記念日	N	Constitution Day (BTS 18)	4	4
	こ	～個	Classifier	classifier for counting small objects	3	5
	ご	五・5	Numbers	5	3	2
	ここ	ここ	N	here	2	7
+	ごい	語彙	N	vocabulary	5	6
+	こうえん	公園	N	park	4	4
+	こうがく	工学	N	engineering	4	2
	こうかん	交換	N	exchange	6	4
+	こうこう	高校	N	high school	3	1
+	ごうしつ	～号室	Classifier	classifier for naming room number	4	5
+	こうじょう	工場	N	factory, workshop	5	4
+	こうちゃ	紅茶	N	black tea	2	3
+	こうはい	後輩	N	junior (BTS 30)	2	8
+	コーヒー	コーヒー	N	coffee	2	3
+	ごご	午後	N	afternoon, p.m.	3	4
	ございます	ございます (-ARU)	V	exists (polite form of あります) The ～て form and the informal forms are rarely used today.	5	5
	ごじゅうおんひょう	五十音表	N	Chart of Fifty Sounds	2	BTL 1
	ごぜん	午前	N	morning, a.m.	3	4
	ごぞんじだ↑	ご存知だ↑	Sp. Exp.	know (honorific)	6	6

	こたえてください。	答えてください。	Inst. Exp	Please answer.	0	0
	こたえてください。	PERSON に答えてください。	Inst. Exp	Please answer PERSON.	2	0
	ごちそうさま。	ごちそうさま。	Sp. Exp.	Thank you. (lit. 'It was a feast.')	1	6
+	ごちそうさまでした。	ごちそうさまでした。	Sp. Exp.	Thank you. (lit. 'It was a feast,' formal)	1	6
	こちら	こちら	N	here, this, in this general area, in this direction, this alternative (of two), the speaker's side of a telephone conversation, this person (polite)	2	4
	こちらこそ	こちらこそ	Sp. Exp.	(the pleasure/fault/etc.) is mine	1	10
	こっち	こっち	N	here, in this general area, in this direction, this alternative (of two)	2	7
	こと	こと	N	matter	4	4
+	ことし	今年	N	this year	4	4
+	こどものひ	こどもの日	N	Children's Day (BTS 18)	4	4
	ことわざ	ことわざ	N	words of wisdom	1	0
	この	この+ N	Sp. Exp.	this N	3	5
+	こばやし	小林	N	[family name]	3	9R
+	ごはん	ご飯	N	cooked rice or a meal	2	3
+	こまる	困る (-U; 困った)	V	be troubled; be bothered; be embarrassed	6	6
+	ゴルフ	ゴルフ	N	golf	3	4
+	これ	これ	N	this (thing)	2	1
+	これから	これから	N	from now	2	2
	ごろ	TIME+ごろ	Sp. Exp.	about [time]	3	2
+	こんがっき	今学期	N	this term	4	6
+	こんげつ	今月	N	this month	4	4
+	コンサート	コンサート	N	concert	4	4
+	こんしゅう	今週	N	this week	4	4
+	こんど	今度	N	this time, next time	3	4
	こんにちは。	こんにちは。	Day 1 Phrase	Hello.	0	0

+	こんばん	今晩	N	this evening	4	4
	こんばんは。	こんばんは。	Day1 Phrase	Good evening.	0	0
+	コンビニ	コンビニ	N	convenience store	2	5
	サークル	サークル	N	club	3	1
+	サーシャ	サーシャ	Name	Sasha [given name]	1	1
+	さいとう	斎藤	N	[family name]	3	9R
+	サイフ	サイフ (財布)	N	wallet	3	5
+	さかもと	坂本	Name	Sakamoto [family name]	1	1
	さかもとせんせい	坂本先生	Name	Prof./Dr. Sakamoto	1	1
+	さき	(お)先	N	ahead, previous	4	3
+	ささき	佐々木	N	[family name]	3	9R
	さすが	さすが (Noun)	Sp. Exp.	true to (your reputation), what I expected, etc.	6	6
+	さつ	～冊	Classifier	classifier for counting bound volumes	3	5
+	サッカー	サッカー	N	soccer	3	4
+	さっき	さっき	N	a while ago	4	4
+	さとう	佐藤	N	[family name]	3	9R
+	さよ(う)なら	さよ(う)なら	Sp. Exp.	goodbye (BTS 11)	1	5
	さん	NAME ～さん	Title	Mr/s. NAME	1	1
	さん	三・3	Numbers	3	3	2
	じ	～時	Classifier	classifier for naming hours on the clock	3	2
	し・よん	四・4	Numbers	4	3	2
	ジェーエルシー	JLC	N	JLC	3	1
+	じかん	時間	N	time	3	4
	じかん	～時間	Classifier	classifier for counting hours	4	6
	じこしょうかい	自己紹介(する)	N	self-introduction	6	1
+	しごと	(お)仕事 (する)	N	work, job	2	2
+	しごとする	仕事する	V	work	3	2
+	した	下	N	bottom, under	6	2
	しち・なな	七・7	Numbers	7	3	2
	しっている	知っている	V	know	6	6
	しつもん	質問(する)	N	(ask a) question	5	2

	しつれいします。	失礼します。	Sp. Exp.	Excuse me.	1	5
+	じてんしゃ	自転車	N	bicycle	4	5
	じはん	X時半	Sp. Exp.	half past (hour X) (2:30)	3	2
	しました	しました	V	did	4	3
+	しみず	清水	N	[family name]	3	9R
	じゃ	じゃ(あ)	Sp. Exp.	So. (informal)	1	9
	じゃあ	じゃあ	Sp. Exp.	well then,	2	8
+	シャーペン	シャーペン	N	mechanical pencil	3	3
+	しゃかいがく	社会学	N	sociology	4	2
	しゃしん	写真	N	photo	6	3
+	しゃちょう	社長	N	company president	6	5
	じゃね。	じゃ(あ)ね。	Sp. Exp.	See you later. (informal)	1	9
	じゃまた。	じゃまた。	Sp. Exp.	See you again. (informal)	1	9
	じゃまたね。	じゃまたね。	Sp. Exp.	See you again. (informal)	1	9
	じゅう	十　(10〜90)	Numbers	tens (10 through 90)	3	5
	じゅう	十・１０	Numbers	10	3	2
	じゅういち	十一・１１	Numbers	11	3	2
+	しゅうかん	〜週間	Classifier	classifier for counting weeks	4	6
+	しゅうかん	州	N	state, as in the US	6	1
	しゅうきょう(がく)	宗教(学)	N	religion (religious studies)	4	2
+	ジュース	ジュース	N	juice	2	3
	じゅうに	十二・１２	Numbers	12	3	2
+	しゅうぶんのひ	秋分の日	N	Autumnal Equinox (BTS 18)	4	4
+	しゅうまつ	週末	N	weekend	3	4
+	じゅぎょう	授業(する)	N	class	3	2
+	しゅくだい	宿題	N	homework	2	2
+	しゅくだいする	宿題する	V	do homework	3	2
+	しゅんぶんのひ	春分の日	N	Vernal Equinox (BTS 18)	4	4
+	しょう	省	N	provinces in China	6	1
+	しょうがつ	(お)正月	N	New Year's Day/Month (BTS 18)	4	4
+	じょうず	上手	N	skillful, good at	6	1

+	しょうわ	昭和	N	Showa era (1926–1989)	4	4
+	しょうわのひ	昭和の日	N	Showa Day (BTS 18)	4	4
	しょだん	初段	N	first or lowest rank black belt in martial arts, calligraphy, *shōgi*, *igo*, etc.	6	2
+	しょちょう	所長	N	head of a laboratory, research center	6	5
+	しらい	白井	Name	Shirai [family name]	1	1
	しらいです。	NAMEです。	Sp. Exp.	My name is NAME.	1	4
+	しる	知る (-U; 知った)	V	find out, know	6	6
	しろ	白	N	white	6	3
+	しろい	白い	Adj	white	3	5
	すき	(お)好き	N	liking, fondness, love	2	3
+	すいよう(び)	水曜(日)	N	Wednesday	4	6
	すうがく	数学	N	mathematics	4	2
+	スーパー	スーパー	N	supermarket	5	4
+	すぎ	過ぎ	N	after, past [time]	3	2
	すぐ	すぐ	N	soon, immediately, right away	5	1
	ずつ	一人ずつ	Sp. Exp.	one (person) at a time	6	2
	すごい	すごい	Adj	amazing	2	1
	すこし	少し	N	a little, a few	5	1
+	すし	(お)すし・寿司	N	sushi	2	3
+	すずき	鈴木	N	[family name]	3	9R
	すすめ	(お)勧め	N	recommendation, suggestion	6	6
	すすめる、Xに	Xに勧める・薦める (-RU; 勧めた・薦めた)	V	recommend to X, advise X, encourage X	6	6
+	スペインご	スペイン語	N	Spanish (language)	3	1
+	スペインじん	スペイン人	N	Spanish (person)	3	1
+	スポーツのひ	スポーツの日	N	Sports Day (BTS 18)	4	4
	スマホ	スマホ	N	smartphone	3	3
	すみません。	すみません・すいません。	Sp. Exp.	Excuse me. I'm sorry. Thank you.	1	3

+	すみませんでした。	すみませんでした・すいませんでした。	Sp. Exp.	Sorry. Thank you (for what has happened).	2	2
+	する	する (IRR; した)	V	do, play (a game or sport)	2	1
	する、Xに	Xにする	Sp. Exp.	decide on X	6	6
	すること	すること	N	something to do	2	8
+	すわる	座る(-U; 座った)	V	sit	6	3
	せ	背	N	back, spine, rear side	6	3
+	セールス	セールス	N	sales	6	2
+	せいじんのひ	成人の日	N	Coming of Age Day (BTS 18)	4	4
	せいぶつ	生物	N	biology	6	2
	せがたかいひと	背が高い人	Sp. Exp.	tall person/people	6	3
+	ぜひ	是非	Sp. Exp.	by all means	5	5
	ゼロ・まる・れい	ゼロ・まる・零	Numbers	zero	3	5
	せわ	(お)世話	N	help, aid, assistance	6	4
	せん・ぜん	千 (1000〜9000)	Numbers	thousands (1000 ~ 9000)	4	1
+	せんがっき	先学期	N	last semester	4	3
+	せんげつ	先月	N	last month	4	3
	せんこう	(ご)専攻(する)	N	major, field of study	4	2
+	せんじつ	先日	N	the other day	4	3
	せんしゅう	先週	N	last week	4	3
	せんせい	NAME 〜先生	Title	Prof./Dr. NAME	1	1
	ぜんぜん	全然	N	not at all, entirely	4	2
+	セント	〜セント	Classifier	cent	3	5
+	せんぱい	先輩	N	senior (BTS 30)	2	8
	ぜんぶ	全部	N	all, everything	5	3
+	ぜんぶで	全部でX	Sp. Exp.	X for everything; X all together	3	5
+	せんもん	(ご)専門	N	specialization, major	4	2
	せんりのみちもいっぽから	千里の道も一歩から	Kotowaza	A journey of a thousand miles begins with a single step.	2	0
	そう	そう	N	that way, so	2	5
	そう、そう。	そう、そう。	Sp. Exp.	Right, right; Yes, yes.	3	3
	そうか。	そうか。	Sp. Exp.	Is that so? (expression of awareness)	4	4

	そうしていただけ ますか?	そうしていただけま すか?	Sp. Exp.	Can I have you do that?	5	6
	そうしましょう。	そうしましょう。	Sp. Exp.	Let's do it that way.	4	5
+	そうだん	(ご)相談(する)	N	consultation	6	5
	そうだんする	Xに・と相談する	Sp. Exp.	consult with X	6	6
	そうですね(え)	そうですね(え)	Sp. Exp.	(hesitation)	2	7
	そうですねえ	そうですねえ	Sp. Exp.	(to express consideration) let's see	5	3
+	そこ	そこ	N	there (near you), that place just mentioned	2	7
+	そちら	そちら	N	there (near you), that (near you), in that general area, in that direction (in your direction), that alternative (of two near you), the other side of a telephone conversation, that person (polite)	2	4
+	そっち	そっち	N	there (near you), in that general area, in that direction (in your direction), that alternative (of two near you)	2	7
+	そと	外	N	outside	6	2
+	その	その+N	Sp. Exp.	that N	3	5
+	そば	そば	N	soba (buckwheat noodles)	2	3
	それ	それ	N	that (thing near you)	2	1
	それほど	それほど	Sp. Exp.	that much; to that extent	4	1
+	そんけいご	尊敬語	N	honorific language (BTS 10)	5	5
+	ぞんじる	存じる↓ (-U 存じた)	V	know, find out (humble)	6	6
	たい	Verb～たい	Adj	want to VERB	6	5
+	だいがく	大学	N	university, college	3	1
+	だいがく、X	X大学	N	X University, X College	3	1
+	だいがくいん	大学院	N	graduate school	3	1
+	たいしょう	大正	N	Taisho era (1912–1926)	4	4
	だいじょうぶ	大丈夫	N	fine, safe, all right	2	1

+	だいすき	大好き	N	very likeable, like very much	2	3
	たいへん	大変(な)	N	tough (to do), awful, terrible	4	3
	たかい	高い	Adj	expensive	2	7
	たかい(せが)	(背が)高い	Adj	tall (in stature)	6	3
+	たかはし	高橋	N	[family name]	3	9R
	だくおん	濁音	N	voiced consonant	5	BTL9
+	たくさん	たくさん	N	a lot, many	3	5
	だくてん	濁点	N	[diacritical marks]	2	BTL 4
	だけ	～だけ	Particle	just, only	4	2
	だす	出す (-U; 出した)	V	submit, take out (of a container), send out (mail)	5	2
	たすかる	助かる (-U; 助かった)	V	be helped, be saved, be rescued	5	4
	ただいま。	ただいま。	Sp. Exp.	I'm home; I'm back.	1	13
	たつ	立つ(-U; 立った)	V	stand	6	3
	たてがき	縦書き	N	vertical writing	1	BTL 3
+	たなか	田中	N	[family name]	3	9R
	たのむ	頼む (-U: 頼んだ)	V	order (at a restaurant, online, etc.), request	6	6
+	たべもの	食べ物	N	food	2	3
	たべる	食べる (-RU; 食べた)	V	eat	2	3
+	だめ	だめ(な)	N	bad, useless, problematic	3	4
	だれ	だれ・誰	N	who	2	6
	チーズ	チーズ	N	cheese	6	3
	チーズ!	チーズ!	Sp. Exp.	Cheese!	6	3
+	ちいさい	小さい	Adj	small	2	7
+	ちか	地下	N	basement, underground	4	5
+	ちかい	近い	Adj	close	2	7
	ちがう	違う(-U; 違った)	V	different from X	3	6
	ちがう・おなじ	(Xと)違う・同じ	Sp. Exp.	different from/same as X	3	6
+	ちかく	近く	N	nearby, vicinity, neighborhood	6	2
	ちかてつ	地下鉄	N	subway	5	4
	ちがわない	Xと違わない	Sp. Exp.	not different from X	6	6

+	チケット	チケット	N	ticket	3	5
+	ちゃいろ	茶色	N	brown	6	3
+	ちゅうごく	中国	N	China	6	1
+	ちゅうごくご	中国語	N	Chinese (language)	3	1
+	ちゅうごくじん	中国人	N	Chinese (person)	3	1
+	ちょう	兆	Numbers	trillions (BTS 4)	4	1
+	ちょう・ジャン	張	N	Zhang (Japanese pronunciation: Cho) [Chinese family name]	3	1
	ちょっと	ちょっと	Sp. Exp.	a little	2	2
	つ	〜つ	Classifier	classifier for counting items	5	3
	ついたち〜さんじゅういちにち	ついたち〜三十一日	Numbers	the first ~ the 31st	4	4
	ついて	N について	Sp. Exp.	with regard to N	6	5
	にごりてん	濁り点	N	[diacritical marks]	2	BTL 4
	つかう	使う(-U; 使った)	V	use	4	2
+	つぎ	次	N	next, following	3	4
+	つくる	作る(-U; 作った)	V	make	4	1
	って	〜って	Particle	[topic particle]	3	1
+	つまらない	つまらない	Adj	boring	2	7
+	つよい	強い	Adj	strong	5	6
	つれていく	連れて行く	V	take (a person) along	5	4
+	つれてくる	連れて来る	V	bring (a person) along	5	4
	で	〜で	Particle	by means of X	5	4
	で	PLACE で	Particle	[location of activity]	3	4
+	ティーシャツ	ティーシャツ	N	T-shirt	3	5
+	ていしょく	定食	N	set meal	6	6
+	ていねいご	丁寧語	N	formal language (BTS 10)	5	5
+	できる	できる (-RU; できた)	V	can do, become complete	2	1
+	でぐち	出口	N	exit	6	3
+	デザイン	デザイン(する)	N	design	6	2
+	テスト	テスト	N	test	2	2
+	てつだう	手伝う (-U; 手伝った)	V	helped	4	3
	テニス	テニス	N	tennis	3	4

	では	では	Sp. Exp.	Well then,	1	5
	では	では	Sp. Exp.	[written equivalent of じゃ]	4	7R
	でも	でも	Sp. Exp.	but, however, and yet	5	1
	でも　じゃなくても	X でも X じゃなくても	Sp. Exp.	whether it's X or not X	5	1
	でも　でも	X でも Y でも	Sp. Exp.	whether it's X or Y	5	1
	でる	出る(-RU; 出た)	V	go out, leave, attend (an event), appear, answer (the phone)	5	4
	てん	点(、)	N	point, dot	2	BTL 2
	でんしゃ	電車	N	train	5	4
	てんてん	点々	N	[diacritical marks]	2	BTL 4
+	てんのうたんじょうび	天皇誕生日	N	Emperor's Birthday (BTS 18)	4	4
+	てんのうへいか	天皇陛下	N	emperor (honorific) (BTS 18)	4	4
	でんわ	電話 (する)	N	telephone	2	2
+	でんわばんごう	(お)電話番号	N	telephone number (your telephone number)	6	4
	と	〜と(X と Y)	Particle	X and Y	3	2
	と	〜と(言います／申します↓／おっしゃいます↑)	Particle	[quotation particle]	6	2
+	ドイツ	ドイツ	N	Germany	6	1
+	トイレ	トイレ	N	toilet	2	5
	どう	どう	N	how	2	7
	どうぞ。	どうぞ。	Sp. Exp.	Go ahead.	1	2
	どうぞよろしく。	どうぞよろしく。	Sp. Exp.	Nice to meet you.	1	4
+	どうぞよろしくおねがいします。	どうぞよろしくお願いします。	Sp. Exp.	Nice to meet you.	1	4
	とうてん	読点	N	point, dot	2	BTL 2
	どうも。	どうも。	Sp. Exp.	Hello.	1	7
+	どうりょう	同僚	N	co-worker, colleague	3	6
+	とおい	遠い	Adj	far	2	7
	とか	〜とか	Particle	(things) like, such as	4	2

	とかも	〜とかも	Particle	also (things) like, such as	4	2
	ときはかねなり	時は金なり	Kotowaza	Time is money.	4	0
	どこ	どこ	N	where	2	7
	ところ	ところ	N	place	4	4
+	としょかん	図書館	N	library	3	4
+	どちら	どちら	N	where, which, which direction, which (of two), which person/who (polite)	2	4
+	どっち	どっち	N	where, which direction, which (of two)	2	7
+	とても	とても	Sp. Exp.	very	2	7
	どなた	どなた	N	who (polite)	2	6
+	となり	隣	N	next door, beside	6	2
+	どの	どの+N	Sp. Exp.	which N	3	5
+	ともだち	ともだち	N	friend	3	6
+	どよう(び)	土曜(日)	N	Saturday	4	6
	とる	取る(-U; 取った)	V	take (a class)	4	2
+	とる	撮る(-U; 撮った)	V	take (a photo)	6	3
+	ドル	〜ドル	Classifier	dollar(s) (U.S. currency)	3	5
+	どれ	どれ	N	which (thing)	2	1
	なあ	〜なあ	S. Particle	[sentence particle indicating shared agreement]	2	6
+	なか	中	N	inside	6	2
+	ながい	長い	Adj	long	5	5
	なかてん	中点(・)	N	raised period	2	BTL 2
+	なかむら	中村	N	[family name]	3	9R
+	なにいろ	何色	N	what color	6	3
	なにか	何か	Sp. Exp.	Something	6	5
	なにか・なんか	なにか・何か	Sp. Exp.	something	2	8
+	なにご	何語	N	which language?	3	1
+	なにじん	何人・なに人	N	what nationality	3	1
	なにも	何も	Sp. Exp.	nothing	6	6
+	なまえ	(お)名前	N	name (your name)	6	4
	なる	なる(-U; なった)	V	become	5	6

	なるべく	なるべく	Sp. Exp.	As . . . as possible	5	1
	なるほど	なるほど	Sp. Exp.	Oh, now I see.	3	1
	なん、なに	何 (なん)	N	what	2	3
	なんじ	何時	N	what time	3	2
	なんでしょう。	何でしょう。	Sp. Exp.	What? What could it be?	5	3
+	なんよう（び）	何曜(日)	N	what day (of the week)?	4	6
	に	〜に	Particle	to, towards X	5	4
	に	〜に	Particle	[inanimate location particle]	3	6
	に	TIME に	Particle	[point of time]	3	4
	に	二・2	Numbers	2	3	2
	にくい	使いにくい	Adj	hard to use	4	5
	にち・か	〜日	Classifier	classifier for naming the days of the month; Scene 4–6 naming and counting	4	4
+	にちよう（び）	日曜(日)	N	Sunday	4	6
+	にっけいじん	日系人	N	person of Japanese heritage	3	1
+	にほん	日本 (にほん・にっぽん)	N	Japan	6	1
	にほんがく	日本学	N	Japanese studies	4	2
	にほんご	日本語	N	Japanese (language)	3	1
	にほんごクラブ	日本語クラブ	N	Japanese Language Club	3	1
	にほんごではなしましょう。	日本語で話しましょう。	Inst. Exp	Let's speak in Japanese.	2	0
+	にほんじん・にっぽんじん	日本人	N	Japanese (person)	3	1
+	ニュース	ニュース	N	news	3	3
	にん・り	〜人	Classifier	[classifier for people]	6	2
	ね	〜ね	S. Particle	[sentence particle indicating agreement]	2	1
	ね?	〜ね?	Particle	[particle checking on whether the other person is following]	2	1
	ねえ	〜ねえ	S. Particle	[sentence particle assuming shared attitude/opinion]	2	3
	ねん	〜年	Classifier	classifier for naming the years; Scene 4-6 naming and counting the years	4	4

+	ねんかん	〜年間	Classifier	classifier for counting years	6	2
+	ねんせい	〜年生	Classifier	grade, class in school	6	1
	の	の	N	one(s)	3	5
+	ノート	ノート	N	notebook	3	5
	こと	X のこと	Sp. Exp.	it's a matter of X; it means X	3	1
+	のみもの	飲み物	N	drink	2	3
+	のむ	飲む・呑む (-U; 飲・呑んだ)	V	drink, swallow (i.e. medicine)	2	3
+	のる	乗る(-U; 乗った)	V	ride, get onboard	5	4
	は	〜は	Particle	[phrase particle indicating contrast]	2	6
	は	Xは	Particle	as for X	3	2
	はい、	はい、	Inst. Exp	Okay,	0	0
	はい。	はい。	Sp. Exp.	Present. (in roll call); Scene 1-2 Here you are. (handing something over); Scene 1-3 Got it. (accepting something)	1	1
	バイ。	バイ。	Sp. Exp.	Bye. (informal)	1	9
	はい、どうぞ。	はい、どうぞ。	Sp. Exp.	Here you go (take it, do it).	1	2
	バイバイ。	バイバイ。	Sp. Exp.	Bye-bye. (informal)	1	9
	はじめまして。	はじめまして。	Sp. Exp.	How do you do.	6	4
	はじめましょう。	始めましょう。	Inst. Exp	Let's begin.	0	0
+	はじめる	始める (-RU; 始めた)	V	begin (something)	2	2
	ばしょ	場所	N	place	4	4
+	バス	バス	N	bus	5	4
+	パソコン	パソコン	N	personal computer, laptop	3	6
	はち	八・8	Numbers	8	3	2
	はつか	20日	N	the twentieth day of the month	4	4
+	はっぴょう	発表	N	presentation	5	5
	はなし	(お)話	N	talk	6	5
+	はなす	話す(-U; 話した)	V	talk	3	4
	はやい	早い	Adj	early	3	4
+	はやし	林	N	[family name]	3	9R

	ばん	〜番	Classifier	classifier for naming the numbers (in a series)	4	4
+	ばん	晩	N	evening	3	4
	ばんきょうしつ	〜番教室	Classifier	classifier for naming a classroom numbers	4	5
	ばんごう	番号	N	number	6	4
+	ばんごはん	晩ごはん	N	dinner	2	3
+	ビール	ビール	N	beer	2	3
+	ひくい(せが)	(背が)低い	Adj	short (in stature)	6	3
+	ひだり	左	N	left	6	2
	ひと	人(ひと)	N	pcrson	6	3
	ひとこと	ひとこと	N	something (to say)	6	1
	ずっと	ずっと	Sp. Exp.	continuously, by far, the whole time	6	5
	ひとりずついって ください。	一人ずつ言ってくだ さい。	Inst. Exp	Please say it one at a time.	0	0
	ひゃく・びゃく・ ぴゃく	百 (100〜900)	Numbers	hundreds (100 through 900)	3	5
+	びょういん	病院	N	hospital	5	4
+	びょうき	病気	N	sick	3	2
	ひらがな	平仮名・ひらがな	N	hiragana syllabary	1	BTL 1
+	ひるごはん	(お)昼ごはん	N	lunch	2	3
+	ピンク	ピンク	N	pink	6	3
	ふうん	ふうん	Sp. Exp.	hmm	4	2
	フォント	フォント	N	font	4	5
	ふくざわだいがく	福沢大学	N	Fukuzawa University	3	1
	ふくしゅう	復習 (する)	N	review	5	6
+	ぶちょう	部長	N	division chief	3	6
+	ぶつり(がく)	物理(学)	N	physics	4	2
	ブライアン・ワン	ブライアン・ワン	Name	Brian Wang	1	1
	ブライアン?	ブライアン?	Sp. Exp.	(Is it/Are you) Brian?	1	7
+	ブラジル	ブラジル	N	Brazil	6	1
+	フランスご	フランス語	N	French (language)	3	1
+	フランスじん	フランス人	N	French (person)	3	1
	ふりがな	振り仮名	N	phonetic guide to reading	1	BTL 4

+	ふるい	古い	Adj	old	4	1
	プレゼン	プレゼン	N	presentation	5	5
	ふん・ぷん	〜分 (ふん・ぷん), 1分〜60分, 何分	Classifier	classifier for naming and counting minute(s)	3	4
+	ぶんがく	文学	N	literature	4	2
+	ぶんがくぶ	文学部	N	faculty of arts and humanities	6	1
+	ぶんかのひ	文化の日	N	Culture Day (BTS 18)	4	4
+	ふんかん・ぷんかん	〜分間	Classifier	classifier for counting minutes	6	2
+	ぶんぽう	文法	N	grammar	5	6
+	へ	〜へ	Particle	to, towards X	5	4
	ページ	〜ページ	Classifier	pages	5	2
+	へいき	平気	N	calm, unconcerned, all right	2	1
+	へいせい	平成	N	Heisei era (1989–2019)	4	4
	へえ	へえ	Sp. Exp.	oh, yes? really?	3	5
	へた	下手	N	unskillful, bad at	6	1
+	べつ	別	N	different, separate, distinct	6	6
	べつに	別に	Sp. Exp.	(not) particularly	2	8
	へや	部屋	N	room	4	5
+	ペン	ペン	N	pen	3	3
+	べんきょう	勉強 (する)	N	study	2	2
+	べんきょうする	勉強する	V	study	3	2
+	べんとう	(お)弁当	N	meal in a box	2	3
	ほか	他・外	N	other, else, besides	6	6
	ほう	方	N	way, alternative (of two)	6	3
+	ほうこく	(ご)報告(する)	N	report	6	5
+	ほうこくする	Xに報告する	Sp. Exp.	make a report to X	6	6
	ぼうせん	棒線	N	long vowel symbol	5	BTL2
	ホームステイ	ホームステイ	N	homestay	6	1
	ぼく	他	N	I (masculine)	1	7
	ぼく、いちろう。	僕、一郎。	Sp. Exp.	I'm Ichiro. (casual)	1	7
+	ポスター	ポスター	N	poster	4	1
+	ホテル	ホテル	N	hotel	4	4

	ほど	ほど	Particle	as much as [comparison particle]	6	6
	カレーほど〜ない	カレーほどすごくない	Sp. Exp.	not as awesome as curry	6	6
+	ほん	本	N	book	3	5
+	ほん・ぼん・ぽん	〜本	Classifier	classifier for counting long objects	3	5
	ほんとう	本当	N	true	4	3
+	ほんや	本屋	N	bookstore	5	4
	ほんをみないでください。	本を見ないでください。	Inst. Exp	Please don't look at the book.	0	0
	まあ	まあ	Sp. Exp.	I guess [Non-committal opinion]	3	1
+	マーケティング	マーケティング	N	marketing	6	2
	まあまあ	まあまあ	Sp. Exp.	so-so	4	1
+	まい	〜枚	Classifier	classifier for counting thin, flat things	3	5
	まいる	参る↓ (-U; 参った)	V	go, come (humble)	5	5
+	まえ	前	N	before [time]; Scene 6–3 front	3	2
	まかせてください。	任せてください。	Sp. Exp.	Leave it to me. Let someone do it.	5	3
	まかせる	任せる (-RU; 任せた)	V	leave it to someone else, let someone else do it	5	3
	また	また	Sp. Exp.	again	1	9
	まだ	まだ	Sp. Exp.	still, yet	6	1
+	またあとで	またあとで	Sp. Exp.	again later	3	4
+	まつ	待つ(-U; 待った)	V	wait	3	2
+	まつもと	松本	N	[family name]	3	9R
	まで	〜まで	Particle	up to, until	4	4
	まで	〜まで	Particle	as far as X	5	4
	までに	TIME〜までに	Particle	by TIME X	5	5
+	まど	窓	N	window	6	3
+	マネージャー	マネージャー	N	manager	6	2

まよう	迷う (-U; 迷った)	V	become confused, lost	6	6
まる	丸 (。)	N	circle, period	2	BTL 2
まん	万	Numbers	10,000s	4	1
+ まんなか	真ん中	N	middle	6	3
+ ミーティング	ミーティング	N	meeting	2	2
+ みえる	見える (-RU; 見えた)	V	appear, be visible	6	3
みぎ	右	N	right	6	2
みぎ、じゃなくひだり	右、じゃなく左	Sp. Exp.	right, I mean left	6	3
みぎからでいい	右からでいい	Sp. Exp.	from the right is good	6	2
みじかい	短い	Adj	short	5	5
+ みず	(お)水	N	water	2	3
+ みせ	店	N	store, shop	6	2
+ みせる	見せる (-RU; 見せた)	V	show	5	5
みてください。	見てください。	Inst. Exp	Please look at it.	2	0
みどり	緑	N	green	6	3
+ みどりのひ	緑の日	N	Green Day (BTS 18)	4	4
みなさん	みなさん	N	everyone (out group); Scene 6-1 (used in addressing a group)	3	7R
+ みる	見る (-RU; 見た)	V	look, watch	3	4
+ ミルク	ミルク	N	milk	2	3
+ みんな	みんな	N	everyone, all	3	4
+ みんなで	みんなで	Sp. Exp.	all together	3	4
みんなでいってください。	みんなで言ってください。	Inst. Exp	Please say it all together.	0	0
+ むこう	向こう	N	opposite side, other side, over there	6	2
+ むずかしい	難しい	Adj	hard, difficult	2	7
むずかしくなりました。	難しくなりました。	Sp. Exp.	It became difficult.	5	6
+ むらさき	紫	N	purple	6	3
め	～目	Classifier	classifier for naming numbers in a series	5	6

+	メキシコ	メキシコ	N	Mexico	6	1
	めいし	名刺	N	business card	6	4
+	めいじ	明治	N	Meiji era (1868–1912	4	4
+	メール	メール	N	email	6	4
	メンバー	メンバー	N	member	6	1
	も	〜も	Particle	also, too	3	6
	もう	もう	Sp. Exp.	already	6	1
	もういちどきいてください。	PERSON にもう一度聞いてください。	Inst. Exp	Please ask PERSON again.	2	0
	もういちまい	もう一枚	Sp. Exp.	one more sheet	6	3
	もういっかいいってください。	もう一回言ってください。	Inst. Exp	Please say it again.	0	0
	もうしわけありません。	申し訳ありません・ないです。	Sp. Exp.	I'm sorry.	5	3
+	もうしわけありませんでした。	申し訳ありませんでした・なかったです。	Sp. Exp.	I'm sorry (for what happened).	5	3
	もうしわけございません↓。	申し訳ございません↓。	Sp. Exp.	I am terribly sorry. (lit. 'I have no excuse.')	6	4
+	もうす	申す↓ (-U; 申した)	V	say (humble)	6	2
+	もうちょっと	もうちょっと	Sp. Exp.	a little more	6	3
+	もくよう(び)	木曜(日)	N	Thursday	4	6
	もちろん	もちろん	Sp. Exp.	of course	5	1
	もつ	持つ (-U)	V	hold, have, carry	5	3
+	もっていく	持っていく	V	take (a thing)	5	3
	もってきていただけますか?	持ってきていただけますか?	Sp. Exp.	Can I have you bring it?	5	3
	もってくる	持ってくる	V	bring (a thing)	5	3
	もっと	もっと	Sp. Exp.	more	6	3
	もっとおおきなこえではなしてください。	もっと大きな声で話してください。	Inst. Exp	Please talk louder.	0	0
	もの	もの	N	thing (tangible)	6	6
+	モリス	モリス	Name	Morris [family name]	1	1

	やぎ	八木	N	Yagi [family name] (Ms. Yagi is Sasha's supervisor)	1	11
+	やきとり	焼き鳥	N	yakitori	2	3
+	やさしい	易しい	Adj	easy	2	7
+	やすい	安い	Adj	inexpensive, cheap	2	7
	やすみ	(お)休み	N	day off, vacation	3	2
+	やすむ	休む (-U; 休んだ)	V	take a break, go on vacation/holiday	6	5
	やっぱり・やはり	やっぱり・やはり	Sp. Exp.	as expected, sure enough	3	2
+	やまぐち	山口	N	[family name]	3	9R
	やましたさん	山下さん	N	Mr/s. Yamashita	4	3
+	やまだ	山田	N	[family name]	3	9R
	やまもと	山本	N	[family name]	3	9R
	やる	やる (-U; やった)	V	do (less formal than する)	5	2
+	ゆうびんきょく	郵便局	N	post office	5	4
+	ゆき	雪	N	snow	3	6
	よ	～よ	S. Particle	[sentence particle indicating certainty]	2	2
	よう(び)	～曜(日)	Classifier	days of the week	4	6
	よかったら	よかったら	Sp. Exp.	if it's all right	2	3
	よくわかりません けど‥‥‥	よくわかりませんけ ど‥‥‥	Sp. Exp.	I'm not sure but . . .	3	6
	よこがき	横書き	N	horizontal writing	1	BTL 3
+	よしだ	吉田	N	[family name]	3	9R
	よしだうんそう	吉田運送	N	Yoshida Transport	6	4
+	よしゅう	予習(する)	N	prepare for a lesson	5	6
	よね	～よね	S. Particle	[sentence particle indicating shared certainty]	3	6
+	よびすて	呼び捨て	N	calling someone without a title (BTS 2)	1	1
	よぶ	呼ぶ (-U; 呼んだ)	V	call, invite	5	5
+	よみ	読み	N	reading	5	6
	よみかき	読み書き	N	reading and writing	5	6
+	よむ	読む (-U; 読んだ)	V	read	2	3
	より	より	Particle	compared to [comparison particle]	6	6

	よる	寄る(-U; 寄った)	V	get close to, drop by, lean on	6	3
	よろこぶ	喜ぶ(-U; 喜んだ)	V	be delighted, be pleased	5	5
	よろこんで	喜んで	Sp. Exp.	delighted	5	5
+	よろしい	よろしい	Adj	good (polite)	2	1
+	よろしかったら	よろしかったら	Sp. Exp.	if it's all right (polite)	2	3
	よろしく	よろしく	Sp. Exp.	thanks; please treat me favorably	2	1
	よろしくおねがいします。	よろしくお願いします。	Sp. Exp.	Nice to meet you.	1	4
	よろしければ	よろしければ	Sp. Exp.	if you would like, if it pleases you	5	5
	よわい	弱い	Adj	weak	5	6
	よんでください。	読んでください。	Inst. Exp	Please read it.	2	0
+	ラーメン	ラーメン	N	ramen (noodles)	2	3
+	らいがっき	来学期	N	next semester	4	4
+	らいげつ	来月	N	next month	4	4
+	らいしゅう	来週	N	next week	4	4
+	らいねん	来年	N	next year	4	4
	ランチ	ランチ	N	lunch, lunch special	6	6
	ランチよりカレーのほうがおすすめ	ランチよりカレーの方がお勧め	Sp. Exp.	curry rather than the special lunch is the recommendation	6	6
+	リーダー	リーダー	N	leader	6	2
+	りゅうがく	留学(する)	N	study abroad	6	1
+	りゅうがくせい	留学生	N	study abroad student	6	1
	りゅうがくせいセンター	留学生センター	N	International Student Center	6	1
+	りょう	寮	N	dormitory	2	5
	りょうかい	了解(する)	N	understanding, consent, agreement	5	1
+	ルームメート	ルームメート	N	roommate	3	6
+	るす	留守	N	away from home or work	6	5
	ルビ	ルビ	N	phonetic guide to reading	1	BTL 4
	れいごうごうにい、はちきゅうのななななにいれい	０５５２、８９の７７２０	Sp. Exp.	(0552) 89-7720	6	4
	れいじ	零時	Numbers	midnight (0 o'clock)	3	2
+	れいわ	令和	N	Reiwa era (2019-present	4	4

	れきし	歴史	N	history	4	2
+	レストラン	レストラン	N	restaurant	4	4
	レセプション	レセプション	N	reception	5	5
+	レポート	レポート	N	report	2	2
+	れんしゅう	練習（する）	N	practice, rehearse	5	6
	れんらく	（ご）連絡	N	contact, communication	4	4
+	れんらくさき	連絡先	N	contact information	6	4
	ろく	六・6	Numbers	6	3	2
+	ロシアご	ロシア語	N	Russian (language)	3	1
+	ロシアじん	ロシア人	N	Russian (person)	3	1
+	ロビー	ロビー	N	lobby	3	4
	わあ	わあ	Sp. Exp.	wow	2	3
	わかりました。	わかりました。	Sp. Exp.	Understood.	2	4
	わかる	わかる (-U; わかった)	V	understand	2	1
+	わたし	私	N	I (gentle)	1	7
+	わたなべ	渡辺	N	[family name]	3	9R
	わりと	わりと	Sp. Exp.	relatively	4	5

Appendix B: Japanese-English glossary by Act and Scene

List of abbreviations

N = Noun
V = Verb
Adj = Adjective
Sp. Exp. = Special Expressions

はい、	はい、	Inst. Exp	Okay,	0	0
はじめましょう。	始めましょう。	Inst. Exp	Let's begin.	0	0
きいてください。	聞いてください。	Inst. Exp	Please listen.	0	0
いってください。	言ってください。	Inst. Exp	Please say it.	0	0
こたえてください。	答えてください。	Inst. Exp	Please answer.	0	0
もういっかいいってください。	もう一回言ってください。	Inst. Exp	Please say it again.	0	0
みんなでいってください。	みんなで言ってください。	Inst. Exp	Please say it all together.	0	0
ひとりずついってください。	一人ずつ言ってください。	Inst. Exp	Please say it one at a time.	0	0
もっとおおきなこえではなしてください。	もっと大きな声で話してください。	Inst. Exp	Please talk louder.	0	0
ほんをみないでください。	本を見ないでください。	Inst. Exp	Please don't look at the book.	0	0
けいたいをみないでください。	携帯を見ないでください。	Inst. Exp	Please don't look at your phone.	0	0
かいてください。	書いてください。	Inst. Exp	Please write it.	0	0
おわります。	終わります。	Inst. Exp	That's all for today (used at the end of a class).	0	0
おはようございます。	おはようございます。	Day1 Phrase	Good morning. (formal)	0	0
こんにちは。	こんにちは。	Day1 Phrase	Hello.	0	0
こんばんは。	こんばんは。	Day1 Phrase	Good evening.	0	0

	ありがとうございました。	ありがとうございました。	Day1 Phrase	Thank you. (past, formal)	0	0
	いちごいちえ	一期一会	Kotowaza	'Once in a lifetime' or 'carpe diem' (seize the day).	1	0
	ことわざ	ことわざ	N	words of wisdom	1	0
	さかもとせんせい	坂本先生	Name	Prof./Dr. Sakamoto	1	1
	ブライアン・ワン	ブライアン・ワン	Name	Brian Wang	1	1
+	モリス	モリス	Name	Morris [family name]	1	1
+	サーシャ	サーシャ	Name	Sasha [given name]	1	1
+	かんだ	神田	Name	Mr/s. Kanda	1	1
+	しらい	白井	Name	Shirai [family name]	1	1
+	さかもと	坂本	Name	Sakamoto [family name]	1	1
	さん	NAME～さん	Title	Mr/s. NAME	1	1
		NAME～先生	Title	Prof./Dr. NAME	1	1
	はい。	はい。	Sp. Exp.	Present. (in roll call); Scene 1-2 Here you are. (handing something over); Scene 1-3 Got it. (accepting something)	1	1
+	ええ	ええ	Sp. Exp.	yes (suggesting agreement or indicating understanding; less formal than *hai*)	1	1
+	よびすて	呼び捨て	N	calling someone without a title (BTS 2)	1	1
	はい、どうぞ。	はい、どうぞ。	Sp. Exp.	Here you go (take it, do it).	1	2
	どうぞ。	どうぞ。	Sp. Exp.	Go ahead.	1	2
	ありがとうございます。	ありがとうございます。	Sp. Exp.	Thank you. (non-past, formal)	1	2
+	ありがとう。	ありがとう。	Sp. Exp.	Thank you. (non-past or past, informal)	1	2
	すみません。	すみません・すいません。	Sp. Exp.	Excuse me. I'm sorry. Thank you.	1	3
	おねがいします。	お願いします。	Sp. Exp.	please help me with this	1	3
	しらいです。	NAMEです。	Sp. Exp.	My name is NAME.	1	4
	どうぞよろしく。	どうぞよろしく。	Sp. Exp.	Nice to meet you.	1	4
	よろしくおねがいします。	よろしくお願いします。	Sp. Exp.	Nice to meet you.	1	4
+	どうぞよろしくおねがいします。	どうぞよろしくお願いします。	Sp. Exp.	Nice to meet you .	1	4
	では	では	Sp. Exp.	Well then,	1	5
	しつれいします	失礼します。	Sp. Exp.	Excuse me.	1	5
+	さよ(う)なら	さよ(う)なら	Sp. Exp.	goodbye (BTS 11)	1	5
	おはよう。	おはよう。	Day1 Phrase	Good morning. (informal)	1	6
	いただきます。	いただきます。	Sp. Exp.	I humbly receive. (eating ritual)	1	6
	ごちそうさま。	ごちそうさま。	Sp. Exp.	Thank you. (lit. 'It was a feast.')	1	6

+	ごちそうさまでした。	ごちそうさまでした。	Sp. Exp.	Thank you. (lit. 'It was a feast,' formal)	1	6
	ぼく	僕	N	I (masculine)	1	7
+	わたし	私	N	I (gentle)	1	7
+	あなた	あなた	N	you	1	7
	いちろう	一郎	N	[given name]	1	7
	ブライアン？	ブライアン？	Sp. Exp.	(Is it/Are you) Brian?	1	7
	どうも。	どうも。	Sp. Exp.	Hello.	1	7
	ぼく、いちろう 。	僕、一郎。	Sp. Exp.	I'm Ichiro. (casual)	1	7
	いちろうくん	一郎君	Sp. Exp.	Ichiro (addressing or referring to)	1	7
+	おれ	俺	N	I (masculine, informal) (BTS 15)	1	7
	いっていらっしゃい。	行って(い)らっしゃい。	Sp. Exp.	See you later. (lit. 'Go and come back.')	1	8
	いってきます 。	行ってきます。	Sp. Exp.	See you later. (lit. 'I'll go and come back.')	1	8
	じゃね。	じゃ(あ)ね。	Sp. Exp.	See you later. (informal)	1	9
	じゃ。	じゃ(あ)	Sp. Exp.	So. (informal)	1	9
	バイバイ。	バイバイ。	Sp. Exp.	Bye-bye. (informal)	1	9
	バイ。	バイ。	Sp. Exp.	Bye. (informal)	1	9
	じゃまた。	じゃまた。	Sp. Exp.	See you again. (informal)	1	9
	じゃまたね。	じゃまたね。	Sp. Exp.	See you again. (informal)	1	9
	また	また	Sp. Exp.	again	1	9
	あ、	あ、	Sp. Exp.	Oh	1	10
	かんださんですか？	神田さんですか？	Sp. Exp.	Are you Mr./Ms. Kanda?	1	10
	こちらこそ	こちらこそ	Sp. Exp.	(the pleasure/fault/etc.) is mine	1	10
	やぎ	八木	N	Yagi [family name] (Ms. Yagi is Sasha's supervisor)	1	11
	おつれさまです。	お疲れ様です。	Sp. Exp.	Good work. Hello.	1	11
	おつれさま。	お疲れ様。	Sp. Exp.	Good work. Hello. (informal)	1	11
	おさきにしつれいします。	お先に失礼します。	Sp. Exp.	I'll be leaving (ahead of you).	1	12
+	おさきに	お先に	Sp. Exp.	I'll be x-ing (ahead of you)	1	12
	おつれさまでした。	お疲れ様でした。	Sp. Exp.	Good work.	1	12
	えり	恵理	N	Eri [female given name] (Eri is Sasha's house mate)	1	13
	ただいま。	ただいま。	Sp. Exp.	I'm home; I'm back.	1	13
	おかえりなさい。	おかえりなさい。	Sp. Exp.	Welcome back.	1	13
	おやすみなさい。	おやすみなさい。	Sp. Exp.	Good night.	1	14
	かな	かな	N	syllabary	1	BTL 1
	ひらがな	平仮名・ひらがな	N	hiragana syllabary	1	BTL 1
	カタカナ	片仮名・カタカナ	N	katakana syllabary	1	BTL 1
	かんじ	漢字	N	kanji	1	BTL 1

	くんよみ	訓読み	N	Japanese-based readings of kanji	1	BTL 2
	おんよみ	音読み	N	Chinese-based readings of kanji	1	BTL 2
	たてがき	縦書き	N	vertical writing	1	BTL 3
	よこがき	横書き	N	horizontal writing	1	BTL 3
	ふりがな	振り仮名	N	phonetic guide to reading	1	BTL 4
	ルビ	ルビ	N	phonetic guide to reading	1	BTL 4
	げんこうようし	原稿用紙	N	Japanese writing paper	1	BTL 5
	せんりのみちもいっぽから	千里の道も一歩から	Kotowaza	A journey of a thousand miles begins with a single step.	2	0
	いってください。	PERSON に言ってください。	Inst. Exp	Please say it to PERSON.	2	0
	きいてください。	PERSON に聞いてください。	Inst. Exp	Please ask PERSON.	2	0
	もういちどきいてください。	PERSON にもう一度聞いてください。	Inst. Exp	Please ask PERSON again.	2	0
	こたえてください。	PERSON に答えてください。	Inst. Exp	Please answer PERSON.	2	0
	にほんごではなしましょう。	日本語で話しましょう。	Inst. Exp	Let's speak in Japanese.	2	0
	よんでください。	読んでください。	Inst. Exp	Please read it.	2	0
	みてください。	見てください。	Inst. Exp	Please look at it.	2	0
	がんばりましょう。	頑張りましょう。	Inst. Exp	Do your best.	2	0
	それ	それ	N	that (thing near you)	2	1
+	これ	これ	N	this (thing)	2	1
+	あれ	あれ	N	that (thing over there)	2	1
+	どれ	どれ	N	which (thing)	2	1
	だいじょうぶ	大丈夫	N	fine, safe, all right	2	1
+	へいき	平気	N	calm, unconcerned, all right	2	1
	わかる	わかる (-U; わかった)	V	understand	2	1
+	できる	できる (-RU; できた)	V	can do, become complete	2	1
+	する	する (IRR; した)	V	do, play (a game or sport)	2	1
+	くる	来る (IRR; 来た)	V	come	2	1
	がんばる	頑張る (-U; 頑張った)	V	will do my best	2	1
	すごい	すごい	Adj	amazing	2	1
+	いい	いい	Adj	good	2	1
+	よろしい	よろしい	Adj	good (polite)	2	1
	ね	～ね	S. Particle	[sentence particle indicating agreement]	2	1
	か?	～か?	S. Particle	[question particle]	2	1
	ね?	～ね?	Particle	[particle checking on whether the other person is following]	2	1

320

	はい	はい	Sp. Exp.	yes; here you are	2	1
	ええ	ええ	Sp. Exp.	yes (casual)	2	1
	いえいえ	いえいえ	Sp. Exp.	no, no	2	1
+	いえ	いえ	Sp. Exp.	no	2	1
+	いいえ	いいえ	Sp. Exp.	no	2	1
	よろしく	よろしく	Sp. Exp.	thanks; please treat me favorably	2	1
	いま	今	N	now	2	2
+	きょう	きょう・今日	N	today	2	2
+	あした	あした・明日	N	tomorrow	2	2
+	これから	これから	N	from now	2	2
	でんわ	電話 (する)	N	telephone	2	2
+	けいたい	携帯/ケータイ	N	cell phone, mobile phone	2	2
+	べんきょう	勉強 (する)	N	study	2	2
+	しごと	(お)仕事 (する)	N	work, job	2	2
+	しゅくだい	宿題	N	homework	2	2
+	テスト	テスト	N	test	2	2
+	レポート	レポート	N	report	2	2
+	きょうかしょ	教科書	N	textbook	2	2
+	ミーティング	ミーティング	N	meeting	2	2
+	いく	行く(-U; 行った)	V	go	2	2
+	いる	いる(-RU; いた)	V	be, exist (animate)	2	2
+	かく	書く(-U; 書いた)	V	write	2	2
+	はじめる	始める(-RU; 始めた)	V	begin (something)	2	2
+	おわる	終わる(-U; 終わった)	V	end	2	2
	よ	～よ	S. Particle	[sentence particle indicating certainty]	2	2
	あのう	あのう	Sp. Exp.	umm (hesitation noise)	2	2
	ええと	ええと	Sp. Exp.	uhh (hesitation noise)	2	2
+	すみませんでした。	すみませんでした・すいませんでした。	Sp. Exp.	Sorry/thank you (for what has happened).	2	2
	ちょっと	ちょっと	Sp. Exp.	a little	2	2
	あとで	あとで	Sp. Exp.	later	2	2
	すき	(お)好き	N	liking, fondness, love	2	3
+	だいすき	大好き	N	very likeable, like very much	2	3
	なん、なに	何 (なん)	N	what	2	3
	クッキー	クッキー	N	cookie	2	3
+	ケーキ	ケーキ	N	cake	2	3
+	ごはん	ご飯	N	cooked rice or a meal	2	3
+	あさごはん	朝ごはん	N	breakfast	2	3
+	ひるごはん	(お)昼ごはん	N	lunch	2	3
+	ばんごはん	晩ごはん	N	dinner	2	3
+	べんとう	(お)弁当	N	meal in a box	2	3
+	すし	(お)すし・寿司	N	sushi	2	3
+	やきとり	焼き鳥	N	yakitori	2	3
+	うどん	うどん	N	udon (wheat noodles)	2	3

+	そば	そば	N	soba (buckwheat noodles)	2	3
+	カレーライス	カレーライス	N	curry rice	2	3
+	ラーメン	ラーメン	N	ramen (noodles)	2	3
+	おちゃ	お茶	N	tea	2	3
+	みず	（お）水	N	water	2	3
+	ビール	ビール	N	beer	2	3
+	ウーロンちゃ	ウーロン茶	N	oolong tea	2	3
+	こうちゃ	紅茶	N	black tea	2	3
+	コーヒー	コーヒー	N	coffee	2	3
+	ミルク	ミルク	N	milk	2	3
+	ジュース	ジュース	N	juice	2	3
+	たべもの	食べ物	N	food	2	3
+	のみもの	飲み物	N	drink	2	3
+	くすり	（お）薬	N	medicine	2	3
	おいしそう	おいしそう	N	look(s) delicious	2	3
+	おもしろそう	おもしろそう	N	look(s) interesting	2	3
+	きれい	きれい（な）	N	pretty, clean	2	3
	たべる	食べる (-RU; 食べた)	V	eat	2	3
+	のむ	飲む・呑む(-U; 飲・呑んだ)	V	drink, swallow (i.e. medicine)	2	3
	いただく	いただく↓(-U; いただいた)	V	eat; receive (humble)	2	3
+	よむ	読む(-U; 読んだ)	V	read	2	3
	おいしい	おいしい	Adj	delicious	2	3
	おもしろい	おもしろい	Adj	interesting	2	3
	ねえ	～ねえ	S. Particle	[sentence particle assuming shared attitude/opinion]	2	3
	わあ	わあ	Sp. Exp.	wow	2	3
	え?	え?	Sp. Exp.	what?	2	3
	よかったら	よかったら	Sp. Exp.	if it's all right	2	3
+	よろしかったら	よろしかったら	Sp. Exp.	if it's all right (polite)	2	3
	こちら	こちら	N	here, this, in this general area, in this direction, this alternative (of two), the speaker's side of a telephone conversation, this person (polite)	2	4
+	そちら	そちら	N	there (near you), that (near you), in that general area, in that direction (in your direction), that alternative (of two near you), the other side of a telephone conversation, that person (polite)	2	4

+	あちら	あちら	N	there (away from both of us), that thing (away from both of us), in that direction (away from both of us), that alternative (of two away from both of us), that place (that we both know about), that person over there (polite)	2	4
+	どちら	どちら	N	where, which, which direction, which (of two), which person/who (polite)	2	4
	いそがしい	（お）忙しい	Adj	busy	2	4
	けど	〜けど	S. Particle	but	2	4
+	が	〜が	S. Particle	but, and	2	4
+	けれど(も)	〜け(れ)ど(も)	S. Particle	but	2	4
	いや	いや	Sp. Exp.	no (informal); uhh (hesitation noise)	2	4
	わかりました。	わかりました。	Sp. Exp.	Understood.	2	4
	かいしゃ	会社	N	office, company	2	5
+	がっこう	学校	N	school	2	5
+	うち	うち	N	house, home	2	5
+	いえ	いえ・家	N	house, home	2	5
+	おたく	お宅	N	home (polite)	2	5
+	りょう	寮	N	dormitory	2	5
+	アパート	アパート	N	apartment	2	5
+	コンビニ	コンビニ	N	convenience store	2	5
+	えき	駅	N	train station	2	5
+	トイレ	トイレ	N	toilet	2	5
	そう	そう	N	that way, so	2	5
	どなた	どなた	N	who (polite)	2	6
	だれ	だれ・誰	N	who	2	6
	かなあ	〜かなあ	S. Particle	[sentence particle indicating a shared question]	2	6
	なあ	〜なあ	S. Particle	[sentence particle indicating shared agreement]	2	6
	は	〜は	Particle	[phrase particle indicating contrast]	2	6
	ここ	ここ	N	here	2	7
+	そこ	そこ	N	there (near you), that place just mentioned	2	7
+	あそこ	あそこ	N	over there, there (away from both of us), that place (that we both know about)	2	7
	どこ	どこ	N	Where	2	7

	どう	どう	N	how	2	7
	こっち	こっち	N	here, in this general area, in this direction, this alternative (of two)	2	7
+	そっち	そっち	N	there (near you), in that general area, in that direction (in your direction), that alternative (of two near you)	2	7
+	あっち	あっち	N	there (away from both of us), in that direction (away from both of us), that alternative (of two away from both of us), that place (that we both know about)	2	7
+	どっち	どっち	N	where, which direction, which (of two)	2	7
	たかい	高い	Adj	expensive	2	7
+	やすい	安い	Adj	inexpensive, cheap	2	7
+	おおきい	大きい	Adj	big	2	7
+	ちいさい	小さい	Adj	small	2	7
+	とおい	遠い	Adj	far	2	7
+	ちかい	近い	Adj	close	2	7
+	むずかしい	難しい	Adj	hard, difficult	2	7
+	やさしい	易しい	Adj	easy	2	7
+	つまらない	つまらない	Adj	boring	2	7
	う～ん	う～ん	Sp. Exp.	well (hesitation)	2	7
	そうですね(え)	そうですね(え)	Sp. Exp.	(hesitation)	2	7
	ああ	ああ	Sp. Exp.	ahh, oh	2	7
+	とても	とても	Sp. Exp.	very	2	7
	すること	すること	N	something to do	2	8
	ある	ある(-U;あった;ない)	V	exist (inanimate)	2	8
	なにか・なんか	なにか・何か	Sp. Exp.	something	2	8
	べつに	別に	Sp. Exp.	(not) particularly	2	8
	じゃあ	じゃあ	Sp. Exp.	well then,	2	8
+	せんぱい	先輩	N	senior (BTS 30)	2	8
+	こうはい	後輩	N	junior (BTS 30)	2	8
	ごじゅうおんひょう	五十音表	N	Chart of Fifty Sounds	2	BTL 1
	くとうてん	句読点	N	punctuation	2	BTL 2
	くてん	句点	N	phrase point, comma	2	BTL 2
	とうてん	読点	N	point, dot	2	BTL 2
	てん	点(、)	N	point, dot	2	BTL 2
	まる	丸(。)	N	circle, period	2	BTL 2
	なかてん	中点(・)	N	raised period	2	BTL 2
	だくてん	濁点	N	[diacritical marks]	2	BTL 4
	にごりてん	濁り点	N	[diacritical marks]	2	BTL 4

てんてん	点々	N	[diacritical marks]	2	BTL	4
いそがばまわれ	急がば回れ	Kotowaza	More haste, less speed. (lit. 'If you are in a hurry, go the long way.')	3	0	
ジェーエルシー	JLC	N	JLC	3	1	
ふくざわだいがく	福沢大学	N	Fukuzawa University	3	1	
+ だいがく	大学	N	university, college	3	1	
+ だいがく、X	X大学	N	X University, X College	3	1	
+ こうこう	高校	N	high school	3	1	
+ だいがくいん	大学院	N	graduate school	3	1	
+ おおがきしょうかい	大垣商会	N	Ogaki Trading Company, Ltd.	3	1	
+ アオイしゅっぱん	アオイ出版	N	Aoi Publishing	3	1	
にほんご	日本語	N	Japanese (language)	3	1	
+ えいご	英語	N	English (language)	3	1	
+ ちゅうごくご	中国語	N	Chinese (language)	3	1	
+ かんこくご	韓国語	N	Korean (language)	3	1	
+ フランスご	フランス語	N	French (language)	3	1	
+ スペインご	スペイン語	N	Spanish (language)	3	1	
+ ロシアご	ロシア語	N	Russian (language)	3	1	
+ なにご	何語	N	which language	3	1	
がくせい	学生	N	student	3	1	
サークル	サークル	N	club	3	1	
+ かい	~会	N	organization, club, association, group	3	1	
クラブ	クラブ	N	club	3	1	
にほんごクラブ	日本語クラブ	N	Japanese Language Club	3	1	
+ ちょう・ジャン	張	N	Zhang (Japanese pronunciation: Choo) [Chinese family name]	3	1	
+ にほんじん・にっぽんじん	日本人	N	Japanese (person)	3	1	
+ アメリカじん	アメリカ人	N	American (person)	3	1	
+ ちゅうごくじん	中国人	N	Chinese (person)	3	1	
+ かんこくじん	韓国人	N	Korean (person)	3	1	
+ フランスじん	フランス人	N	French (person)	3	1	
+ スペインじん	スペイン人	N	Spanish (person)	3	1	
+ ロシアじん	ロシア人	N	Russian (person)	3	1	
+ なにじん	何人・なに人	N	what nationality	3	1	
+ にっけいじん	日系人	N	person of Japanese heritage	3	1	
+ がいこくじん	外国人	N	foreigner	3	1	
+ がいじん	外人	N	foreigner (can be derogatory)	3	1	
いう	いう・言う(-U; 言った)	V	is called, say	3	1	
って	~って	Particle	[topic particle]	3	1	
こと	X のこと	Sp. Exp.	it's a matter of X; it means X	3	1	

	なるほど	なるほど	Sp. Exp.	Oh, now I see.	3	1
	まあ	まあ	Sp. Exp.	I guess [Non-committal opinion]	3	1
	なんじ	何時	N	what time	3	2
+	まえ	前	N	before [time]	3	2
+	すぎ	過ぎ	N	after, past [time]	3	2
+	じゅぎょう	授業	N	class	3	2
+	かいぎ	会議	N	meeting	3	2
+	やすみ	(お)休み	N	day off, vacation	3	2
+	びょうき	病気	N	sick	3	2
+	かえる	帰る(-U; 帰った)	V	return [home]	3	2
+	まつ	待つ(-U; 待った)	V	wait	3	2
+	べんきょうする	勉強する	V	study	3	2
+	しごとする	仕事する	V	work	3	2
+	しゅくだいする	宿題する	V	do homework	3	2
+	じゅぎょうする	授業する	V	conduct a class	3	2
+	かいぎする	会議する	V	hold a meeting	3	2
	れいじ	零時	Numbers	midnight (0 o'clock)	3	2
	いち	一・1	Numbers	1	3	2
	に	二・2	Numbers	2	3	2
	さん	三・3	Numbers	3	3	2
	し・よん	四・4	Numbers	4	3	2
	ご	五・5	Numbers	5	3	2
	ろく	六・6	Numbers	6	3	2
	しち・なな	七・7	Numbers	7	3	2
	はち	八・8	Numbers	8	3	2
	きゅう・く	九・9	Numbers	9	3	2
	じゅう	十・10	Numbers	10	3	2
	じゅういち	十一・11	Numbers	11	3	2
	じゅうに	十二・12	Numbers	12	3	2
	と	〜と(XとY)	Particle	X and Y	3	2
	は	Xは	Particle	as for X	3	2
	じ	〜時	Classifier	classifier for naming hours on the clock	3	2
	やっぱり・やはり	やっぱり・やはり	Sp. Exp.	as expected, sure enough	3	2
	ごろ	TIME +ごろ	Sp. Exp.	about [time]	3	2
	じはん	X時半	Sp. Exp.	half past (hour X) (2:30)	3	2
	スマホ	スマホ	N	smartphone	3	3
+	えんぴつ	鉛筆	N	pencil	3	3
+	ペン	ペン	N	pen	3	3
+	シャーペン	シャーペン	N	mechanical pencil	3	3
+	アプリ	アプリ	N	app, application	3	3
+	ニュース	ニュース	N	news	3	3
	そう、そう。	そう、そう。	Sp. Exp.	Right, right; Yes, yes.	3	3
	がいらいご	外来語	N	loan words (BTS 14)	3	3
+	じかん	時間	N	time	3	4
	あさって	あさって	N	day after tomorrow	3	4

Appendix B

326

+	こんど	今度	N	this time, next time	3	4
+	つぎ	次	N	next, following	3	4
+	しゅうまつ	週末	N	weekend	3	4
	ごぜん	午前	N	morning, a.m.	3	4
+	ごご	午後	N	afternoon, p.m.	3	4
+	あさ	朝	N	morning	3	4
+	ばん	晩	N	evening	3	4
+	だめ	だめ (な)	N	bad, useless, problematic	3	4
	いっしょ	一緒	N	together	3	4
+	みんな	みんな	N	everyone, all	3	4
	テニス	テニス	N	tennis	3	4
+	ゴルフ	ゴルフ	N	golf	3	4
+	サッカー	サッカー	N	soccer	3	4
	げんち	現地	N	the place, destination	3	4
+	としょかん	図書館	N	library	3	4
+	ロビー	ロビー	N	lobby	3	4
+	はなす	話す (-U; 話した)	V	talk	3	4
+	あう	会う (-U; 会った)	V	see, meet	3	4
+	みる	見る (-RU; 見た)	V	look, watch	3	4
	はやい	早い	Adj	early	3	4
+	おそい	遅い	Adj	late	3	4
	で	PLACE で	Particle	[location of activity]	3	4
	に	TIME に	Particle	[point of time]	3	4
	ふん・ぷん	〜分 (ふん・ぷん), 1 分〜60分, 何分	Classifier	classifier for naming and counting minute(s)	3	4
+	みんなで	みんなで	Sp. Exp.	all together	3	4
+	またあとで	またあとで	Sp. Exp.	again later	3	4
	オッケー	オッケー	Sp. Exp.	okay	3	4
	おもいやり	思いやり	N	consideration	3	4
	ゼロ・まる・れい	ゼロ・まる・零	Numbers	zero	3	5
	じゅう	十 (10〜90)	Numbers	tens (10 through 90)	3	5
	ひゃく・びゃく・ぴゃく	百 (100〜900)	Numbers	hundreds (100 through 900)	3	5
	の	の	N	one(s)	3	5
+	サイフ	サイフ (財布)	N	wallet	3	5
+	チケット	チケット	N	ticket	3	5
+	ティーシャツ	ティーシャツ	N	T-shirt	3	5
+	ほん	本	N	book	3	5
+	ノート	ノート	N	notebook	3	5
	いくら	いくら	N	how much	3	5
+	たくさん	たくさん	N	a lot, many	3	5
	あかい	赤い	Adj	red	3	5
+	あおい	青い	Adj	blue	3	5
+	くろい	黒い	Adj	black	3	5
+	しろい	白い	Adj	white	3	5
	かわいい	かわいい	Adj	cute	3	5
	へえ	へえ	Sp. Exp.	oh, yes? really?	3	5

+	ぜんぶで	全部でX	Sp. Exp.	X for everything; X all together	3	5
	あかいの	赤いの	Sp. Exp.	the red one	3	5
	この	この+ N	Sp. Exp.	this N	3	5
+	その	その+ N	Sp. Exp.	that N	3	5
+	あの	あの+ N	Sp. Exp.	that N over there	3	5
+	どの	どの + N	Sp. Exp.	which N	3	5
	えん	～円	Classifier	yen (Japanese currency)	3	5
+	ドル	～ドル	Classifier	dollar(s) (U.S. currency)	3	5
+	セント	～セント	Classifier	cent	3	5
+	こ	～個	Classifier	classifier for counting small objects	3	5
+	まい	～枚	Classifier	classifier for counting thin, flat things	3	5
+	ほん・ぼん・ぽん	～本	Classifier	classifier for counting long objects	3	5
+	さつ	～冊	Classifier	classifier for counting bound volumes	3	5
	かさ	傘	N	umbrella	3	6
+	かばん	かばん	N	bag, briefcase	3	6
+	けしゴム	消しゴム	N	(pencil) eraser	3	6
+	パソコン	パソコン	N	personal computer, laptop	3	6
+	かみ	紙	N	paper	3	6
+	ともだち	ともだち	N	friend	3	6
+	ぶちょう	部長	N	division chief	3	6
+	どうりょう	同僚	N	co-worker, colleague	3	6
+	クラスメート	クラスメート	N	classmate	3	6
+	ルームメート	ルームメート	N	roommate	3	6
	あめ	雨	N	rain	3	6
+	ゆき	雪	N	snow	3	6
+	おなじ	同じ	N	same	3	6
	ちがう	違う(-U; 違った)	V	different from X	3	6
	に	～に	Particle	[inanimate location particle]	3	6
	も	～も	Particle	also, too	3	6
	よね	～よね	S. Particle	[sentence particle indicating shared certainty]	3	6
	よくわかりません けど……	よくわかりません けど……	Sp. Exp.	I'm not sure but . . .	3	6
	ちがう・おなじ	(Xと)違う・同じ	Sp. Exp.	different from/same as X	3	6
	みなさん	みなさん	N	everyone (out group)	3	7R
+	さとう	佐藤	N	[family name]	3	9R
+	すずき	鈴木	N	[family name]	3	9R
+	たかはし	高橋	N	[family name]	3	9R
+	たなか	田中	N	[family name]	3	9R

+	いとう	伊藤	N	[family name]	3	9R
+	わたなべ	渡辺	N	[family name]	3	9R
+	やまもと	山本	N	[family name]	3	9R
+	なかむら	中村	N	[family name]	3	9R
+	こばやし	小林	N	[family name]	3	9R
+	かとう	加藤	N	[family name]	3	9R
+	よしだ	吉田	N	[family name]	3	9R
+	やまだ	山田	N	[family name]	3	9R
+	ささき	佐々木	N	[family name]	3	9R
+	やまぐち	山口	N	[family name]	3	9R
+	まつもと	松本	N	[family name]	3	9R
+	いのうえ	井上	N	[family name]	3	9R
+	きむら	木村	N	[family name]	3	9R
+	はやし	林	N	[family name]	3	9R
+	さいとう	斎藤	N	[family name]	3	9R
+	しみず	清水	N	[family name]	3	9R
	ときはかねなり	時は金なり	Kotowaza	Time is money.	4	0
+	ポスター	ポスター	N	poster	4	1
	せん・ぜん	千 (1000〜9000)	Numbers	thousands (1000 ~ 9000)	4	1
	まん	万	Numbers	10,000s	4	1
+	つくる	作る (-U; 作った)	V	make	4	1
+	かう	買う (-U; 買った)	V	buy	4	1
+	あたらしい	新しい	Adj	new	4	1
+	ふるい	古い	Adj	old	4	1
	それほど	それほど	Sp. Exp.	that much; to that extent	4	1
	まあまあ	まあまあ	Sp. Exp.	so-so	4	1
	ぐらい・くらい	X ぐらい・くらい	Sp. Exp.	about X	4	1
+	おく	億	Numbers	hundred millions (BTS 4)	4	1
+	ちょう	兆	Numbers	trillions (BTS 4)	4	1
	せんこう	(ご)専攻(する)	N	major field of study	4	2
+	せんもん	(ご)専門	N	specialization, major	4	2
	すうがく	数学	N	mathematics	4	2
	れきし	歴史	N	history	4	2
	にほんがく	日本学	N	Japanese studies	4	2
	しゅうきょう(がく)	宗教(学)	N	religion (religious studies)	4	2
+	しゃかいがく	社会学	N	sociology	4	2
+	けいざい(がく)	経済(学)	N	economics	4	2
+	ぶんがく	文学	N	literature	4	2
+	げんごがく	言語学	N	linguistics	4	2
+	こうがく	工学	N	engineering	4	2
+	ぶつり(がく)	物理(学)	N	physics	4	2
	ぜんぜん	全然	N	not at all, entirely	4	2
	つかう	使う (-U; 使った)	V	use	4	2
	とる	取る (-U; 取った)	V	take (a class)	4	2
	とか	〜とか	Particle	(things) like, such as	4	2
	とかも	〜とかも	Particle	also (things) like, such as	4	2

	だけ	～だけ	Particle	just, only	4	2
	ふうん	ふうん	Sp. Exp.	hmm	4	2
	けっこう	けっこう	Sp. Exp.	a fair amount	4	2
+	あまり・あんまり	あまり・あんまり + negative	Sp. Exp.	not very much	4	2
+	あと	あと	Sp. Exp.	lastly, remaining, and then	4	2
	あいまい	曖昧(な)	N	ambiguity (BTS 12)	4	2
	いつ	いつ	N	when?	4	3
	せんしゅう	先週	N	last week	4	3
+	きのう	きのう	N	yesterday	4	3
+	おととい	おととい	N	the day before yesterday	4	3
+	せんげつ	先月	N	last month	4	3
+	せんがっき	先学期	N	last semester	4	3
+	せんじつ	先日	N	the other day	4	3
+	きょねん	去年	N	last year	4	3
+	さき	(お)先	N	ahead, previous	4	3
	ほんとう	本当	N	true	4	3
	たいへん	大変(な)	N	tough (to do), awful, terrible	4	3
	やましたさん	山下さん	N	Mr/s. Yamashita	4	3
	しました	しました	V	did	4	3
+	かんがえる	考える (-RU; 考えた)	V	think about, consider	4	3
+	てつだう	手伝う (-U; 手伝った)	V	helped	4	3
	が	～が	Particle	[subject particle]	4	3
	れんらく	(ご)連絡	N	contact, communication	4	4
+	イベント	イベント	N	event	4	4
+	コンサート	コンサート	N	concert	4	4
	こと	こと	N	matter	4	4
	ばしょ	場所	N	place	4	4
	ところ	ところ	N	place	4	4
	いつも	いつも	N	always, usual(ly)	4	4
	かいぎしつ	会議室	N	meeting room	4	4
+	きょうしつ	教室	N	classroom	4	4
+	レストラン	レストラン	N	restaurant	4	4
+	カフェ	カフェ	N	café	4	4
+	ホテル	ホテル	N	hotel	4	4
+	こうえん	公園	N	park	4	4
+	らいげつ	来月	N	next month	4	4
+	こんげつ	今月	N	this month	4	4
+	こんしゅう	今週	N	this week	4	4
+	らいしゅう	来週	N	next week	4	4
+	ことし	今年	N	this year	4	4
+	らいねん	来年	N	next year	4	4
+	らいがっき	来学期	N	next semester	4	4

+	めいじ	明治	N	Meiji era (1868–1912)	4	4
+	たいしょう	大正	N	Taisho era (1912–1926)	4	4
+	しょうわ	昭和	N	Showa era (1926–1989)	4	4
+	へいせい	平成	N	Heisei era (1989–2019)	4	4
+	れいわ	令和	N	Reiwa era (2019-present)	4	4
	けさ	今朝	N	this morning	4	4
+	こんばん	今晩	N	this evening	4	4
+	さっき	さっき	N	a while ago	4	4
	はつか	２０日	N	the twentieth day of the month	4	4
	きく	聞く (-U; 聞いた)	V	hear; listen	4	4
	から	～から	Particle	from (starting point)	4	4
	まで	～まで	Particle	up to, until	4	4
	にち・か	～日	Classifier	classifier for naming the day of the month	4	4
	ついたち～さんじゅういちにち	ついたち～三十一日	Numbers	the first ~ the 31st	4	4
	がつ	～月(がつ)	Classifier	classifier for naming the months of the year	4	4
	ばん	～番	Classifier	classifier for naming the numbers (in a series)	4	4
	ねん	～年	Classifier	classifier for naming the years	4	4
	そうか。	そうか。	Sp. Exp.	Is that so? (expression of awareness)	4	4
	いつものN	いつものN	Sp. Exp.	the usual N (e.g., *basho* 場所 place, *jikan* 時間 time, *tokoro* ところ place,	4	4
+	がんねん	元年	N	first year (of a new era) (BTS 18)	4	4
+	てんのうへいか	天皇陛下	N	emperor (honorific) (BTS 18)	4	4
+	がんじつ	元日	N	New Year's Day (BTS 18)	4	4
+	しょうがつ	（お）正月	N	New Year's Day/Month (BTS 18)	4	4
+	せいじんのひ	成人の日	N	Coming of Age Day (BTS 18)	4	4
+	けんこくきねんび	建国記念日	N	Foundation Day (BTS 18)	4	4
+	しゅんぶんのひ	春分の日	N	Vernal Equinox (BTS 18)	4	4
+	しょうわのひ	昭和の日	N	Showa Day (BTS 18)	4	4
+	けんぽうきねんび	憲法記念日	N	Constitution Day (BTS 18)	4	4
+	みどりのひ	緑の日	N	Green Day (BTS 18)	4	4
+	こどものひ	こどもの日	N	Children's Day (BTS 18)	4	4
+	うみのひ	海の日	N	Marine Day (BTS 18)	4	4
+	けいろうのひ	敬老の日	N	Respect for the Aged Day (BTS 18)	4	4
+	しゅうぶんのひ	秋分の日	N	Autumnal Equinox (BTS 18)	4	4

+	スポーツのひ	スポーツの日	N	Sports Day (BTS 18)	4	4
+	ぶんかのひ	文化の日	N	Culture Day (BTS 18)	4	4
+	きんろうかんしゃのひ	勤労感謝の日	N	Labor/Thanksgiving Day (BTS 18)	4	4
+	てんのうたんじょうび	天皇誕生日	N	Emperor's Birthday (BTS 18)	4	4
	へや	部屋	N	room	4	5
	オフィス	オフィス	N	office	4	5
	フォント	フォント	N	font	4	5
+	じてんしゃ	自転車	N	bicycle	4	5
+	ちか	地下	N	basement, underground	4	5
	つかいやすい	使いやすい	Adj	easy to use	4	5
	つかいにくい	使いにくい	Adj	hard to use	4	5
	かい	〜階	Classifier	classifier for naming and counting floors	4	5
	ばんきょうしつ	〜番教室	Classifier	classifier for naming a classroom number	4	5
+	ごうしつ	〜号室	Classifier	classifier for naming room numbers	4	5
	そうしましょう	そうしましょう	Sp. Exp.	Let's do it that way.	4	5
	わりと	わりと	Sp. Exp.	relatively	4	5
+	いちばん	一番	Sp. Exp.	most, best	4	5
	ほとんど	ほとんど	N	almost; barely (plus negative)	4	6
+	げつよう(び)	月曜(日)	N	Monday	4	6
+	かよう(び)	火曜(日)	N	Tuesday	4	6
+	すいよう(び)	水曜(日)	N	Wednesday	4	6
+	もくよう(び)	木曜(日)	N	Thursday	4	6
+	きんよう(び)	金曜(日)	N	Friday	4	6
+	どよう(び)	土曜(日)	N	Saturday	4	6
+	にちよう(び)	日曜(日)	N	Sunday	4	6
+	なんよう(び)	何曜(日)	N	what day (of the week)?	4	6
+	こんがっき	今学期	N	this term	4	6
	かかる	かかる(-U; かかった)	V	take (time/money)	4	6
+	いる	いる(-U; いった)	V	need	4	6
	にち・か	〜日	Classifier	classifier for naming and counting days	4	6
	よう(び)	〜曜(日)	Classifier	days of the week	4	6
	じかん	〜時間	Classifier	classifier for counting hours	4	6
+	しゅうかん	〜週間	Classifier	classifier for counting weeks	4	6
+	かげつ	〜ヶ月・〜カ月	Classifier	classifier for counting months	4	6
+	ねん	〜年	Classifier	classifier for naming and counting years	4	6

+	がっき	〜学期	Classifier	school/academic term	4	6
	では	では	Particle	[written equivalent of じゃ]	4	7R
	きくはいっときの はじ、きかぬはい っしょうのはじ	聞くは一時の恥、聞 かぬは一生の恥	Kotowaza	To ask may lead to shame for a moment, but not to ask leads to shame for a lifetime.	5	0
	すぐ	すぐ	N	soon, immediately, right away	5	1
	あす	あす	N	tomorrow (slightly more formal than あした)	5	1
	すこし	少し	N	a little, a few	5	1
	りょうかい	了解(する)	N	understanding, consent, agreement	5	1
	きめる	決める (-RU; 決 めた)	V	dccide (something)	5	1
+	いそぐ	急ぐ(-U; 急いだ)	V	hurry	5	1
	かまう	構う(-U; 構った)	V	mind, care, be concerned about (most commonly occurs in the negative)	5	1
	もちろん	もちろん	Sp. Exp.	of course	5	1
	なるべく	なるべく	Sp. Exp.	As . . . as possible	5	1
	でも	でも	Sp. Exp.	but, however, and yet	5	1
	でも　でも	Xでもy でも	Sp. Exp.	whether it's X or Y	5	1
	でも　じゃなくても	XでもXじゃなくても	Sp. Exp.	whether it's X or not X	5	1
	しつもん	質問(する)	N	(ask a) question	5	2
	やる	やる(-U; やった)	V	do (less formal than する	5	2
	だす	出す(-U; 出した)	V	submit, take out (of a container), send out (mail)	5	2
	ページ	〜ページ	Classifier	pages	5	2
	きょうまでだったで しょう?	今日までだったでし ょう?	Sp. Exp.	It was until today, wasn't it?	5	2
	ぜんぶ	全部	N	all, everything	5	3
	いちおう	一応	N	for the time being, tentatively, more or less	5	3
	もつ	持つ (-U)	V	hold, have, carry	5	3
	もってくる	持ってくる	V	bring (a thing)	5	3
+	もっていく	持っていく	V	take (a thing)	5	3
+	かりる	借りる (-RU; 借りた)	V	borrow	5	3
	おねがいできる	お願いできる (-RU)	V	can request	5	3
	いただける	いただける (-RU; い ただけた)	V	can/may have someone do X	5	3
	まかせる	任せる(-RU; 任せ た)	V	leave it to someone else, let someone else do it	5	3
	つ	〜つ	Classifier	classifier for counting items	5	3
	いくつ	(お)いくつ	Classifier	how many things/items	5	3

もうしわけありません。	申し訳ありません・ないです。	Sp. Exp.	I'm sorry.	5	3
+ もうしわけありませんでした。	申し訳ありませんでした・なかったです。	Sp. Exp.	I'm sorry (for what happened).	5	3
そうですねえ	そうですねえ	Sp. Exp.	(to express consideration) let's see	5	3
なんでしょう。	何でしょう。	Sp. Exp.	What? What could it be?	5	3
もってきていただけますか?	持ってきていただけますか?	Sp. Exp.	Can I have you bring it?	5	3
まかせてください。	任せてください。	Sp. Exp.	Leave it to me. Let someone do it.	5	3
おねがいできますか?	お願いできますか?	Sp. Exp.	Can I ask a favor of you?	5	3
ぎんこう	銀行	N	bank	5	4
+ ほんや	本屋	N	bookstore	5	4
+ スーパー	スーパー	N	supermarket	5	4
+ ゆうびんきょく	郵便局	N	post office	5	4
+ びょういん	病院	N	hospital	5	4
+ こうじょう	工場	N	factory, workshop	5	4
+ かいもの	買い物	N	shopping	5	4
くるま	車	N	car	5	4
+ バス	バス	N	bus	5	4
ちかてつ	地下鉄	N	subway	5	4
でんしゃ	電車	N	train	5	4
つれていく	連れて行く	V	take (a person) along	5	4
+ つれてくる	連れて来る	V	bring (a person) along	5	4
でる	出る(-RU; 出た)	V	go out, leave, attend (an event), appear, answer (the phone)	5	4
たすかる	助かる(-U; 助かった)	V	be helped, be saved, be rescued	5	4
あるく	歩く(-U; 歩いた)	V	walk	5	4
+ のる	乗る(-U; 乗った)	V	ride, get onboard	5	4
に	〜に	Particle	to, towards X	5	4
+ へ	〜へ	Particle	to, towards X	5	4
で	〜で	Particle	by means of X	5	4
あるいて	歩いて	Sp. Exp.	on foot	5	4
レセプション	レセプション	N	reception	5	5
プレゼン	プレゼン	N	presentation	5	5
+ はっぴょう	発表	N	presentation	5	5
うち	うち	N	our company	5	5
よぶ	呼ぶ(-U; 呼んだ)	V	call, invite	5	5
うかがう	伺う↓(-U; 伺った)	V	visit (humble)	5	5
よろこぶ	喜ぶ(-U; 喜んだ)	V	be delighted, be pleased	5	5

ございます	ございます (-ARU)	V	exists (polite form of あります) The 〜て form and the informal forms are rarely used today.	5	5
+ おしえる	教える (-RU; 教えた)	V	tell, teach	5	5
+ みせる	見せる (-RU; 見せた)	V	show	5	5
まいる	参る↓ (-U; 参った)	V	go, come (humble)	5	5
いらっしゃる↑	いらっしゃる↑／いらっしゃって↑ or いらして↑ (-ARU; いらっしゃった or いらした)	V	go, come (honorific)	5	5
みじかい	短い	Adj	short	5	5
+ ながい	長い	Adj	long	5	5
までに	TIME〜までに	Particle	by TIME X	5	5
から	REASON 〜から	S. Particle	because of REASON X	5	5
うち	うちのX	Sp. Exp.	our company's X	5	5
よろこんで	喜んで	Sp. Exp.	delighted	5	5
よろしければ	よろしければ	Sp. Exp.	if you would like, if it pleases you	5	5
+ ぜひ	是非	Sp. Exp.	by all means	5	5
くださってありがとう (ございます)。	Xくださって↑ありがとう (ございます)。	Sp. Exp.	Thank you for doing X.	5	5
+ けいご	敬語	N	politeness, polite language (BTS 10)	5	5
+ そんけいご	尊敬語	N	honorific language (BTS 10)	5	5
+ けんじょうご	謙譲語	N	humble language (BTS 10)	5	5
+ ていねいご	丁寧語	N	formal language (BTS 10)	5	5
おじかん	お時間	N	your time	5	6
+ アドバイス	アドバイス	N	advice	5	6
よみかき	読み書き	N	reading and writing	5	6
+ よみ	読み	N	reading	5	6
+ かき	書き	N	writing	5	6
かいわ	会話	N	conversation	5	6
+ ぶんぽう	文法	N	grammar	5	6
+ ごい	語彙	N	vocabulary	5	6
+ ききとり	聞き取り	N	listening	5	6
+ かきとり	書き取り	N	dictation	5	6
あと	あと・後	N	time after	5	6
+ れんしゅう	練習 (する)	N	practice, rehearse	5	6
+ よしゅう	予習 (する)	N	prepare for a lesson	5	6
ふくしゅう	復習 (する)	N	review	5	6
なる	なる (-U; なった)	V	become	5	6

	よわい	弱い	Adj	weak	5	6
+	つよい	強い	Adj	strong	5	6
	め	〜目	Classifier	classifier for naming numbers in a series	5	6
	むずかしくなりました。	難しくなりました。	Sp. Exp.	It became difficult.	5	6
	あとで	あとで	Sp. Exp.	later, N のあとで = 'after N'	5	6
	そうしていただけますか?	そうしていただけますか?	Sp. Exp.	Can I have you do that?	5	6
	ぼうせん	棒線	N	long vowel symbol	5	BTL2
	だくおん	濁音	N	voiced consonant	5	BTL9
	あすのひゃくよりきょうのごじゅう	明日の百より今日の五十	Kotowaza	A bird in the hand is worth two in the bush.	6	0
	みなさん	みなさん	N	everyone (used in addressing a group)	6	1
	メンバー	メンバー	N	member	6	1
	ひとこと	ひとこと	N	something (to say)	6	1
	じこしょうかい	自己紹介(する)	N	self-introduction	6	1
	アメリカ	アメリカ	N	America	6	1
+	にほん	日本(にほん・にっぽん)	N	Japan	6	1
+	カナダ	カナダ	N	Canada	6	1
+	メキシコ	メキシコ	N	Mexico	6	1
+	ブラジル	ブラジル	N	Brazil	6	1
+	ちゅうごく	中国	N	China	6	1
+	かんこく	韓国	N	Korea	6	1
+	イギリス	イギリス	N	England, U. K.	6	1
+	ドイツ	ドイツ	N	Germany	6	1
+	ケニア	ケニア	N	Kenya	6	1
	オレゴンしゅう	オレゴン州	N	Oregon	6	1
+	しゅうかん	州	N	state, as in the U.S.	6	1
+	しょう	省	N	provinces in China	6	1
+	かんとんしょう	広東省	N	Guangdong Province	6	1
	りゅうがくせいセンター	留学生センター	N	International Student Center	6	1
+	りゅうがくせい	留学生	N	study abroad student	6	1
+	りゅうがく	留学(する)	N	study abroad	6	1
+	がくぶ	学部	N	academic division, college	6	1
+	ぶんがくぶ	文学部	N	faculty of arts and humanities	6	1
	ホームステイ	ホームステイ	N	homestay	6	1
	あいきどう	合気道	N	aikido (martial art)	6	1
	へた	下手	N	unskillful, bad at	6	1
+	じょうず	上手	N	skillful, good at	6	1

+	ねんせい	～年生	Classifier	classifier for naming grade, class in school	6	1
	くん	NAME ～君	Sp. Exp.	[informal title]	6	1
	もう	もう	Sp. Exp.	already	6	1
	まだ	まだ	Sp. Exp.	still, yet	6	1
	みぎ	右	N	right	6	2
+	ひだり	左	N	left	6	2
	しょだん	初段	N	first or lowest rank black belt in martial arts, calligraphy, *shōgi*, *igo*, etc.	6	2
+	ちかく	近く	N	nearby, vicinity, neighborhood	6	2
+	むこう	向こう	N	opposite side, other side, over there	6	2
+	となり	隣	N	next door, beside	6	2
+	うえ	上	N	top, over	6	2
+	した	下	N	bottom, under	6	2
+	なか	中	N	inside	6	2
+	そと	外	N	outside	6	2
+	みせ	店	N	store, shop	6	2
	せいぶつ	生物	N	biology	6	2
	きょうし	教師	N	instructor, teacher	6	2
+	マネージャー	マネージャー	N	manager	6	2
+	リーダー	リーダー	N	leader	6	2
+	いしゃ	医者	N	(medical) doctor	6	2
+	かいはつ	開発(する)	N	development	6	2
+	きかく	企画(する)	N	plan, project, design	6	2
+	デザイン	デザイン(する)	N	design	6	2
+	マーケティング	マーケティング	N	marketing	6	2
+	セールス	セールス	N	sales	6	2
+	もうす	申す↓(-U; 申した)	V	say (humble)	6	2
+	おっしゃる	おっしゃる↑(-ARU; おっしゃった)	V	say (honorific)	6	2
	と	～と(言います／申します↓／おっしゃいます↑)	Particle	[quotation particle]	6	2
	にん・り	～人	Classifier	classifier for counting people	6	2
+	ふんかん・ぷんかん	～分間	Classifier	classifier for counting minutes	6	2
+	かかん・にちかん・にち	～日間	Classifier	classifier for counting days	6	2
+	ねんかん	～年間	Classifier	classifier for counting years	6	2
	ひとりずつ	一人ずつ	Sp. Exp.	one (person) at a time	6	2
	みぎからでいい	右からでいい	Sp. Exp.	from the right is good	6	2

	あいだ	Amount of time 〜間	Sp. Exp.	number of hours, days, weeks, years	6	2
	しゃしん	写真	N	photo	6	3
	ほう	方	N	way, alternative (of two)	6	3
	せ	背	N	back, spine, rear side	6	3
	うしろ	後ろ	N	back, behind	6	3
+	まえ	前	N	front	6	3
+	まんなか	真ん中	N	middle	6	3
+	でぐち	出口	N	exit	6	3
+	いりぐち	入り口／入口	N	entrance	6	3
+	まど	窓	N	window	6	3
	ひと	人(ひと)	N	person	6	3
+	かた	方(かた)	N	person (honorific)	6	3
+	おんなのひと	女の人	N	woman	6	3
+	おとこのひと	男の人	N	man	6	3
	チーズ	チーズ	N	cheese	6	3
	みどり	緑	N	green	6	3
+	むらさき	紫	N	purple	6	3
+	ちゃいろ	茶色	N	brown	6	3
+	きいろ	黄色	N	yellow	6	3
+	グレー	グレー	N	gray	6	3
+	ピンク	ピンク	N	pink	6	3
+	あか	赤	N	red	6	3
	しろ	白	N	white	6	3
+	あお	青	N	blue, green	6	3
+	くろ	黒	N	black	6	3
+	いろ	色	N	color	6	3
+	なにいろ	何色	N	what color	6	3
+	とる	撮る(-U; 撮った)	V	take (a photo)	6	3
+	みえる	見える (-RU; 見えた)	V	appear, be visible	6	3
	たつ	立つ(-U; 立った)	V	stand	6	3
+	すわる	座る(-U; 座った)	V	sit	6	3
	よる	寄る(-U; 寄った)	V	get close to, drop by, lean on	6	3
	たかい(せが)	(背が)高い	Adj	tall (in stature)	6	3
+	ひくい(せが)	(背が)低い	Adj	short (in stature)	6	3
	せがたかいひと	背が高い人	Sp. Exp.	tall person/people	6	3
	もっと	もっと	Sp. Exp.	more	6	3
	もういちまい	もう一枚	Sp. Exp.	one more sheet	6	3
+	もうちょっと	もうちょっと	Sp. Exp.	a little more	6	3
	みぎ、じゃなくひだり	右、じゃなく左	Sp. Exp.	right, I mean left	6	3
	いきますよ。	行きますよ。	Sp. Exp.	Here we go!	6	3
	いち、に、さん!	いち、に、さん!	Sp. Exp.	One, two, three!	6	3
	チーズ!	チーズ!	Sp. Exp.	Cheese!	6	3
	めいし	名刺	N	business card	6	4

	こうかん	交換	N	exchange	6	4
	せわ	（お）世話	N	help, aid, assistance	6	4
	よしだうんそう	吉田運送	N	Yoshida Transport	6	4
	ばんごう	番号	N	number	6	4
+	でんわばんごう	（お）電話番号	N	telephone number (your telephone number)	6	4
+	なまえ	（お）名前	N	name (your name)	6	4
+	メール	メール	N	email	6	4
+	アドレス	アドレス	N	(email) address	6	4
+	れんらくさき	連絡先	N	contact information	6	4
	おる	おる↓(-U; おった)	V	be (humble form of います 'be') The 〜て form is rarely used today.	6	4
+	いらっしゃる	いらっしゃる↑(-ARU; いらっしゃった)	V	be (honorific form of います 'be')	6	4
	はじめまして。	はじめまして。	Sp. Exp.	How do you do.	6	4
	いつもおせわになっております↓。	いつもお世話になっております↓。	Sp. Exp.	I/we are always in your debt.	6	4
	もうしわけございません↓。	申し訳ございません↓。	Sp. Exp.	I am terribly sorry. (lit. 'I have no excuse.')	6	4
	れいごうごうにい、はちきゅうのななななにいれい	０５５２、８９の７７２０	Sp. Exp.	(0552) 89-7720	6	4
+	かちょう	課長	N	section chief	6	5
+	しゃちょう	社長	N	company president	6	5
+	しょちょう	所長	N	head of a laboratory, research center	6	5
+	がくちょう	学長	N	school president	6	5
	はなし	（お）話	N	talk	6	5
+	そうだん	（ご）相談（する）	N	consultation	6	5
+	ほうこく	（ご）報告（する）	N	report	6	5
+	アポ	アポ	N	appointment	6	5
+	るす	留守	N	away from home or work	6	5
	おはなしする↓	お話しする↓	V	talk (humble)	6	5
	あく	空く・あく (-U; 空いた)	V	become free, empty	6	5
+	やすむ	休む (-U; 休んだ)	V	take a break, go on vacation/holiday	6	5
+	いたす	いたす(-U; いたした)	V	do (humble)	6	5
	たい	Verb〜たい	Adj	want to VERB	6	5
	いつか	いつか	Sp. Exp.	sometime	6	5
	なにか	何か	Sp. Exp.	something	6	5
	について	N について	Sp. Exp.	with regard to N	6	5

いかが	いかが	Sp. Exp.	how (polite)	6	5
ずっと	ずっと	Sp. Exp.	continuously, by far, the whole time	6	5
ランチ	ランチ	N	lunch, lunch special	6	6
+ ていしょく	定食	N	set meal	6	6
すすめ	(お)勧め	N	recommendation, suggestion	6	6
ほか	他・外	N	other, else, besides	6	6
+ べつ	別	N	different, separate, distinct	6	6
もの	もの	N	thing (tangible)	6	6
グルメ	グルメ	N	gourmet, connoisseur	6	6
たのむ	頼む (-U: 頼んだ)	V	order (at a restaurant, online, etc.), request	6	6
まよう	迷う (-U; 迷った)	V	become confused, lost	6	6
+ こまる	困る (-U; 困った)	V	be troubled; be bothered; be embarrassed	6	6
+ ぞんじる	存じる↓ (-U 存じた)	V	know, find out (humble)	6	6
+ しる	知る (-U; 知った)	V	find out, know	6	6
しっている	知っている	V	know	6	6
すすめる、Xに	Xに勧める・薦める (-RU; 勧めた・薦めた)	V	recommend to X, advise X, encourage X	6	6
より	より	Particle	compared to, [comparison particle]	6	6
ほど	ほど	Particle	as much as, [comparison particle]	6	6
おまたせしました。	お待たせしました。	Sp. Exp.	Sorry to make you wait.	6	6
なにも	何も	Sp. Exp.	nothing	6	6
カレーかきょうのランチか	カレーか今日のランチか	Sp. Exp.	curry or today's lunch special	6	6
ランチよりカレーのほうがおすすめ	ランチよりカレーの方がお勧め	Sp. Exp.	curry rather than the lunch special is the recommendation	6	6
カレーほどすごくない	カレーほどすごくない	Sp. Exp.	not as awesome as curry	6	6
ちがわない	Xと違わない	Sp. Exp.	not different from X	6	6
さすが	さすが (Noun)	Sp. Exp.	true to (your reputation), what I expected, etc.	6	6
ごぞんじだ↑	ご存知だ↑	Sp. Exp.	know (honorific)	6	6
+ する、する	Xにする	Sp. Exp.	decide on X	6	6
+ きく、Xに	Xに聞く	Sp. Exp.	ask X	6	6
そうだんする	Xに・と相談する	Sp. Exp.	consult with X	6	6
+ ほうこくする	Xに報告する	Sp. Exp.	make a report to X	6	6

340

Index